Census Records for Latin America
and the Hispanic United States

Census Records

for

LATIN AMERICA and the
HISPANIC UNITED STATES

Lyman D. Platt

Published by Genealogical Publishing Co., Inc.
1001 N. Calvert St., Baltimore, MD 21202
Library of Congress Catalog Card Number 97-78047
International Standard Book Number 0-8063-1555-5
Made in the United States of America

CONTENTS

INTRODUCTION

Prior to the Spanish invasion of the Indies and the subsequent conquest of the various native cultures that existed throughout the Caribbean and throughout North, Central and South America, some tribal groups made and kept census records, usually in pictographic formats, of their families, lands, etc. For the most part, however, these were kept hidden from the eyes of the invading Spaniards and the priests who accompanied them, and have either not been preserved or are still not for viewing by the general public.[1] There is ample evidence that pre-conquest records still exist, however. An analysis of this whole area of study forms part of another work currently in progress.[2]

In every colony of the Spanish Empire at least one major census was taken during the colonial period (1492–1825), although not all of these documents have been preserved. However, the stream of colonial reports on local population submitted to Spain for administrative, fiscal, military and religious purposes swelled to a flood as the Spanish colonial administrative apparatus was reformed and expanded during the Intendency Period (1763–1825). The amount of material available to genealogists and family historians during this period of time is the largest accumulation of demographic information available for any major region of the world.

Excellent details on family names, ages, relationships and civil status are available in the extant censuses. It should be kept in mind, however, that when using any census return the information contained therein might not be unique to that census alone. In most Spanish colonial censuses there exists the possibility that the returns originally made for one census were used in subsequent surveys. While it was the local priest or *alcalde*[3] to whom fell the actual task of counting the population, it is to be expected that such enumerations would have been used by any level of administration to satisfy more than one of the growing demands made upon them for information.[4]

---

[1] Silvio A. Zavala, *La Encomienda Indiana.* 2nd ed., rev. & enlarged (México, D.F.: 1973), page 124.

[2] Volume 1 of this work has been published by the author as *The World Book of Generations: A Genealogical History* (St. George, Utah: The Teguayo Press, 1996). Volumes 2 and 3 will contain further information on the records of the pre-conquest Americas, with ample documentation and actual photographs of some of the discoveries that have been made in the last twenty years.

[3] Municipal judge, mayor or justice of the peace.

[4] David G. Browning and David J. Robinson, *The Origins and Comparability of Peruvian Population Data: 1776–1815.* Discussion paper series #23, Department of Geography, Syracuse, New York, 1976, pages 1–3.

Beginning in the late 1700s the Council of Indies, the administrative arm of the Crown in Spain, initiated an Empire-wide project of population control through systematic and regular census reports. All persons in a given area, together with information about their age, sex, residence, and marital status, were to be listed, by name, usually within family grouping, showing an implied or written relationship to the head of the household. The women were almost always recorded in these listings with their maiden names, as is common in all Latin American records. The first such census was initially ordered as the 1768 census of Spain, which in 1776, under the direction of the illustrious José de Gálvez, Minister of the Indies, was expanded to include the rest of Spain's territories. Similarly, the 1786 Spanish census became the 1790 territorial returns, not all taken exactly in 1790, but generally ranging between the period of 1788–1794. A final colonial census was taken in 1812 and during that immediate time period.[5]

The first series of censuses beginning in 1776 resulted from orders issued to both civil and ecclesiastical officials that each take separate counts. The results were sporadic, but they were fairly extensive, and a goodly number of them have survived in one archive or another in Latin America or Spain. Some have been microfilmed by the Family History Library (FHL) in Salt Lake City and by other entities, although during a critical period of filming in the late 1970s and early 1980s, those *padrones*[6] archived in the parishes were not part of the microfilming policy of the FHL. In the following study, occasionally a record or series of records has been identified that is found only in its original archive. Most, however, have been preserved on microfilm and can be consulted in family history centers of the FHL throughout the world. The most complete collection of censuses identifed in this study will be those of the 1790 time period.

In Mexico the viceroy Juan Francisco Güemes y Orcasitas, the 1st Conde de Revillagigedo, ordered censuses taken throughout the viceroyalty in 1791 and again in 1792. The actual returns came in during the 1791–1794 period. A large number of these are accompanied by geographical descriptions and maps of the smaller civil divisions (provinces, intendencies, *partidos*)[7]. This collection is housed at the Archivo General de la Nación (AGN) in the Old Penitenciary in Mexico City, one of the finest archives in the world, and is also available at the University of Texas at Austin, Nettie Lee Benson Latin American Collection, at the University of California at San Diego, at the University of California at Berkeley, Bancroft Library, at the Family History Library in Salt Lake

---

[5] *Ibid.*, pages 4–6.

[6] Ecclesiastical census records, one of the five official records of the Catholic Church: baptism, confirmation, marriage, burial, and *padrón*.

[7] A *partido* was a sub-division of an Intendency, and as the political system developed, these *partidos* often became the municipalities of the Independence time period, subdivisions of provinces and later of the states.

City and in a number of other scattered collections, principally in Spain in their original form. The FHL microfilm collection is a separate filming from the others in Texas and California, and the copy at the AGN is from the FHL filming.

Special attention has been given to Aguascalientes in this study to show what can be done as this analysis reaches further levels of development. Also, the state of Hidalgo has been completely indexed in this book to show the detail that is available in these censuses. To do this for all records listed herein would require several volumes at least. The Guadalajara *padrones* and those from Morelia are voluminous in and of themselves, and would double the size of this current analysis.

Most of the following census references are listed in their modern jurisdictions, both by province (or department or state) and by country. Many of the boundaries of these jurisdictions have changed over the years, however, and the modern names and boundaries simply don't apply. For example, the Province of Cuyo first belonged to Chile, then later became part of Argentina. A census for Cuyo must remain intact as a reference even though Cuyo is not a modern province. Within Cuyo was Uspallata, which in 1777 has a census reference under its own listing in Argentina, but by 1810 Uspallata was only a *partido* in the province of Mendoza; therefore, the reference to that census is found under Mendoza.

When reviewing the following index, remember that some of the entries, although listed under "Locality" and appearing to be a city or a parish, are in fact a wider census of the colonial jurisdictions by those names, which included all the surrounding pueblos, haciendas, ranchos, estancias and smaller jurisdictions within the control of that provincial capital. **It is critical to remember the broad coverage of these one-line entries.** For example, Otumba, México, México refers to the colonial province of Otumba. It includes the city of Otumba, as well as two pueblos: Axapusco and Ostoticpac, along with eleven haciendas and twenty-seven ranchos in the 1791 *padrón* of that province.

The modern states of California, Arizona, New Mexico and Texas are found under Mexico in this volume because they belonged to Mexico during the period in which most of the censuses were taken. Florida and Louisiana, on the other hand, are considered as separate entities because of their loose ties to Mexico.

Within Mexico an area like the Provincias Internas should be consulted for its sub-divisions, like Alta California, Sonora, Chihuahua, Durango, Coahuila, and so forth, because the actual territories of some of these larger censuses have not been broken down in this study into the respective provincial jurisdictions, given that the actual records have not been available for consultation. Although each jurisdiction should be included in these large censuses, it is not known for sure that they are and hence they have not been listed separately. For the Province of Nombre de Dios, look under Nueva Vizcaya. For Campeche,

Tabasco and the other colonial provinces of the Yucatán peninsula, all have been combined under Yucatán. Panamá, which was a province of Colombia until 1903, is listed twice for obvious reasons, and for easy historical reference.

Many more censuses will be found in the future in parishes, Latin American provincial and national archives, and throughout Spain's rich archival treasures. Collections like those mentioned in Cuba, Mexico and Perú will be more accurately detailed. Other researchers may have used censuses not found in this work that will come to light by referring to recent publications in the field. However, approximately 4,000 listings are included in this work, making it the largest and most complete survey of census records available for Latin America and the Hispanic United States. Many of the entries found here, even though they cite microfilm sources in the Family History Library collection in Salt Lake City, Utah, are unique to this work due to oversights in the FHL's cataloging, particularly in the Morelia, Guadalajara, and Revillagigedo collections. (Note that numbers given in the "Reference" column, in the text, are Family History Library microfilm numbers.) Finally, some of the entries included here may not actually contain information on the families themselves, but only statistics; however, they have been included as a guide to the researcher to be aware that a *padrón* does exist, or has existed, that should be found as part of a complete investigation of the families of that area.

Lyman D. Platt, Ph.D.
President of the Institute of Genealogy and History for Latin America
316 W. 500 N., St. George, Utah 84770.

ACRONYMS AND BIBLIOGRAPHY FOR ARCHIVES AND PUBLICATIONS WHERE CENSUSES ARE LOCATED

811	University of Arizona, 811 microfilm series
AAA	Archivo del Antiguo Ayuntamiento de México, now called Archivo Histórico del Ayuntamiento de la Ciudad de México, Mexico City
AAG	Archivo del Arzobispado de Guadalajara, México
AAL	Archbishop's Archives, Lima, Perú
AAO	Archivo de la Arquiodiócesis de Oaxaca, México
ACC	Academia Costarricense de Ciencias Genealógicas. *Revista.*
ACG	Archivo de la Curia Metropolitana de Guayaquil, Ecuador
ACH	Academia Chilena de Historia. *Boletín.*
ACM	Archivo de la Curia Metropolitana de Cuenca, Ecuador
ACV	Academia Nacional de Historia. *Actas Capitulares de la Villa de Concepción del Río Cuarto, 1798–1812.* Buenos Aires, 1947.
ADA	Archivo Diocesano de Arica, Chile
ADC	Archivo Diocesano de Chiapas in San Cristóbal de las Casas, Mexico
AES	Archivo Histórico del Estado de Sonora, Hermosillo, Mexico
AF	Archivo Franciscano, Biblioteca Nacional, Mexico City
AGC	Archivo General de Centroamérica, Guatemala City, Guatemala
AGE	Academia Guatemalteca de Estudios Genealógicos, Heráldicos e Históricos
AGEC	Archivo General del Estado, Coahuila, México
AGEM	Cathedral, Hermosillo, Sonora, México (Arizona microfilm series 422 - 40 rolls)
AGI	Archivo General de Indias, Seville, Spain
AGN	Archivo General de la Nación, followed by the country: Mexico, Argentina, Perú, Venezuela.
AGP	Archivo General de los Puertorriqueño, San Juan, Puerto Rico
AGS	Archivo General de Simancas, Simancas, Spain
AHA	Archivo Histórico de Antioquia, Colombia
AHA1	Gómez Canedo, Lino. *Los Archivos Históricos de América, Período Colonial Español.* 2 volumes. México, D.F., 1961.

AHB	Archivo Histórico, Baja California Sur, La Paz, Baja California Sur
AHC	Archivo Histórico de Córdoba, Argentina
AHC	Archivo Histórico de Cuzco, Perú
AHH	Archivo Histórico de Hacienda, AGN, Mexico City
AHN	Archivo Histórico Nacional, Madrid, Spain
AHP	Archivo Administrativo e Histórico de la Provincia de Mendoza, Argentina
AHS	Arizona Historical Society
AM	Archivo Municipal, followed by place name
AMH	Academia Mexicana de la Historia. *Memorias.*
AN	Archivo Nacional, followed by the country: Chile, Ecuador.
ANH	Academia Nacional de la Historia
AOI	Archivo del Obispado de Iquique, Chile
AP	Audiencia of Panamá, Archivo General de Indias, Seville
ASG	Arizona State Genealogical Society. *Copper State Bulletin.*
BAG	Archivo General de la Nación. *Boletín.*
BNE	Biblioteca Nacional, Madrid, Spain
BNM	Biblioteca Nacional de México, Mexico City
BNP	Bibliothèque Nationale, Paris. All references to this library are for the Fonds mexicains (FM).
BPT	Biblioteca Pública de Toledo, Spain, usually referring to the Colección Borbón-Lorenzana, Manuscript 45
CA	Ramo de Californias, AGN, Mexico City
CAG	Colección Amigos de la Genealogía, Ecuador
CAL	Los Californianos. *Antepasados.*
CCM	Aguirre, Carlos and Sánchez de Tagle, Rosa María. *Padrones y Censos de la Ciudad de México.* N.P., n.d.
CEG	Centro de Estudios Genealógicos de Buenos Aires. *Revista.*
DEA	Vasco de Escudero, Grecia. *Directorio Ecuatoriano de Archivos.* Quito, 1979.
DEI	Rodríguez Demorizi, Emilio. *Los Dominicos y las Encomiendas de Indios en la Isla Española.* Santo Domingo, 1971
EGC	Centro de Estudios Genealógicos de Córdoba. *Boletín.*
FHQ	*Florida Historical Quarterly*
FV	Fondo Varios of the National Archive, Santiago, Chile
GGC	Haigh, Roger M. *Bibliographic Guide to the Guatemalan Collection.* Salt Lake City, 1981.
GGS	Colker, William S., and Inglis, Douglas. *Genealogical Guide to Spanish Pensacola.* Pensacola, 1980.

GHG   Platt, Lyman D. *Genealogical Historical Guide to Latin America.* Detroit, 1978.

GLC   Genealogical Library Catalog of the Genealogical Society of Utah, Salt Lake City, Utah

HAH   *Hispanic American Historical Review.*

HER   Pérez, Cesar B. *Historia de Entre Ríos.* Paraná: 1936.

HI   Ramo de Historia, AGN, Mexico City

HOP   Perera, Ambrosio. *Historia de la Organización de Pueblos Antiguos de Venezuela.* Madrid, 1964.

IAC   *Genealogía,* Revista del Instituto Argentino de Ciencias Genealógicas

IEG   Instituto de Estudios Genealógicos Uruguayos. *Revista.*

IEI   Instituto de Estudios Iberoamericanos

IGHL   Instituto Genealógico e Histórico Latinoamericano. *Revista.*

IHE   Instituto de Historia Eclesiástica Ecuatoriana

INA   Archivo Histórico del Instituto Nacional de Antropología e Historia

IPI   Instituto Peruano de Investigaciones Genealógicas. *Revista.*

IVG   Instituto Venezolano de Genealogía. *Revista.*

JAH   *Journal of Arizona History*

LEA   Azarola Gil, Luis Enrique. *Crónicas y Linajes de la Gobernación del Plata: Documentos Inéditos de los Siglos XVII y XVIII.* Buenos Aires, 1927.

LEI   Zavala, Silvio A. *La Encomienda Indiana.* 2nd ed., rev. & enlarged. México, D. F., 1973.

LGH   *Louisiana Genealogical Register*

LOY   Loyola University, New Orleans, Louisiana

MAQ   Municipal Archives of Quito, Quito, Ecuador

MBL   Hammond, George P. *A Guide to the Manuscript Collection of the Bancroft Library.* Berkeley & Los Angeles, 1972.

NMHR   *New Mexico Historical Review*

OCP   Browning, David G., and Robinson, David J. *The Origins and Comparability of Peruvian Population Data: 1776–1815.* Discussion paper series #23, Dept. of Geography, Syracuse, N. Y., 1976.

ODM   González Sánchez, Isabel. *El Obispado de Michoacán en 1765.* México, D.F., 1985.

MI   Ramo de Misiones, AGN, Mexico City

PA1   Sierras, Eugene L. *Mexican Census—Pre-Territorial Pimería Alta 1801.* Tucson, 1986.

PA2   Sierras, Eugene L. *Mexican Census—Pre-Territorial Pimería Alta 1852*. Tucson, 1986.

PAD   Ramo de Padrones, AGN, Mexico City

PCO   Esparza, Manuel. *Padrón de Capitación de la Ciudad de Oaxaca, 1875*. Oaxaca, 1986.

PGH   Esparza, Manuel. *Padrón General de los Habitantes de la Ciudad de Oaxaca, 1842*. Oaxaca: Instituto Nacional de Antropología e Historia, 1981.

PI   Ramo de Provincias Internas, AGN, Mexico City

RAH   Real Academia de la Historia, Madrid, Spain

RAN   *Revista del Archivo Nacional del Perú*

RC   Ramo de Reales Cédulas, AGN, Mexico City

RCH   *Revista Chilena de Historia y Geografía*

REH   *Revista de Estudios Históricos*. Santiago, Chile.

ROT   The University of Texas. *Residents of Texas, 1782–1836*. 3 volumes: vol. 1 (1782–1806); vol. 2 (1807–1834); vol. 3 (1835). San Antonio, Texas, 1984.

SAC   Saint Albert's College, Oakland, California. Also available on microfilm at Bancroft.

SBM   Santa Barbara Mission Archive, Santa Barbara, California

SDH   San Diego Historical Society

SLU   St. Louis University, St. Louis, Missouri

SMC   Olmsted, Virginia Langham. *New Mexico, Spanish and Mexican Censuses, 1790, 1823, 1845*. Tucson, 1977.

SSC   Historical Society of Southern California. *Quarterly.*

TSG   Texas State Genealogical Society. *Quarterly.*

TSL   Texas State Library, Mexico Collection, Austin, Texas

UA   University of Arizona, Tucson, Arizona

UMSA   Universidad Mayor de San Andrés, La Paz, Bolivia

UNM   University of New Mexico, Albuquerque, New Mexico

URU   Ministerio de Instrucción Pública. *Fondos documentales relativos a la historia del Uruguay obrantes en los Archivos extranjeros*. Madrid, 1930.

UT   University of Texas at Austin, Nettie Lee Benson Library

VHP   Argas, José María. *Visita hecha a la Provincias de Chucuito por Garci Díez de San Miguel en el año 1567*. Lima, 1964.

WAA   Duaine, Carl Laurence. *With All Arms A Study of a Kindred Group*. Edinburg, Texas, 1987.

CENSUSES OF LATIN AMERICA AND THE HISPANIC UNITED STATES

The censuses that follow are organized first on the national level, if there are any, as in the case of Argentina which follows immediately, then on the provincial level, beginning with those lacking localities, and finally alphabetically by province and within province alphabetically by localities.

ARGENTINA

Locality	Province	Country	Year(s)	Reference
		Argentina[8]	1869	GLC
		Argentina[9]	1895	GLC
	Misiones	Argentina	1657	GHG 131 (AGN)
	Misiones	Argentina	1676	GHG 131 (AGN)
	Misiones	Argentina	1677	GHG 131 (AGN)
	Misiones	Argentina	1735	GHG 131-132 (AGN)
	Misiones	Argentina	1772	GHG 132 (AGN)
B. Aires & province	B.A.	Argentina	1838	GHG 131 (AGN)
	Catamarca	Argentina	1786	GHG 133 (AGN)
	Catamarca	Argentina	1791	GHG 133 (AGN)
	Catamarca	Argentina	1806	GHG 133 (AGN)
Belén	Catamarca	Argentina	1869	671697
Catamarca	Catamarca	Argentina	1869	671692
San Pedro	Catamarca	Argentina	1869	671701
Corrientes	Corrientes	Argentina	?	IAC 11:165-174
Anguiñán	Córdoba	Argentina	1795	1162416:11
Calamuchita	Córdoba	Argentina	1779	1162415:6
Córdoba	Córdoba	Argentina	1778–1779	1162415:9
Córdoba	Córdoba	Argentina	1779	AHC, Caja 19
Córdoba—annexes	Córdoba	Argentina	1779	1162415:7

---

[8] First National Census of Argentina.
[9] Second National Census of Argentina.

Locality	Province	Country	Year(s)	Reference
Córdoba	Córdoba	Argentina	1795	1162416:1
Córdoba—annexes	Córdoba	Argentina	1795	1162416:3
Córdoba[10]	Córdoba	Argentina	1813	GHG 134 (AHC)
Córdoba	Córdoba	Argentina	1822	GHG 134 (AHC)
Guandacol	Córdoba	Argentina	1795	1162416:10
Ischilín	Córdoba	Argentina	1779	1162415:1
Ischilín[11]	Córdoba	Argentina	1793	1162416:4
Los Llanos	Córdoba	Argentina	1795	1162416:13
Punilla	Córdoba	Argentina	1779	1162415:5
Punilla (La)	Córdoba	Argentina	1795	1162416:5
Río Cuarto	Córdoba	Argentina	1779	1162415:13
Río Cuarto	Córdoba	Argentina	1794	ACV, 17-21
Río Seco	Córdoba	Argentina	1778	CEG 6:18
Río Seco (partido)	Córdoba	Argentina	1779	1162415:10
Río Segundo	Córdoba	Argentina	1779	1162415:4
Río Tercero	Córdoba	Argentina	1778	1162415:3
Río Tercero Abajo	Córdoba	Argentina	1795	1162416:8
Río Tercero Arriba	Córdoba	Argentina	1796	1162416:7
S.Blas de los Sauces, Villa Arauco	Córdoba	Argentina	1795	1162416:12
S.Javier	Córdoba	Argentina	1795	1162416:6
Tegua	Córdoba	Argentina	1779	1162415:2
Traslasierra	Córdoba	Argentina	1779	1162415:12
Traslasierra	Córdoba	Argentina	1795	1162416:14
Tulumba	Córdoba	Argentina	1795	1162416:2
Tulumba (partido)	Córdoba	Argentina	1779	1162415:11
	Cuyo	Argentina	1778	AN, Chile, Contaduría
Canota	Cuyo	Argentina	1777	AAHP,28:3[12]; (IGHL 4:55)
Cruz Alta	Cuyo	Argentina	1698	AHP, 29-30:13; (IGHL 4:55)
Las Barrancas	Cuyo	Argentina	1778	AHP, 28:5; (IGHL 4:55)
Mendoza	Cuyo	Argentina	1777	AHP, 28:2; (IGHL 4:55)
Río Diamanta	Cuyo	Argentina	1777	AHP, 29-30:37; (IGHL 4:55)
San Carlos	Cuyo	Argentina	1778	AHP, 28:6; (IGHL 4:55)
San Carlos	Cuyo	Argentina	1794	AHP, 28:10; (IGHL 4:55)
San Carlos	Cuyo	Argentina	1795	AHP, 28:12; (IGHL 4:55)
Uspallata	Cuyo	Argentina	1777	AHP, 28:3; (IGHL 4:55)
B. Aires	D.F.	Argentina	1778	GHG 130 (AGN)

[10] This entry and the following entry are from the city and the surrounding area: ciudad y campaña.

[11] Nuestra Señora del Rosario de Ischilín.

[12] Archivo Histórico Provincial, Epoca Colonial, File or *Carpeta* 28, document 3 as an example of all similiar references that follow in this section.

Locality	Province	Country	Year(s)	Reference
B. Aires	D.F.	Argentina	1810	IAC 13
B. Aires	D.F.	Argentina	1815	GHG 130 (AGN)
B. Aires	D.F.	Argentina	1827	GHG 131 (AGN)
B. Aires	D.F.	Argentina	1854	GHG 131 (AGN)
B. Aires—Balvanera	D.F.	Argentina	1855	760008-760009
B. Aires—Barrancas Norte	D.F.	Argentina	1855	759520
B. Aires—Catedral N.	D.F.	Argentina	1855	760007
B. Aires—Catedral S.	D.F.	Argentina	1855	759519
B. Aires—Catedral S.	D.F.	Argentina	1855	759521
B. Aires—Concepción	D.F.	Argentina	1855	759514
B. Aires—Concepción	D.F.	Argentina	1855	760011
B. Aires—Monserrat	D.F.	Argentina	1855	759517-759518
B. Aires—Piedad	D.F.	Argentina	1855	759516
B. Aires—San Miguel	D.F.	Argentina	1855	760006
B. Aires—San Nicolás	D.F.	Argentina	1855	760010
B. Aires—Socorro	D.F.	Argentina	1855	759515
Alcarez	Entre Ríos	Argentina	1805	HER, 393-404
Entre Ríos	Entre Ríos	Argentina	1745	HER, 315-320
Gualeguay	Entre Ríos	Argentina	1803	HER, 363-392
Paraná	Entre Ríos	Argentina	1803	HER, 321-361
	Jujuy	Argentina	1779	1162415:8
	Jujuy	Argentina	1786	GHG 133 (AGN)
	Jujuy-part	Argentina	1791	GHG 133 (AGN)
	Jujuy	Argentina	1806	GHG 133 (AGN)
La Ríoja & annexes	La Ríoja	Argentina	1795	1162416:9
Alto Verde (partido)	Mendoza	Argentina	1855	AHP,:844; IGHL 4:50
Arbol Solo	Mendoza	Argentina	1810	AHP,:777; IGHL 2:68
Asuncion de las Lagunas de Rosario	Mendoza	Argentina	1814	AHP,:893; IGHL 4:53
Barrancas (partido)	Mendoza	Argentina	1855	AHP,:844; IGHL 4:50
Barrancas, cuartel 22	Mendoza	Argentina	1823	AHP,:811; IGHL 4:45
Barrancas, cuartel 32	Mendoza	Argentina	1823	AHP,:812; IGHL 4:45
Buen Orden (partido)	Mendoza	Argentina	1855	AHP,:844; IGHL 4:50
Carbón	Mendoza	Argentina	1810	AHP,:779; IGHL 2:68
Chinva (partido)	Mendoza	Argentina	1855	AHP,:844; IGHL 4:50
Costa de Tunuyan	Mendoza	Argentina	1810	AHP,:778; IGHL 2:68
Cuarteles 10-15, 2º Dpto. de Campaña	Mendoza	Argentina	1855	AHP,:845; IGHL 4:50
Guaymallén, 1st dist.	Mendoza	Argentina	1859	AHP,:851; IGHL 4:51
Guaymallén, 2nd dist.	Mendoza	Argentina	1859	AHP,:853; IGHL 4:51
Guaymallén[13]	Mendoza	Argentina	1859	AHP,:854; IGHL 4:51
Jocoli	Mendoza	Argentina	1810	AHP,:777; IGHL 2:68

[13] This census is for the 3rd district, cuarteles four through thirteen.

Locality	Province	Country	Year(s)	Reference
La Barrancas	Mendoza	Argentina	1810	AHP,:778; IGHL 2:68
Libertado (partido)	Mendoza	Argentina	1855	AHP,:844; IGHL 4:50
Lulunta, cuartel 31	Mendoza	Argentina	1823	AHP,:818; IGHL 4:46
Mendoza[14]	Mendoza	Argentina	1855	AHP,:847; IGHL 4:50
Mendoza outskirts[15]	Mendoza	Argentina	1823	AHP,:813; IGHL 4:45
Mendoza[16]	Mendoza	Argentina	1814	AHP,:806; IGHL 3:75
Mendoza, cuartel —	Mendoza	Argentina	1814	AHP,:797; IGHL 3:74
Mendoza, cuartel —	Mendoza	Argentina	1823	AHP,:820; IGHL 4:46
Mendoza, cuartel 1	Mendoza	Argentina	1824	AHP,:840; IGHL 4:49
Mendoza, cuartel 2	Mendoza	Argentina	1814	AHP,:793; IGHL 3:73
Mendoza, cuartel 2	Mendoza	Argentina	1814	AHP,:804; IGHL 3:75
Mendoza, cuartel 3	Mendoza	Argentina	1814	AHP,:798; IGHL 3:74
Mendoza, cuartel 3	Mendoza	Argentina	1823	AHP,:835; IGHL 4:48
Mendoza, cuartel 3	Mendoza	Argentina	1814	AHP,:784; IGHL 2:69
Mendoza, cuartel 4	Mendoza	Argentina	1814	AHP,:787; IGHL 2:69
Mendoza, cuartel 4	Mendoza	Argentina	1814	AHP,:799; IGHL 3:74
Mendoza, cuartel 4	Mendoza	Argentina	1823	AHP,:836; IGHL 4:48
Mendoza, cuartel 5	Mendoza	Argentina	1814	AHP,:785; IGHL 2:69
Mendoza, cuartel 5	Mendoza	Argentina	1824	AHP,:841; IGHL 4:49
Mendoza, cuartel 5	Mendoza	Argentina	1814	AHP,:803; IGHL 3:75
Mendoza, cuartel 6	Mendoza	Argentina	1814	AHP,:782; IGHL 2:69
Mendoza, cuartel 6	Mendoza	Argentina	1814	AHP,:800; IGHL 3:74
Mendoza, cuartel 6	Mendoza	Argentina	1823	AHP,:825; IGHL 4:47
Mendoza, cuartel 6	Mendoza	Argentina	1823	AHP,:833; IGHL 4:48
Mendoza, cuartel 7	Mendoza	Argentina	1814	AHP,:805; IGHL 3:74
Mendoza, cuartel 7	Mendoza	Argentina	1823	AHP,:808; IGHL 4:45
Mendoza, cuartel 7	Mendoza	Argentina	1824	AHP,:839; IGHL 4:49
Mendoza, cuartel 7	Mendoza	Argentina	1814	AHP,:801; IGHL 3:75
Mendoza, cuartel 8	Mendoza	Argentina	1814	AHP,:794; IGHL 3:74
Mendoza, cuartel 10	Mendoza	Argentina	1814	AHP,:802; IGHL 3:75
Mendoza, cuartel 10	Mendoza	Argentina	1823	AHP,:807; IGHL 4:45
Mendoza, cuartel 11	Mendoza	Argentina	1823	AHP,:814; IGHL 4:45
Mendoza, cuartel 12	Mendoza	Argentina	1814	AHP,:786; IGHL 2:69
Mendoza, cuartel 12	Mendoza	Argentina	1823	AHP,:828; IGHL 4:47
Mendoza, cuartel 13	Mendoza	Argentina	1814	AHP,:796; IGHL 3:74
Mendoza, cuartel 13	Mendoza	Argentina	1823	AHP,:821; IGHL 4:46
Mendoza, cuartel 17	Mendoza	Argentina	1814	AHP,:789; IGHL 3:73
Mendoza, cuartel 17	Mendoza	Argentina	1823	AHP,:816; IGHL 4:46
Mendoza, cuartel 18	Mendoza	Argentina	1823	AHP,:809; IGHL 4:45
Mendoza, cuartel 19	Mendoza	Argentina	1823	AHP,:810; IGHL 4:45
Mendoza, cuartel 21	Mendoza	Argentina	1823	AHP,:815; IGHL 4:46

[14] This census is for the seventeen cuartels of Mendoza.

[15] This census is for the ten cuartels of Mendoza.

[16] This census is for men 18–60.

Locality	Province	Country	Year(s)	Reference
Mendoza, cuartel 23	Mendoza	Argentina	1823	AHP,:823; IGHL 4:47
Mendoza, cuartel 24	Mendoza	Argentina	1814	AHP,:791; IGHL 3:73
Mendoza, cuartel 24	Mendoza	Argentina	1823	AHP,:817; IGHL 4:46
Mendoza, cuartel 25	Mendoza	Argentina	1814	AHP,:790; IGHL 3:73
Mendoza, cuartel 26	Mendoza	Argentina	1823	AHP,:832; IGHL 4:48
Mendoza, cuartel 27	Mendoza	Argentina	1814	AHP,:792; IGHL 3:73
Mendoza, cuartel de Lujan	Mendoza	Argentina	1814	AHP,:795; IGHL 3:74
Mendoza, outskirts (2)	Mendoza	Argentina	1823	AHP,:838; IGHL 4:49
Mendoza, outskirts (5)	Mendoza	Argentina	1823	AHP,:834; IGHL 4:48
Mendoza, outskirts (9)	Mendoza	Argentina	1823	AHP,:822; IGHL 4:47
Mendoza, outskirts (14)	Mendoza	Argentina	1823	AHP,:819; IGHL 4:46
Mendoza, outskirts (16)	Mendoza	Argentina	1823	AHP,:826; IGHL 4:47
Mendoza, outskirts (19)	Mendoza	Argentina	1823	AHP,:831; IGHL 4:48
Mendoza, outskirts (20)	Mendoza	Argentina	1823	AHP,:827; IGHL 4:47
Mendoza, outskirts (27)	Mendoza	Argentina	1823	AHP,:837; IGHL 4:48
Mendoza, outskirts (30)	Mendoza	Argentina	1823	AHP,:824; IGHL 4:47
Mendoza, outskirts (33)	Mendoza	Argentina	1823	AHP,:830; IGHL 4:48
Mendoza, rural, cuartel 25	Mendoza	Argentina	1823	AHP,:829; IGHL 4:47
Monte Caseros (partido)	Mendoza	Argentina	1855	AHP,:844; IGHL 4:49
Moyano (partido)	Mendoza	Argentina	1855	AHP,:844; IGHL 4:50
N. Constitucion (partido)	Mendoza	Argentina	1855	AHP,:844; IGHL 4:50
N. Independencia (partido)	Mendoza	Argentina	1855	AHP,:844; IGHL 4:50
N. de San Isidro (partido)	Mendoza	Argentina	1855	AHP,:844; IGHL 4:50
Pasaje de la Ramada	Mendoza	Argentina	1810	AHP,:780; IGHL 2:68
Plumerillo	Mendoza	Argentina	1810	AHP,:777; IGHL 2:68
Reduccion (partido)	Mendoza	Argentina	1855	AHP,:844; IGHL 4:50
Ríobamba (partido)	Mendoza	Argentina	1855	AHP,:844; IGHL 4:50
Rivadavia	Mendoza	Argentina	1855	AHP,:844; IGHL 4:49
Rodeo del Retamo	Mendoza	Argentina	1810	AHP,:778; IGHL 2:68
S. Constitución (partido)	Mendoza	Argentina	1855	AHP,:844; IGHL 4:50

Locality	Province	Country	Year(s)	Reference
S. Independencia (partido)	Mendoza	Argentina	1855	AHP,:844; IGHL 4:50
S. de San Isidro (partido)	Mendoza	Argentina	1855	AHP,:844; IGHL 4:50
San Carlos, cuartel 3	Mendoza	Argentina	1859	AHP,:850; IGHL 4:50
San Martín	Mendoza	Argentina	1855	AHP,:844; IGHL 4:49
San Miguel, cuartel 10	Mendoza	Argentina	1814	AHP,:783; IGHL 2:69
San Rafael	Mendoza	Argentina	1855	AHP,:846; IGHL 4:50
San Rafael	Mendoza	Argentina	1852	AHP,:843; IGHL 4:49
San Rafael (Indians)	Mendoza	Argentina	1852	AHP,:842; IGHL 4:49
San Vicente, cuartel 28	Mendoza	Argentina	1814	AHP,:788; IGHL 3:73
Santa Rosa	Mendoza	Argentina	1855	AHP,:844; IGHL 4:49
Santa Rosa (partido)	Mendoza	Argentina	1855	AHP,:844; IGHL 4:50
Uspallata (partido)	Mendoza	Argentina	1810	AHP,:779; IGHL 2:68
V. de San Martín (partido)	Mendoza	Argentina	1855	AHP,:844; IGHL 4:49
Valle Hermoso (partido)	Mendoza	Argentina	1855	AHP,:844; IGHL 4:50
Valle Hermoso S. (partido)	Mendoza	Argentina	1855	AHP,:844; IGHL 4:50
Valle de Huco	Mendoza	Argentina	1810	AHP,:781; IGHL 2:68
Valle de Uco	Mendoza	Argentina	1855	AHP,:848; IGHL 4:50
Villa La Paz (Dpto)	Mendoza	Argentina	1859	AHP,:852; IGHL 4:51
	Salta	Argentina	1588–1811	GHG 140 (AGN)
	Salta	Argentina	1785–1792	GHG 140 (AGN)
Santa Fe	Santa Fé	Argentina	1622	IAC 16:51-66
Famailla	Tucumán	Argentina	1711	?
Tucumán	Tucumán	Argentina	1607	ANH 15
Sacramento	Tucumán	Argentina	?	IAC 11:106-122

BOLIVIA

Locality	Province	Country	Year(s)	Reference
		Bolivia	1645–1686	GHG 140[17]
		Bolivia	1774–1788	GHG 140
	Misiones	Bolivia	1735–1802	GHG 140
	Misiones	Bolivia	1759–1800	GHG 140
	Misiones	Bolivia	1778–1807	GHG 140
	Cochabamba	Bolivia	1683	GHG 141
	Cochabamba	Bolivia	1714–1770	GHG 141
	Cochabamba	Bolivia	1733–1738	GHG 141
	Cochabamba	Bolivia	1771–1786	GHG 141
Arani	Cochabamba	Bolivia	1783–1820	1157904
Arque	Cochabamba	Bolivia	1787–1792	GHG 141
Arque	Cochabamba	Bolivia	1794–1797	GHG 142
Arque	Cochabamba	Bolivia	1804–1808	GHG 142
Ayopaya	Cochabamba	Bolivia	1792	GHG 142
Ayopaya	Cochabamba	Bolivia	1797–1799	GHG 142
Ayopaya	Cochabamba	Bolivia	1804–1808	GHG 142
Cliza	Cochabamba	Bolivia	1792	GHG 142
Cliza	Cochabamba	Bolivia	1794–1797	GHG 142
Cliza	Cochabamba	Bolivia	1800–1803	GHG 142
Cochabamba	Cochabamba	Bolivia	1787–1792	GHG 141
Cochabamba	Cochabamba	Bolivia	1792	GHG 142
Cochabamba	Cochabamba	Bolivia	1794–1797	GHG 142
Cochabamba	Cochabamba	Bolivia	1800–1803	GHG 142
Mizque	Cochabamba	Bolivia	1792	GHG 142
Mizque	Cochabamba	Bolivia	1797–1799	GHG 142
Mizque	Cochabamba	Bolivia	1804–1808	GHG 142
Pacca	Cochabamba	Bolivia	1787	GHG 141
Punata	Cochabamba	Bolivia	1785	1157870
Sacaba	Cochabamba	Bolivia	1787	GHG 141
Sacaba	Cochabamba	Bolivia	1797–1799	GHG 142
Sacaba	Cochabamba	Bolivia	1804–1808	GHG 142
Tapacari	Cochabamba	Bolivia	1618–1619	GHG 141
Tapacari	Cochabamba	Bolivia	1787	GHG 141

---

[17] All of the GHC references in this section of Bolivia refer to records which are housed in the Archivo General de la Nación, Buenos Aires. At one time the part of Bolivia covered by these censuses was part of the Viceroyalty of Río de la Plata; consequently the records are in Buenos Aires, former capital of the Viceroyalty.

Locality	Province	Country	Year(s)	Reference
Tapacari	Cochabamba	Bolivia	1792	GHG 142
Tapacari	Cochabamba	Bolivia	1797–1799	GHG 142
Tapacari	Cochabamba	Bolivia	1804–1808	GHG 142
Valle Grande	Cochabamba	Bolivia	1787–1792	GHG 141
Valle Grande	Cochabamba	Bolivia	1792	GHG 142
Valle Grande	Cochabamba	Bolivia	1797–1799	GHG 142
Valle Grande	Cochabamba	Bolivia	1804–1808	GHG 142
	La Paz	Bolivia	1579–1684	GHG 140
	La Paz	Bolivia	1602–1705	GHG 140
	La Paz	Bolivia	1681–1685	GHG 140
	La Paz	Bolivia	1720–1726	GHG 140
	La Paz	Bolivia	1721–1724	GHG 140
	La Paz	Bolivia	1751	GHG 140
	La Paz	Bolivia	1751–1752	GHG 140
	La Paz	Bolivia	1760–1761	GHG 140
	La Paz	Bolivia	1770	GHG 140
Caupolicán	La Paz	Bolivia	1786–1788	GHG 141
Caupolicán	La Paz	Bolivia	1792–1794	GHG 141
Caupolicán	La Paz	Bolivia	1802–1803	GHG 141
Chulumani	La Paz	Bolivia	1784–1792	GHG 140
Chulumani	La Paz	Bolivia	1786	GHG 140
Chulumani	La Paz	Bolivia	1797–1798	GHG 141
Chulumani	La Paz	Bolivia	1802–1803	GHG 141
Chulumani Indians	La Paz	Bolivia	1771–1780	GHG 140
Chuma	La Paz	Bolivia	1714	UMSA:63
La Paz	La Paz	Bolivia	1580–1620	GHG 140
La Paz	La Paz	Bolivia	1784–1792	GHG 140
La Paz	La Paz	Bolivia	1786	GHG 140
La Paz	La Paz	Bolivia	1786–1788	GHG 141
La Paz	La Paz	Bolivia	1792	GHG 141
La Paz	La Paz	Bolivia	1797	GHG 141
La Paz	La Paz	Bolivia	1797–1798	GHG 141
La Paz	La Paz	Bolivia	1804–1807	GHG 141
La Paz (cuarteles 1,2,5,8)	La Paz	Bolivia	1823–1824	UMSA:277
Larecaja	La Paz	Bolivia	1786–1788	GHG 141
Larecaja	La Paz	Bolivia	1792	GHG 141
Larecaja	La Paz	Bolivia	1797	GHG 141
Larecaja	La Paz	Bolivia	1804–1807	GHG 141
Larecaja	La Paz	Bolivia	1786	GHG 140
Omasuyos	La Paz	Bolivia	1780	GHG 140
Omasuyos	La Paz	Bolivia	1786	GHG 140
Omasuyos	La Paz	Bolivia	1792–1794	GHG 141
Omasuyos	La Paz	Bolivia	1797	GHG 141
Omasuyos	La Paz	Bolivia	1803	GHG 141

Locality	Province	Country	Year(s)	Reference
Pacajes	La Paz	Bolivia	1767	GHG 141
Pacajes	La Paz	Bolivia	1786	GHG 140
Pacajes	La Paz	Bolivia	1792	GHG 141
Pacajes	La Paz	Bolivia	1797–1798	GHG 141
Pacajes	La Paz	Bolivia	1802–1803	GHG 141
Pacajes	La Paz	Bolivia	1804–1807	GHG 141
Sicasica	La Paz	Bolivia	1580–1620	GHG 140
Sicasica	La Paz	Bolivia	1786	GHG 140
Sicasica	La Paz	Bolivia	1786–1788	GHG 141
Sicasica	La Paz	Bolivia	1792	GHG 141
Sicasica	La Paz	Bolivia	1797	GHG 141
Sicasica	La Paz	Bolivia	1802–1803	GHG 141
Andamarca	La Plata	Bolivia	1796–1806	GHG 142
Carabaya	La Plata	Bolivia	1770–1779	GHG 142
Carangas	La Plata	Bolivia	1683	GHG 142
Carangas	La Plata	Bolivia	1720–1725	GHG 142
Carangas	La Plata	Bolivia	1770–1779	GHG 142
Carangas	La Plata	Bolivia	1786–1787	GHG 142
Carangas	La Plata	Bolivia	1796–1806	GHG 142
Challacollo	La Plata	Bolivia	1770–1779	GHG 142
Challapata	La Plata	Bolivia	1770–1779	GHG 142
Cinti	La Plata	Bolivia	1786–1787	GHG 142
Cinti	La Plata	Bolivia	1793–1795	GHG 142
Cinti	La Plata	Bolivia	1796–1806	GHG 142
Condocondo	La Plata	Bolivia	1770–1779	GHG 142
Guari	La Plata	Bolivia	1770–1779	GHG 142
La Plata	La Plata	Bolivia	1589–1683	GHG 142
La Plata	La Plata	Bolivia	1596–1684	GHG 142
La Plata	La Plata	Bolivia	1616–1725	GHG 142
La Plata	La Plata	Bolivia	1683	GHG 142
La Plata	La Plata	Bolivia	1720–1725	GHG 142
Paria	La Plata	Bolivia	1616–1725	GHG 142
Paria	La Plata	Bolivia	1725–1754	GHG 142
Paria	La Plata	Bolivia	1764–1770	GHG 142
Paria	La Plata	Bolivia	1770–1779	GHG 142
Paria	La Plata	Bolivia	1793–1795	GHG 142
Paspaya	La Plata	Bolivia	1764–1770	GHG 142
Paspaya	La Plata	Bolivia	1786–1787	GHG 142
Paspaya	La Plata	Bolivia	1793–1795	GHG 142
Paspaya	La Plata	Bolivia	1725–1754	GHG 142
Pilaya	La Plata	Bolivia	1725–1754	GHG 142
Pilaya	La Plata	Bolivia	1764–1770	GHG 142
Pilaya	La Plata	Bolivia	1770–1779	GHG 142
Pilaya	La Plata	Bolivia	1786–1787	GHG 142
Pilaya	La Plata	Bolivia	1793–1795	GHG 142

Locality	Province	Country	Year(s)	Reference
Pomabamba	La Plata	Bolivia	1770–1779	GHG 142
Pomabamba	La Plata	Bolivia	1786	GHG 142
Pomabamba	La Plata	Bolivia	1807	GHG 142
Poopo	La Plata	Bolivia	1807	GHG 142
Tomina	La Plata	Bolivia	1725–1754	GHG 142
Tomina	La Plata	Bolivia	1770–1779	GHG 142
Tomina	La Plata	Bolivia	1786	GHG 142
Tomina	La Plata	Bolivia	1793–1795	GHG 142
Tomina	La Plata	Bolivia	1807	GHG 142
Yamparaes	La Plata	Bolivia	1596–1684	GHG 142
Yamparaes	La Plata	Bolivia	1720–1725	GHG 142
Yamparaes	La Plata	Bolivia	1770–1779	GHG 142
Yamparaes	La Plata	Bolivia	1786	GHG 142
	Mizque	Bolivia	1733–1738	GHG 141
	Mizque	Bolivia	1771–1786	GHG 141
	Oruro	Bolivia	1604–1786	GHG 140
Atacama	Potosí	Bolivia	1787–1789	GHG 143
Atacama	Potosí	Bolivia	1791–1792	GHG 143
Atacama	Potosí	Bolivia	1797–1798	GHG 143
Atacama	Potosí	Bolivia	1804	GHG 143
Chayanta	Potosí	Bolivia	1606–1612	GHG 143
Chayanta	Potosí	Bolivia	1612–1619	GHG 143
Chayanta	Potosí	Bolivia	1612–1686	GHG 143
Chayanta	Potosí	Bolivia	1670–1694	GHG 143
Chayanta	Potosí	Bolivia	1725–1726	GHG 143
Chayanta	Potosí	Bolivia	1743–1756	GHG 143
Chayanta	Potosí	Bolivia	1764–1766	GHG 143
Chayanta	Potosí	Bolivia	1773–1784	GHG 143
Chayanta	Potosí	Bolivia	1781–1786	GHG 143
Chayanta	Potosí	Bolivia	1786–1787	GHG 143
Chayanta	Potosí	Bolivia	1787–1789	GHG 143
Chayanta	Potosí	Bolivia	1792–1793	GHG 143
Chayanta	Potosí	Bolivia	1797–1798	GHG 143
Chayanta	Potosí	Bolivia	1804–1805	GHG 143
Chichas	Potosí	Bolivia	1670–1694	GHG 143
Chichas	Potosí	Bolivia	1723–1726	GHG 143
Chichas	Potosí	Bolivia	1764–1766	GHG 143
Chichas	Potosí	Bolivia	1786–1787	GHG 143
Chichas	Potosí	Bolivia	1791–1792	GHG 143
Chichas	Potosí	Bolivia	1797–1798	GHG 143
Chichas	Potosí	Bolivia	1804	GHG 143
Lipes	Potosí	Bolivia	1602–1684	GHG 142
Lipes	Potosí	Bolivia	1791–1792	GHG 143
Lipes	Potosí	Bolivia	1797–1798	GHG 143
Lipes	Potosí	Bolivia	1804	GHG 143

Locality	Province	Country	Year(s)	Reference
Moscari	Potosí	Bolivia	1791–1792	GHG 143
Porco	Potosí	Bolivia	1670–1694	GHG 143
Porco	Potosí	Bolivia	1701–1712	GHG 143
Porco	Potosí	Bolivia	1712–1713	GHG 143
Porco	Potosí	Bolivia	1723–1726	GHG 143
Porco	Potosí	Bolivia	1729–1730	GHG 143
Porco	Potosí	Bolivia	1729–1735	GHG 143
Porco	Potosí	Bolivia	1743–1756	GHG 143
Porco	Potosí	Bolivia	1764–1766	GHG 143
Porco	Potosí	Bolivia	1781–1786	GHG 143
Porco	Potosí	Bolivia	1786–1787	GHG 143
Porco	Potosí	Bolivia	1792–1793	GHG 143
Porco	Potosí	Bolivia	1799	GHG 143
Porco	Potosí	Bolivia	1804–1805	GHG 143
Potosí	Potosí	Bolivia	1575–1612	GHG 142
Potosí	Potosí	Bolivia	1781–1786	GHG 143
Potosí	Potosí	Bolivia	1787–1789	GHG 143
Tarija	Potosí	Bolivia	1670–1694	GHG 143
Tarija	Potosí	Bolivia	1725–1726	GHG 143
Tarija	Potosí	Bolivia	1763–1765	GHG 143
Tarija	Potosí	Bolivia	1764–1766	GHG 143
Tarija	Potosí	Bolivia	1787–1789	GHG 143
Tarija	Potosí	Bolivia	1792–1793	GHG 143
Tarija	Potosí	Bolivia	1804	GHG 143
Santa Cruz de la Sierra	Santa Cruz	Bolivia	1787	GHG 141
Santa Cruz de la Sierra	Santa Cruz	Bolivia	1800–1803	GHG 142
Santa Cruz de la Sierra	Santa Cruz	Bolivia	1804–1808	GHG 142

CHILE

Locality	Province	Country	Year(s)	Reference
		Chile	1777–1778	1162403-1162405
Guechullami	?	Chile	1579	ACH 62:52-107
San José Logrono	?	Chile	1790	AN, FV:451:378-448
Aconcagua	Aconcagua	Chile	1813	AN
La Ligua	Aconcagua	Chile	1813	AN
Los Andes	Aconcagua	Chile	1788	1410431:2
Los Andes	Aconcagua	Chile	1813	AN
Petorca	Aconcagua	Chile	1788	1410431:2
Petorca	Aconcagua	Chile	1813	AN
Petorca	Aconcagua	Chile	1815–1816	1410431:2
Putaendo	Aconcagua	Chile	?	AN, FV:450
Putaendo	Aconcagua	Chile	1788	1410431:2
San Felipe	Aconcagua	Chile	1787	AN, FV:450
Teno	Aconcagua	Chile	1784	1410432:2
Isla de Laja	Arauco	Chile	1813	AN
	Arica	Chile	1698	AHP 29-30:12[18]
	Atacama	Chile	1698	AHP 29-30:12
Copiapó	Atacama	Chile	1788	1410431:2
Copiapó	Atacama	Chile	1813	AN
Huasco	Atacama	Chile	1778	1162405
Huasco	Atacama	Chile	1779	AN, FV:458
Huasco	Atacama	Chile	1813	AN
S. Fco. de la Selva	Atacama	Chile	1779	AN, FV:450
Castro	Chiloé	Chile	1784	AN
Chacao	Chiloé	Chile	1784	AN
	Colchagua	Chile	1786	AN, FV:452
Barriales	Colchagua	Chile	1786	AN, FV:452:53-56
Chimbarongo	Colchagua	Chile	1778	1162403
Chimbarongo	Colchagua	Chile	1784	1410432:2
Chimbarongo	Colchagua	Chile	1786	AN, FV:696
Colchagua	Colchagua	Chile	1777	1410432:1
Colchagua	Colchagua	Chile	1778	1162403
Colchagua	Colchagua	Chile	1813	AN
Cuenca	Colchagua	Chile	1786	AN, FV:452:49-52
Nancagua	Colchagua	Chile	1778	1162403

---

[18] Archivo Administrative e Histórico de la Provincia de Mendoza, Epoca Colonial [Colonial Period], Sección Gobierno [Gobierno Section], Indios [Indians], Bundle or *Carpeta* 29–30, document 12 (as an example of the references noted).

Locality	Province	Country	Year(s)	Reference
Nancagua	Colchagua	Chile	1784	1410432:2
Nancagua	Colchagua	Chile	1786	AN, FV:696
Quilicura	Colchagua	Chile	1788	1410431:3
San Fernando	Colchagua	Chile	1778	1162403
San Fernando	Colchagua	Chile	1786	AN, FV:452:28-48
San Roque de Roma	Colchagua	Chile	1786	AN, FV:452:49-52
Talcanegua	Colchagua	Chile	1786	AN, FV:452:49-52
	Concepción	Chile	1791	AN
Concepción	Concepción	Chile	1812	AN
Concepción	Concepción	Chile	1813	AN
Rere	Concepción	Chile	1813	AN
Andacolla	Coquimbo	Chile	1778	1162405
Combarbala	Coquimbo	Chile	1778	1162405
La Serena	Coquimbo	Chile	1813	AN
Limari	Coquimbo	Chile	1778	1162405
San Ildefonso, Elqui	Coquimbo	Chile	1778	1162405
San Joseph	Coquimbo	Chile	1778	1162405
Serena (La)	Coquimbo	Chile	1778	1162405
Sotaqui	Coquimbo	Chile	1778	1162405
Curicó	Curicó	Chile	1777	1410432:1
Curicó	Curicó	Chile	1778	1162405
Curicó	Curicó	Chile	1788	AN, FV:452:204-298
Curicó	Curicó	Chile	1813	AN
Lampa	Lampa	Chile	1788	1410431:3
Linares	Linares	Chile	1813	AN
Loncomilla	Linares	Chile	1579	ACH 62:52-107
Parral	Linares	Chile	1813	AN
Calbuco	Llanquihue	Chile	1784	AN
Cauquenes	Maule	Chile	1813	AN
Maule	Maule	Chile	1777	1410432:1
Paredones	Maule	Chile	1778	1162403
Rauquen	Maule	Chile	1778	1162405
San Agustín, Talca	Maule	Chile	1778	1162405
Vichuquén	Maule	Chile	1579	ACH 62:52-107
Vichuquén	Maule	Chile	1778	1162405
	Melipilla	Chile	1787	AN, FV:451:295-375
Chillán	Ñublé	Chile	1813	AN
San Carlos	Ñublé	Chile	1813	AN
	O'Higgins	Chile	1786	AN, FV:452
	O'Higgins	Chile	1788	AN, FV:451:128-293
Apaltas	O'Higgins	Chile	1786	AN, FV:452:72-81
Chanqueahue	O'Higgins	Chile	1786	AN, FV:452:72-81
Malloa	O'Higgins	Chile	1786	AN, FV:452:57-58
Olivar	O'Higgins	Chile	1787	AN, FV:452:82-87
Pelequén	O'Higgins	Chile	1786	AN, FV:452:59-68

Locality	Province	Country	Year(s)	Reference
Rancagua	O'Higgins	Chile	1788	1410431:3
Rancagua	O'Higgins	Chile	1813	AN
Osorno	Osorno	Chile	1813	AN
	Santiago	Chile	1791	AN
Catedral	Santiago	Chile	1778	1162405
Chualoco	Santiago	Chile	1579	ACH 62:52-107
Colina	Santiago	Chile	1778	1162405
Curacavi	Santiago	Chile	?	REH 4-5:113-60
Francisco de Borja	Santiago	Chile	1778	1162405
Maipó	Santiago	Chile	1788	1410431:3
Melipilla	Santiago	Chile	1788	1410431:3
Melipilla	Santiago	Chile	1813	AN
Niltonquigue	Santiago	Chile	1579	ACH 62:52-107
Zuñoa	Santiago	Chile	1778	1162405
Puchacay	Santiago	Chile	1813	AN
Renca (doctrina)	Santiago	Chile	1778	1162405
San Isidro	Santiago	Chile	1778	1162405
Santa Ana	Santiago	Chile	1778	1162405
Santiago (indios)	Santiago	Chile	1698	AHP 29-30:12[19]
Tango (doctrina)	Santiago	Chile	1778	1162405
	Talca	Chile	1835	AN, Contaduría
Almendral	Talca	Chile	1784	1410432:2
Almendral	Talca	Chile	1786	AN, FV:696
Boldomahvida	Talca	Chile	1784	1410432:2
Boldomahvida	Talca	Chile	1786	AN, FV:696
Curimón	Talca	Chile	1788	1410431:2
Itata	Talca	Chile	1813	AN
Lontué	Talca	Chile	1778	1162405
Lontué	Talca	Chile	1784	1410432:2
Lontué	Talca	Chile	1787	AN, FV:696
Mesclaro	Talca	Chile	1786	AN, FV:452:63-71
Palmas	Talca	Chile	1784	1410432:2
Palmas	Talca	Chile	1786	AN, FV:696
Pencahue (Penquehue)	Talca	Chile	1786	AN, FV:452:61-62
Pencahue (Penquehue)	Talca	Chile	1788	1410431:2
Popeta	Talca	Chile	1786	AN, FV:452:63-71
Talca	Talca	Chile	1777	1410432:1
Talca	Talca	Chile	1788	AN, FV:452:299-356
Talca	Talca	Chile	1813	AN
Teno	Talca	Chile	1786	AN, FV:696
	Tarapacá	Chile	1698	AHP 29-30:12[20]

[19] *Ibid.*
[20] *Ibid.*

Locality	Province	Country	Year(s)	Reference
Coscaya	Tarapacá	Chile	1845	RAN 4-5:137
Guavina	Tarapacá	Chile	1845	RAN 4-5:136-37
Huantajaya	Tarapacá	Chile	1845	RAN 4-5:132-34
Laonsana	Tarapacá	Chile	1845	RAN 4-5:136
Limaccina	Tarapacá	Chile	1845	RAN 4-5:143-44
Macaya	Tarapacá	Chile	1845	RAN 4-5:140-41
Mamina	Tarapacá	Chile	1845	RAN 4-5:138-39
Mocha	Tarapacá	Chile	1845	RAN 4-5:142-43
Noasa	Tarapacá	Chile	1845	RAN 4-5:139
Pica	Tarapacá	Chile	1845	RAN 4-5:145-53
Santa Rosa	Tarapacá	Chile	1845	RAN 4-5:129-32
Sibaya	Tarapacá	Chile	1845	RAN 4-5:141-42
Tarapacá	Tarapacá	Chile	1845	RAN 4-5:117-28
Valdivia	Valdivia	Chile	1787	AN, FV:451:449-484
Valdivia	Valdivia	Chile	1813	AN
Llongocura (doctrina)	Valparaíso	Chile	1778	1162405
N. Señora de Puerto Claro	Valparaíso	Chile	1778	1162405
Quillota	Valparaíso	Chile	1813	AN
Valparaíso	Valparaíso	Chile	1777	AN, FV:450
Valparaíso	Valperaíso	Chile	1788	1410431:2
Valparaíso	Valparaíso	Chile	1813	AN

COLOMBIA

Locality	Province	Country	Year(s)	Reference
		Colombia[21]	1812	GHG 173[22]
		Colombia[23]	1825	GHG 173
		Colombia[24]	1835	GHG 173
		Colombia[25]	1843	GHG 173
		Colombia[26]	1851	GHG 173
		Colombia[27]	1905	Cent. Nac. de Estadística
		Colombia[28]	1912	Cent. Nac. de Estadística
		Colombia[29]	1920	Cent. Nac. de Estadística
Isla Bocachicha	?	Colombia	1777	1162417:4
Mahates	?	Colombia	1777	1162417:4
Sativa	?	Colombia	1777	1162417:4
Tacaloa	?	Colombia	1777	1162417:4
Tacamocho	?	Colombia	1777	1162417:4
	Antioquia	Colombia	1784	GHG 172
	Antioquia	Colombia	1790	GHG 172
	Antioquia	Colombia	1798	GHG 172
Buritica	Antioquia	Colombia	1804	GHG 173
Canasgordas	Antioquia	Colombia	1804	GHG 173
Candelaria del Yucal	Antioquia	Colombia	1745	GHG 170
Cuiloto	Antioquia	Colombia	1799	GHG 172
El Peñón	Antioquia	Colombia	1804	GHG 173
Estrella	Antioquia	Colombia	1804	GHG 173
Medellín	Antioquia	Colombia	1786–1787	AHA 1:340:6503
Rosario[30]	Antioquia	Colombia	1745	GHG 170
S.Antonio de Pereira	Antioquia	Colombia	1804	GHG 173
Sabanalarga	Antioquia	Colombia	1804	GHG 173
Sopetran	Antioquia	Colombia	1804	GHG 173
Tenerife	Antioquia	Colombia	1804	GHG 173
Valledupar	Antioquia	Colombia	1804	GHG 173

---

[21] First National Census of Colombia.
[22] All of the censuses referenced as GHG are located in Archivo Nacional in Bogotá.
[23] Second National Census of Colombia.
[24] Third National Census of Colombia.
[25] Fourth National Census of Colombia.
[26] Fifth National Census of Colombia.
[27] Sixth National Census of Colombia.
[28] Seventh National Census of Colombia.
[29] Eighth National Census of Colombia.
[30] Rosario del Buen Retiro.

Locality	Province	Country	Year(s)	Reference
Zabaletas	Antioquia	Colombia	1804	GHG 173
Zaragoza	Antioquia	Colombia	1794	GHG 172
Soata	Boyacá	Colombia	1777	1162417:4
Banco	Cartagena	Colombia	1751	GHG 171
Barrancas[31]	Cartagena	Colombia	1751	GHG 170
Barranquilla	Cartagena	Colombia	1778	GHG 171
Cartagena[32]	Cartagena	Colombia	1777	1162416:17
Cartagena[33]	Cartagena	Colombia	1777	1162416:18
Cartagena[34]	Cartagena	Colombia	1777	1162417:1
Cartagena[35]	Cartagena	Colombia	1777	1162417:1
Ceñón	Cartagena	Colombia	1751	GHG 171
Chillao (S.Juan)	Cartagena	Colombia	1751	GHG 171
El Palmar[36]	Cartagena	Colombia	1777	1162416:16
Isla de San Andrés	Cartagena	Colombia	1793	GHG 172
Ladera de S.Fernando	Cartagena	Colombia	1751	GHG 171
Menchiquejo (S.José)	Cartagena	Colombia	1751	GHG 171
Menchiquejo[37]	Cartagena	Colombia	1751	GHG 171
Real de la Cruz	Cartagena	Colombia	1777	1162416:16
S.Antonio de Padua	Cartagena	Colombia	1777	1162416:16
S.Fernando[38]	Cartagena	Colombia	1751	GHG 171
S.Francisco Javier	Cartagena	Colombia	1777	1162416:16
S.Joseph[39]	Cartagena	Colombia	1777	1162416:16
S.Luis[40]	Cartagena	Colombia	1777	1162416:16
S.Sebastián de Rábago	Cartagena	Colombia	1751	GHG 170
Sabana Grande[41]	Cartagena	Colombia	1777	1162416:16
Sabana Larga	Cartagena	Colombia	1777	1162416:16
Santa Ana[42]	Cartagena	Colombia	1777	1162416:16
Santa Ana[43]	Cartagena	Colombia	1751	GHG 170
Santa Bárbara de Pinto	Cartagena	Colombia	1751	GHG 170
Santa Catalina	Cartagena	Colombia	1777	1162416:16
Santa Rosa (Altas)	Cartagena	Colombia	1777	1162416:16
Santiago	Cartagena	Colombia	1751	GHG 171

[31] Nuestra Señora del Carmen de Barrancas.
[32] Cartagena: Barrio Gigimani.
[33] Cartagena: La Merced.
[34] Cartagena: San Sebastián.
[35] Cartagena: Santo Toribio.
[36] El Palmar de la Candelaria.
[37] San Sebastián de Menchiquejo.
[38] San Fernando de Caravajal.
[39] San Joseph de Puerto Alegre.
[40] San Luis de Pueblo Nuevo.
[41] Santa Rita de Sabana Grande.
[42] Santa Ana de Baranoa.
[43] Santa Ana de Buena Vista.

Locality	Province	Country	Year(s)	Reference
Santo Tomás	Cartagena	Colombia	1777	1162416:16
Tacasoluma	Cartagena	Colombia	1777	1162416:16
Tamalamequito[44]	Cartagena	Colombia	1751	GHG 171
Tentón	Cartagena	Colombia	1780	GHG 172
	Casanare	Colombia	1804	GHG 173
	Chocó	Colombia	1778	GHG 171
	Chocó	Colombia	1779	GHG 172
	Chocó	Colombia	1781	GHG 172
	Chocó	Colombia	1782	GHG 172
Citará	Chocó	Colombia	1783	GHG 172
Citará	Chocó	Colombia	1803	GHG 172
Notiva	Chocó	Colombia	1803	GHG 172
Ambalema	Cundinamarca	Colombia	1669	GHG 170
Ambalema	Cundinamarca	Colombia	1720	GHG 170
Bogotá	Cundinamarca	Colombia	1595	GHG 170
Bogotá	Cundinamarca	Colombia	1718	GHG 170
Chanchón	Cundinamarca	Colombia	1690	GHG 170
Cucunuba	Cundinamarca	Colombia	1690	GHG 170
Espiritu Santo	Cundinamarca	Colombia	1586	GHG 170
Moniquira	Cundinamarca	Colombia	1697	GHG 170
Pare	Cundinamarca	Colombia	1690	GHG 170
S.Sebastián de Madrid	Cundinamarca	Colombia	1776	GHG 171
Sorcota	Cundinamarca	Colombia	1697	GHG 170
Ubate	Cundinamarca	Colombia	1708	GHG 170
	Llanos	Colombia	1804	GHG 173
Río Hacha	Magdalena	Colombia	1777	1162417:3
Neiva	Neiva	Colombia	1772	GHG 171
Neiva	Neiva	Colombia	1779	GHG 172
Otaz	Neiva	Colombia	1778	GHG 171
S.Juan del Retiro	Neiva	Colombia	1770	GHG 171
Darién	Panamá	Colombia	1787	GHG 172
Darién	Panamá	Colombia	1789	GHG 172
Natá	Panamá	Colombia	1740	GHG 170
San Lucas	Panamá	Colombia	1740	GHG 170
Portobelo	Panamá	Colombia	1777	1162417:2
Veraguas	Panamá	Colombia	1756	AGI, AP:130
	Popayán	Colombia	1779	GHG 172
Caloto	Popayán	Colombia	1800	GHG 172
Caloto	Popayan	Colombia	1803	GHG 172
Caloto	Popayan	Colombia	1791	GHG 172

---

[44] Santa Bárbara Tamalamequito.

Locality	Province	Country	Year(s)	Reference
Cartago	Popayan	Colombia	1771	GHG 171
Ondulaga	Popayan	Colombia	1602	1389116
Pasto	Popayan	Colombia	1780	GHG 172
Popayan	Popayan	Colombia	1807	1389116
Quebralomo[45]	Popayan	Colombia	1771	GHG 171
Quelechas	Popayan	Colombia	1791	GHG 172
Quelechas	Popayan	Colombia	1800	GHG 172
	Río Hacha	Colombia	1778	GHG 171
Mamatoco	S.Marta	Colombia	1804	GHG 173
Masinga[46]	S.Marta	Colombia	1804	GHG 173
Santa Ana de Banda	S.Marta	Colombia	1804	GHG 172
Taganga	S.Marta	Colombia	1804	GHG 173
	Tunja	Colombia	1780	GHG 172
Baja	Tunja	Colombia	1778	GHG 171
Betas de Pamplona	Tunja	Colombia	1778	GHG 172
Betas de Pamplona	Tunja	Colombia	1779	GHG 172
Bucaramanga	Tunja	Colombia	1778	GHG 172
Cocata de Surata	Tunja	Colombia	1778	GHG 172
Cucuta[47]	Tunja	Colombia	1792	GHG 172
Cucuta (San José)	Tunja	Colombia	1792	GHG 172
Mérida	Tunja	Colombia	1586	GHG 170
Ocana	Tunja	Colombia	1804	GHG 173
Pedral	Tunja	Colombia	1778	GHG 172
Pedral	Tunja	Colombia	1779	GHG 172
Piedecuesta	Tunja	Colombia	1778	GHG 172
Piedecuesta	Tunja	Colombia	1779	GHG 172
Piedecuesta	Tunja	Colombia	1780	GHG 172
Puerto Botijas	Tunja	Colombia	1778	GHG 172
Puerto Botijas	Tunja	Colombia	1779	GHG 172
S.Cristóbal	Tunja	Colombia	1586	GHG 170
S.Juan de Girón	Tunja	Colombia	1778	GHG 172
S.Juan de Girón	Tunja	Colombia	1779	GHG 172
S.Juan de Girón	Tunja	Colombia	1780	GHG 172
S.Juan de Girón	Tunja	Colombia	1782	GHG 172
S.Juan de Girón	Tunja	Colombia	1782	GHG 172
S.Roque	Tunja	Colombia	1778	GHG 172
S.Roque	Tunja	Colombia	1779	GHG 172
S.Roque	Tunja	Colombia	1780	GHG 172
Salazar de las Palmas	Tunja	Colombia	1784	1162416:15
Vélez	Tunja	Colombia	1664	GHG 170

[45] San Sebastián de Quebralomo.
[46] Santa Cruz de Masinga.
[47] Nuestra Señora del Rosario de Cucuta.

COSTA RICA

Locality	Province	Country	Year(s)	Reference
Alajuela	Alajuela	Costa Rica	1793	?

CUBA

Locality	Province	Country	Year(s)	Reference
Various towns-undetermined		Cuba	?	GHG 186 (AN)

DOMINICAN REPUBLIC

Locality	Province	Country	Year(s)	Reference
		D.R.	1514	DEI, 74-248

ECUADOR

Locality	Province	Country	Year(s)	Reference
		Ecuador	1772–1793	1083258-1083264[48]
	Azuay	Ecuador	1776–1871	AN 1:21; 2:8; 3:14; 4:10
	Chimborazo	Ecuador	1827–1871	AN 8:12; 9:15; 10:8
Catacachi	Cotacachi	Ecuador	1871	1481727
Imantag	Cotacachi	Ecuador	1871	1481727
Intag	Cotacachi	Ecuador	1871	1481727
	Cotopaxi	Ecuador	1737–1861	AN 5:21; 6:14; 7:14
	Esmeraldas	Ecuador	1855–1871	AN 11:34
Atuntaqui	Esperanza	Ecuador	1871	1481726
Mira	Esperanza	Ecuador	1871	1481726
S. P. de Pisquer	Esperanza	Ecuador	1871	1481726
Salinas	Esperanza	Ecuador	1871	1481726
	Guayas	Ecuador	1846–1871	AN 12:13; 13:11; 14:9
Balzar	Guayas	Ecuador	1832	CAG 22:141-143
Guayaquil (Matriz)	Guayas	Ecuador	1832	CAG 22:25-87
Guayaquil	Guayas	Ecuador	1871	AN
Santa Lucía	Guayas	Ecuador	1832	CAG 22:135-140
Ambuqui	Ibarra	Ecuador	1871	1481726
Angochagua	Ibarra	Ecuador	1871	1481726
Caranqui	Ibarra	Ecuador	1871	1481726
Ibarra	Ibarra	Ecuador	1871	1481726
San Antonio	Ibarra	Ecuador	1871	1481726
San Pablo	Ibarra	Ecuador	1871	1481726
Urcuqui	Ibarra	Ecuador	1871	1481727
	Imbabura	Ecuador	1776–1871	AN 15:16; 16:13
Latacunga	Latacunga	Ecuador	1831	GHG 199 (MAQ)
	Loja	Ecuador	1869–1871	AN 19:18; 20:4
Amaluza	Loja	Ecuador	1861	1481727
Cariamanga	Loja	Ecuador	1861	1481728
Cariamanga	Loja	Ecuador	1871	1481730
Chuquiribamba	Loja	Ecuador	1861	1481728
Chuquiribamba	Loja	Ecuador	1871	1481730
El Cisne	Loja	Ecuador	1861	1481727
El Sagrario	Loja	Ecuador	1871	1481730
Gonzanama	Loja	Ecuador	1861	1481728
La Concepción	Loja	Ecuador	1871	1481730

[48] Censuses of Ecuador and Peru, microfilmed in Bogotá, Colombia by the Family History Library of Salt Lake City, Utah.

Locality	Province	Country	Year(s)	Reference
La Paz	Loja	Ecuador	1871	1481730
La Victoria	Loja	Ecuador	1871	1481730
Loja	Loja	Ecuador	1861	1481728
Loja	Loja	Ecuador	1871	1481730
Loja	Loja	Ecuador	1776	1481727
Loja	Loja	Ecuador	1839–1840	1481727
Malacatuso	Loja	Ecuador	1861	1481727
Matriz	Loja	Ecuador	1861	1481728
Paquishapa	Loja	Ecuador	1871	1481730
San Antonio	Loja	Ecuador	1861	1481729
San Juan del Valle	Loja	Ecuador	1871	1481730
San Pablo de Tenta	Loja	Ecuador	1871	1481730
San Pedro	Loja	Ecuador	1871	1481730
Santiago	Loja	Ecuador	1861	1481728
Saraguro	Loja	Ecuador	1861	1481727
Saraguro	Loja	Ecuador	1869	1481730
Valladolid	Loja	Ecuador	1871	1481730
Valle	Loja	Ecuador	1861	1481727
Vilcabamba	Loja	Ecuador	1861	1481728
Zaruma	Loja	Ecuador	1776	1481727
Zozoranga	Loja	Ecuador	1861	1481728
Zozoranga	Loja	Ecuador	1871	1481730
Zumba	Loja	Ecuador	1861	1481727
	Los Ríos	Ecuador	1861–1871	AN 21:15; 22:22; 23:18; 24:15
	Manabi	Ecuador	1861–1872	AN 25:20
Jordán	Otavalo	Ecuador	1871	1481726
	Pichincha	Ecuador	1779–1862	AN 26:9
Cuenca	Quito	Ecuador	1780	GHG 172 (AN)
Guayaquil	Quito	Ecuador	1790	GHG 172 (AN)
Quito	Quito	Ecuador	1783	GHG 172 (AN)
Quito	Quito	Ecuador	1831	GHG 199 (MAQ)
Quito	Quito	Ecuador	1833	GHG 198 (AN)
	Tungurahua	Ecuador	1779–1862	AN 27:15; 28:9
	Tungurahua	Ecuador	1861–1871	AN 29:12; 30:9; 31:8
Ambato	Tungurahua	Ecuador	1831	GHG 199 (MAQ)
Ambato	Tungurahua	Ecuador	1861	AN
Ambato	Tungurahua	Ecuador	1864	AN
Ambato	Tungurahua	Ecuador	1871	AN

In the Archivo Nacional de Ecuador (AN), Colección Empadronamiento (previously called Censos), there are thirty-two boxes of 451 expedientes covering the period 1776–1871. These have not been evaluated as to exact locations of each padrón, except as indicated by province in the analysis above.

FLORIDA

Locality	Province	Country	Year(s)	Reference
		Florida	1784–1820	GGS
		Florida	1792	AGI, Cuba
		Florida	1793	AGI, Cuba
		Florida	1812	AGI, Cuba
		Florida	1814	AGI, Cuba
Escambia River	?	Florida	1820	GGS
	Pensacola	Florida	1784	LGR 27:367
	Pensacola	Florida	1788	LGR 27:367
	Pensacola	Florida	1802	LGR 27:368
	Pensacola	Florida	1805	LGR 27:368
	Pensacola	Florida	1819	LGR 27:368
	Pensacola	Florida	1820	LGR 27:368
	S.Augustine	Florida	1783	1014120
	S.Augustine	Florida	1786	FHQ 18:11-31; 1014120
	S.Augustine	Florida	1789	AGI, Cuba
	S.Augustine[49]	Florida	1793	1014120
	S.Augustine	Florida	1805	LGR 27:368
	S.Augustine	Florida	1812	LGR 27:368
	S.Augustine[50]	Florida	1814	1014120
	West Florida	Florida	1805	LGR 27:368

NOTE: The censuses listed above in LGR are located at Loyola University, New Orleans, and at AGI, Seville.

---

[49] Indexed.
[50] Mosquito Territory.

37

GUATEMALA

The census records of Guatemala for 1778, 1880, 1893 and 1921 were used as scrap paper and no longer exist, nor were they preserved in any other format except for their statistical information. The 1940 census was burned.[51]

Locality	Province	Country	Year(s)	Reference
		Guatemala	15-19 C.	GHG 212
		Guatemala	1698–1746	746825:3
		Guatemala	1711	746867:5
		Guatemala	1713–1718	746827:5
		Guatemala	1721–1818	746829
		Guatemala	1732	746867
		Guatemala	1734–1768	746826
		Guatemala	1740–1741	747060:10
		Guatemala	1741	747058:1
		Guatemala	1749	747296:8
		Guatemala	1750–1811	746868:2-3
		Guatemala	1750–1751	748128:6
		Guatemala	1750	747058:16
		Guatemala	1751	748128:5
		Guatemala	1751–1752	748125:1-2
		Guatemala	1753–1759	748126
		Guatemala	1755	746865:20
		Guatemala	1756–1758	746869:2
		Guatemala	1759–1760	746870:1
		Guatemala	1759–1760	747058:17-18
		Guatemala	1768–1816	746827:1
		Guatemala	1768	747058:5
		Guatemala	1772	746870:2
		Guatemala	1778	746870:3
		Guatemala	1778–1782	747296:16
		Guatemala	1781–1791	747059:1
		Guatemala	1790–1811	746865:11
		Guatemala	1791–1820	748130:5
		Guatemala	1792	747296:11
		Guatemala	1794–1795	746865:21
		Guatemala	1797–1800	746865:5
		Guatemala	1801	746865:7
		Guatemala	1803	747296:10,18

[51] Personal investigations of Lyman D. Platt at the census office in Guatemala City.

Locality	Province	Country	Year(s)	Reference
		Guatemala	1807	748130:7
		Guatemala	1809	747296:19
		Guatemala	1811–1813	747296:21-23
		Guatemala	1813	748131-748132
		Guatemala	1813, 1821	747056:2
		Guatemala	1813, 1821	747057
		Guatemala	1813–1821	747059:10
		Guatemala	1814	746865:22
		Guatemala	1816–1818	746865:13
		Guatemala	1817–1818	746830
		Guatemala	1818	746865:14-15
		Guatemala	1821	748133
		Guatemala	1824–1836	746873
		Guatemala	1825	746871:3
		Guatemala	1887	747294-747295
	A.Verapaz	Guatemala	1818–1819	746871:2
Cahabón	A.Verapaz	Guatemala	1816–1817	746827:2
Cobán	A.Verapaz	Guatemala	1816	746870
Lanquín	A.Verapaz	Guatemala	1816	746827
San Cristóbal Verapaz	A.Verapaz	Guatemala	1741	746826
San Cristobal Verapaz	A.Verapaz	Guatemala	1816	746327
San Cristobal Verapaz	A.Verapaz	Guatemala	1821	748132
San Juan Chamelco	A.Verapaz	Guatemala	1740	746828
San Juan Chamelco	A.Verapaz	Guatemala	1762	763390
San Juan Chamelco	A.Verapaz	Guatemala	1762	773996
San Juan Chamelco	A.Verapaz	Guatemala	1765	748127
San Juan Chamelco	A.Verapaz	Guatemala	1815	746870
San Juan Chamelco	A.Verapaz	Guatemala	1816	746870
Santa Cruz Verapaz	A.Verapaz	Guatemala	1748	747061
Santa Cruz Verapaz	A.Verapaz	Guatemala	1821	748132
Tactic	A.Verapaz	Guatemala	1815–1817	746827
Tactic	A.Verapaz	Guatemala	1751	748125
Tamahu	A.Verapaz	Guatemala	1821	748132
Tucuru	A.Verapaz	Guatemala	1816	746827
Tucuru	A.Verapaz	Guatemala	1821	748133
	B.Verapaz	Guatemala	1700–1702	746827:4
	B.Verapaz	Guatemala	1748	746868:1
	B.Verapaz	Guatemala	1754–1756	746869:1
	B.Verapaz	Guatemala	1767–1768	746827:3
	B.Verapaz	Guatemala	1795–1797	746865:3
	B.Verapaz	Guatemala	1804–1816	746870:4
	B.Verapaz	Guatemala	1824	746821:2
	B.Verapaz	Guatemala	1824	746871:4
	B.Verapaz	Guatemala	1824–1825	746822
	B.Verapaz	Guatemala	1824–1825	746872:1

Locality	Province	Country	Year(s)	Reference
Cubulco	B.Verapaz	Guatemala	1732	746825
Cubulco	B.Verapaz	Guatemala	1762	746826
Cubulco	B.Verapaz	Guatemala	1767	746866
Cubulco	B.Verapaz	Guatemala	1813	748132
Cubulco	B.Verapaz	Guatemala	1815	746827
Cubulco	B.Verapaz	Guatemala	1816–1817	746827
El Chol	B.Verapaz	Guatemala	1778	748128
El Chol	B.Verapaz	Guatemala	1816	746827
El Chol	B.Verapaz	Guatemala	1820	748132
Granados	B.Verapaz	Guatemala	1825	746825
Rabinal	B.Verapaz	Guatemala	1813	748131
Rabinal	B.Verapaz	Guatemala	1816	746870
Salama	B.Verapaz	Guatemala	1711	746867
Salama	B.Verapaz	Guatemala	1762	746866
Salama	B.Verapaz	Guatemala	1762	763390
Salama	B.Verapaz	Guatemala	1762	773996
Salama	B.Verapaz	Guatemala	1803	747296
Salama	B.Verapaz	Guatemala	1821	748133
San Jerónimo	B.Verapaz	Guatemala	1821	748132
San Miguel Chicaj	B.Verapaz	Guatemala	1813	748131
San Miguel Chicaj	B.Verapaz	Guatemala	1815	746827
San Miguel Chicaj	B.Verapaz	Guatemala	1816	746827
	Chimaltenango	Guatemala	1673	747059:18
Comalapa	Chimaltenango	Guatemala	1636	747059
Comalapa	Chimaltenango	Guatemala	1718	746827
Comalapa	Chimaltenango	Guatemala	1735	747060:7
Comalapa	Chimaltenango	Guatemala	1821	748129
Chimaltenango	Chimaltenango	Guatemala	1673	747059
Chimaltenango	Chimaltenango	Guatemala	1778	741739
Patzicía	Chimaltenango	Guatemala	1813	748132
Patzún	Chimaltenango	Guatemala	1810	773999
Pochuta	Chimaltenango	Guatemala	1751	741889
Pochuta	Chimaltenango	Guatemala	1751	746868
San Andrés Itzapa	Chimaltenango	Guatemala	1752	746868
San Andrés Itzapa	Chimaltenango	Guatemala	1756	746869
San Martín Jilotepeque	Chimaltenango	Guatemala	1815	747059
San Martín Jilotepeque	Chimaltenango	Guatemala	1821	747059
Santa Cruz Balanya	Chimaltenango	Guatemala	1821	748129
Semetabaj	Chimaltenango	Guatemala	1768	746867
	Chiquimula	Guatemala	1767–1768	746827
	Chiquimula	Guatemala	1776	748128:3
	Chiquimula	Guatemala	1804–1816	746870:4
	Chiquimula	Guatemala	1824	746821:2
	Chiquimula	Guatemala	1824–1825	746822
Achuapas	Chiquimula	Guatemala	1826	746824

Locality	Province	Country	Year(s)	Reference
Anguiatu	Chiquimula	Guatemala	1813	748131
Anguiatu	Chiquimula	Guatemala	1825	746823
Azacualpa	Chiquimula	Guatemala	1902	737251
Camotán	Chiquimula	Guatemala	1746	748130
Camotán	Chiquimula	Guatemala	1750	741889
Camotán	Chiquimula	Guatemala	1816	746829
Camotán	Chiquimula	Guatemala	1818	773999
Camotán	Chiquimula	Guatemala	1824	746821
Chiquimula	Chiquimula	Guatemala	1743	747058:4
Chiquimula	Chiquimula	Guatemala	1745	747060
Chiquimula	Chiquimula	Guatemala	1749	748128
Chiquimula	Chiquimula	Guatemala	1749–1750	748124:1-2
Chiquimula	Chiquimula	Guatemala	1750	748124
Chiquimula	Chiquimula	Guatemala	1753	748130:4
Chiquimula	Chiquimula	Guatemala	1753	747058
Chiquimula	Chiquimula	Guatemala	1755	748130
Chiquimula	Chiquimula	Guatemala	1757	747296:7
Chiquimula	Chiquimula	Guatemala	1775–1776	748128:2
Chiquimula	Chiquimula	Guatemala	1781	741892
Chiquimula	Chiquimula	Guatemala	1813	748131
Chiquimula	Chiquimula	Guatemala	1817	746830
Chiquimula	Chiquimula	Guatemala	1820	763389
Chiquimula	Chiquimula	Guatemala	1825	746822-746823
Concepción	Chiquimula	Guatemala	1813	748131
Cubiletes	Chiquimula	Guatemala	1813	748131
Ermita	Chiquimula	Guatemala	1813	748131
Esquipulas	Chiquimula	Guatemala	1750	748124
Esquipulas	Chiquimula	Guatemala	1754	746868
Esquipulas	Chiquimula	Guatemala	1764	748127
Esquipulas	Chiquimula	Guatemala	1810	746865
Esquipulas	Chiquimula	Guatemala	1813	747059
Esquipulas	Chiquimula	Guatemala	1820	747059
Esquipulas	Chiquimula	Guatemala	1822	746821
Esquipulas	Chiquimula	Guatemala	1824	746821
Ipala	Chiquimula	Guatemala	1741	747060
Ipala	Chiquimula	Guatemala	1745	747060
Ipala	Chiquimula	Guatemala	1816	746829
Jocotán	Chiquimula	Guatemala	1750	741889
Jocotán	Chiquimula	Guatemala	1768–1775	748128
Jocotan	Chiquimula	Guatemala	1816–1817	746829
Jocotán	Chiquimula	Guatemala	1824	746821
Limones	Chiquimula	Guatemala	1825	746823
Quezaltepeque	Chiquimula	Guatemala	1741	746825
Quezaltepeque	Chiquimula	Guatemala	1768–1775	748128
Quezaltepeque	Chiquimula	Guatemala	1817	746829

Locality	Province	Country	Year(s)	Reference
Quezaltepeque	Chiquimula	Guatemala	1824	746821
Quezaltepeque	Chiquimula	Guatemala	1826	746823
San Esteban	Chiquimula	Guatemala	1817	748130
San Esteban	Chiquimula	Guatemala	1825	746822
San Jacinto	Chiquimula	Guatemala	1742	747060
San Jacinto	Chiquimula	Guatemala	1751	748124
San Jacinto	Chiquimula	Guatemala	1757	747296
San Jacinto	Chiquimula	Guatemala	1770–1776	748128
San Jacinto	Chiquimula	Guatemala	1817	746830
San Jacinto	Chiquimula	Guatemala	1824	746821
San Jacinto	Chiquimula	Guatemala	1826	746823
San José de la Rada	Chiquimula	Guatemala	1825	746825
San Juan Ermita	Chiquimula	Guatemala	1768–1775	748128
San Juan Ermita	Chiquimula	Guatemala	1816	746829
San Juan Ermita	Chiquimula	Guatemala	1824	746821
Santa Elena	Chiquimula	Guatemala	1754	741890
Santa Elena	Chiquimula	Guatemala	1768–1775	748128
Santa Elena	Chiquimula	Guatemala	1816	746827
Santa Elena	Chiquimula	Guatemala	1817	746830
Santa Elena	Chiquimula	Guatemala	1825	746822
Ticanlu	Chiquimula	Guatemala	1825	746822
Valeriano	Chiquimula	Guatemala	1813	748131
Acasaguastlan[52]	El Progreso	Guatemala	1700	747060
Acasaguastlan	El Progreso	Guatemala	1742	747060
Acasaguastlan	El Progreso	Guatemala	1750	748124
Acasaguastlan	El Progreso	Guatemala	1758	748126
Acasaguastlan	El Progreso	Guatemala	1825	746822
Acasaguastlan	El Progreso	Guatemala	1826	746824
Acasaguastlan[53]	El Progreso	Guatemala	1741–1742	747060
Acasaguastlan	El Progreso	Guatemala	1758	748126
Acasaguastlan	El Progreso	Guatemala	1817	746829
Acasaguastlan	El Progreso	Guatemala	1825	746823
Acasaguastlan	El Progreso	Guatemala	1826	746824
El Progreso	El Progreso	Guatemala	1813	748132
El Progreso	El Progreso	Guatemala	1824	746822
El Progreso	El Progreso	Guatemala	1826	746824
Magdalena	El Progreso	Guatemala	1750	748124
Magdalena	El Progreso	Guatemala	1826	746824
Morazán	El Progreso	Guatemala	1821	748133
Morazán	El Progreso	Guatemala	1826	746824
S. Antonio de la Paz	El Progreso	Guatemala	1813	748131
S. Clemente	El Progreso	Guatemala	1826	746824

---

[52] The following six entries are for San Agustín Acasaguastlán.
[53] The following five entries are for San Cristóbal Acasaguastlán.

Locality	Province	Country	Year(s)	Reference
Sanarate	El Progreso	Guatemala	1826	746824
Sansare	El Progreso	Guatemala	1826	746824
	Escuintla	Guatemala	1748–1749	746867:4
	Escuintla	Guatemala	1755	747296:6
	Escuintla	Guatemala	1760–1767	746866:1
	Escuintla	Guatemala	1801	747296:6
Aguacatepequez	Escuintla	Guatemala	1744	747060
Aguacatepequez	Escuintla	Guatemala	1760	746826
Chipilapa	Escuintla	Guatemala	1813	748131
Chipilapa	Escuintla	Guatemala	1817	746830
Cotzumalguapa	Escuintla	Guatemala	1734	746826
Cotzumalguapa	Escuintla	Guatemala	1744	747060-747061
Cotzumalguapa	Escuintla	Guatemala	1754	746869
Cotzumalguapa	Escuintla	Guatemala	1755	741890, 748126
Cotzumalguapa	Escuintla	Guatemala	1756	746869
Cotzumalguapa	Escuintla	Guatemala	1767	748128
Cotzumalguapa	Escuintla	Guatemala	1817	746830
Escuintla	Escuintla	Guatemala	1748	746867
Escuintla	Escuintla	Guatemala	1751	748124
Escuintla	Escuintla	Guatemala	1760	747058
Escuintla	Escuintla	Guatemala	1817	746830
Escuintla	Escuintla	Guatemala	1821	748131
Escuintla	Escuintla	Guatemala	1825	746873
Guanagazapa	Escuintla	Guatemala	1743	747060
Guanagazapa	Escuintla	Guatemala	1756	746871
Guanagazapa	Escuintla	Guatemala	1813	748131
Guanagazapa	Escuintla	Guatemala	1816	746870
Guanagazapa	Escuintla	Guatemala	1836	746873
La Democracia	Escuintla	Guatemala	1755	741890
La Democracia	Escuintla	Guatemala	1817	746830
La Gomera	Escuintla	Guatemala	1821	748133
La Gomera	Escuintla	Guatemala	1836	746873
Masagua	Escuintla	Guatemala	1750	746868
Masagua	Escuintla	Guatemala	1813	748131
Masagua	Escuintla	Guatemala	1817	746830
Masagua	Escuintla	Guatemala	1825	746825
San Juan Mixtán	Escuintla	Guatemala	1813	748131
San Juan Mixtán	Escuintla	Guatemala	1817	746830
San Juan Mixtán	Escuintla	Guatemala	1836	746873
Santa Ana Mixtán	Escuintla	Guatemala	1736	746826
Santa Ana Mixtán	Escuintla	Guatemala	1744	747060
Santa Ana Mixtán	Escuintla	Guatemala	1821	748133
Santa Ana Mixtán	Escuintla	Guatemala	1836	746873
Sinquinala	Escuintla	Guatemala	1726	763388
Sinquinala	Escuintla	Guatemala	1744	747060

Locality	Province	Country	Year(s)	Reference
Sinquinala	Escuintla	Guatemala	1756	741890
Sinquinala	Escuintla	Guatemala	1756	746865
Sinquinala	Escuintla	Guatemala	1817	746830
Texcuaco	Escuintla	Guatemala	1817	746829
Texcuaco	Escuintla	Guatemala	1836	746873
Amatitlán	Guatemala	Guatemala	1676–1680	747059:19
Amatitlán	Guatemala	Guatemala	1731	746825
Amatitlán	Guatemala	Guatemala	1756	746869
Amatitlán	Guatemala	Guatemala	1781	747059
Amatitlán	Guatemala	Guatemala	1784	747059:2
Amatitlán	Guatemala	Guatemala	1813	748132
Amatitlán	Guatemala	Guatemala	1835	746873
Canalitas	Guatemala	Guatemala	1777	747059
Canalitas	Guatemala	Guatemala	1845	747292
Chinautla	Guatemala	Guatemala	1727	746828
Chinautla	Guatemala	Guatemala	1740	746826
Chinautla	Guatemala	Guatemala	1781	747059
Chinautla	Guatemala	Guatemala	1817	746870
Chiquimula	Guatemala	Guatemala	1742–1743	747060:11
Chiquimula	Guatemala	Guatemala	1745–1749	747061
Chiquimula	Guatemala	Guatemala	1774–1791	748128:4
Guatemala City	Guatemala	Guatemala	1579–1713	744588:1
Guatemala City	Guatemala	Guatemala	1599	747059:11
Guatemala City	Guatemala	Guatemala	1607	747059:12
Guatemala City	Guatemala	Guatemala	1636	747059:13
Guatemala City	Guatemala	Guatemala	1639	747059:14
Guatemala City	Guatemala	Guatemala	1648	747059:15
Guatemala City	Guatemala	Guatemala	1652	747059:16
Guatemala City	Guatemala	Guatemala	1678	747059:8
Guatemala City	Guatemala	Guatemala	1687–1690	747060:1
Guatemala City	Guatemala	Guatemala	1692	747060:2
Guatemala City	Guatemala	Guatemala	1700–1703	747060:3-4
Guatemala City	Guatemala	Guatemala	1723–1740	746828:3
Guatemala City	Guatemala	Guatemala	1733	747059:3
Guatemala City	Guatemala	Guatemala	1735	746828
Guatemala City	Guatemala	Guatemala	1741	747060:9
Guatemala City	Guatemala	Guatemala	1742–1743	747060:11
Guatemala City	Guatemala	Guatemala	1743	747059
Guatemala City	Guatemala	Guatemala	1744–1745	747060:12
Guatemala City	Guatemala	Guatemala	1744–1761	748128:7
Guatemala City	Guatemala	Guatemala	1745	747058:3
Guatemala City	Guatemala	Guatemala	1745–1749	747061
Guatemala City	Guatemala	Guatemala	1748–1803	733411
Guatemala City	Guatemala	Guatemala	1753–1765	748127
Guatemala City	Guatemala	Guatemala	1764–1776	748128:1

Locality	Province	Country	Year(s)	Reference
Guatemala City	Guatemala	Guatemala	1765	747059
Guatemala City	Guatemala	Guatemala	1774–1791	748128:4
Guatemala City	Guatemala	Guatemala	1778	741739
Guatemala City	Guatemala	Guatemala	1778	741891
Guatemala City	Guatemala	Guatemala	1791	747059:6
Guatemala City	Guatemala	Guatemala	1796	747296:2-3
Guatemala City	Guatemala	Guatemala	1802	746827
Guatemala City	Guatemala	Guatemala	1803–1806	733412
Guatemala City	Guatemala	Guatemala	1804	747059:7-8
Guatemala City	Guatemala	Guatemala	1805	747296:1
Guatemala City	Guatemala	Guatemala	1807	733413
Guatemala City	Guatemala	Guatemala	1807–1808	733414
Guatemala City	Guatemala	Guatemala	1809	733415
Guatemala City	Guatemala	Guatemala	1809–1810	733526
Guatemala City	Guatemala	Guatemala	1809–1811	733527
Guatemala City	Guatemala	Guatemala	1811–1812	733528
Guatemala City	Guatemala	Guatemala	1813	747296:4
Guatemala City	Guatemala	Guatemala	1813	733529
Guatemala City	Guatemala	Guatemala	1813–1814	733530
Guatemala City	Guatemala	Guatemala	1813–1814	733571
Guatemala City	Guatemala	Guatemala	1813–1816	746828:2
Guatemala City	Guatemala	Guatemala	1814	733527
Guatemala City	Guatemala	Guatemala	1815–1818	733572
Guatemala City	Guatemala	Guatemala	1816	741893
Guatemala City	Guatemala	Guatemala	1818–1819	733573
Guatemala City	Guatemala	Guatemala	1819	746865:17
Guatemala City	Guatemala	Guatemala	1819	747296:5
Guatemala City	Guatemala	Guatemala	1820	733574
Guatemala City	Guatemala	Guatemala	1820–1830	733575
Guatemala City	Guatemala	Guatemala	1824	746871
Guatemala City	Guatemala	Guatemala	1824	746872
Guatemala City	Guatemala	Guatemala	1824–1825	746872
Guatemala City	Guatemala	Guatemala	1830–1832	733576
Guatemala City	Guatemala	Guatemala	1831	747058:9-10
Guatemala City	Guatemala	Guatemala	1835	748134
Guatemala City	Guatemala	Guatemala	1835–1855	733577
Guatemala City	Guatemala	Guatemala	1844	747292:1
Guatemala City	Guatemala	Guatemala	1856–1880	733578
Guatemala City	Guatemala	Guatemala	1877	747292:2
Guatemala City	Guatemala	Guatemala	1877	747293
Guatemala City	Guatemala	Guatemala	1877	744850-744855
Guatemala City	Guatemala	Guatemala	1877	GHG 211
Guatemala City	Guatemala	Guatemala	1898	748134
Guatemala City	Guatemala	Guatemala	1902	748134
Mixco	Guatemala	Guatemala	1804	746865

Locality	Province	Country	Year(s)	Reference
Palencia	Guatemala	Guatemala	1813	748132
Palencia	Guatemala	Guatemala	1821	748133
Petapa	Guatemala	Guatemala	1781	747059
Petapa	Guatemala	Guatemala	1817	746830
S. José Pinula	Guatemala	Guatemala	1825	746872
S. Juan Sacatepéquez	Guatemala	Guatemala	1732–1734	747060:6
S. Juan Sacatepéquez	Guatemala	Guatemala	1781	763388
S. Juan Sacatepéquez	Guatemala	Guatemala	1813	748132
S. Juan Sacatepéquez	Guatemala	Guatemala	1818	746830
S. Pedro Sacatepéquez	Guatemala	Guatemala	1780	747059
S. Pedro Sacatepéquez	Guatemala	Guatemala	1818	746829
S. Raimundo	Guatemala	Guatemala	1781	747059
S. Raimundo	Guatemala	Guatemala	1813	748132
S. Raimundo	Guatemala	Guatemala	1818	746830
S. Raimundo	Guatemala	Guatemala	1898	748134
S. Raimundo	Guatemala	Guatemala	1902	748134
Santa Catarina Pinula	Guatemala	Guatemala	1778–1781	747059
Santa Catarina Pinula	Guatemala	Guatemala	1803	746870
Santa Catarina Pinula	Guatemala	Guatemala	1817	747058:2
Santa Inés Petapa	Guatemala	Guatemala	1762	747059:9
Santa Inés Petapa	Guatemala	Guatemala	1763	748127
Santa Inés Petapa	Guatemala	Guatemala	1765	748127
Santa Inés Petapa	Guatemala	Guatemala	1781	747059
	Huehuetenango	Guatemala	1742	746867:7
	Huehuetenango	Guatemala	1810	747296:20
	Huehuetenango	Guatemala	1818–1819	747055
	Huehuetenango	Guatemala	1824–1825	746820:1-3
Aguacatán	Huehuetenango	Guatemala	1745	746829
Cancuc	Huehuetenango	Guatemala	1816	744581
Chalchitan	Huehuetenango	Guatemala	1819	747056
Chiantla	Huehuetenango	Guatemala	1738	747060
Chiantla	Huehuetenango	Guatemala	1796	748130:6
Chiantla	Huehuetenango	Guatemala	1803	747296
Chiantla	Huehuetenango	Guatemala	1810	747296
Chiantla	Huehuetenango	Guatemala	1813	748131
Chiantla	Huehuetenango	Guatemala	1819	747056
Chiantla	Huehuetenango	Guatemala	1825	746830
Colotenango	Huehuetenango	Guatemala	1819	747055
Concepción	Huehuetenango	Guatemala	1819	747055
Cuchumatán	Huehuetenango	Guatemala	1738	747060
Cuchumatán	Huehuetenango	Guatemala	1738	748128
Cuchumatán	Huehuetenango	Guatemala	1819	747056
Cuilco	Huehuetenango	Guatemala	1780	747296
Cuilco	Huehuetenango	Guatemala	1803	747296
Cuilco	Huehuetenango	Guatemala	1810	747296

Locality	Province	Country	Year(s)	Reference
Cuilco	Huehuetenango	Guatemala	1819	747055
Cuilco	Huehuetenango	Guatemala	1825	746820
Huehuetenango	Huehuetenango	Guatemala	1738	747060
Huehuetenango	Huehuetenango	Guatemala	1742	746867
Huehuetenango	Huehuetenango	Guatemala	1803	747296
Huehuetenango	Huehuetenango	Guatemala	1810	747296
Huehuetenango	Huehuetenango	Guatemala	1813	748131
Ixtahuacán	Huehuetenango	Guatemala	1748	746826
Ixtahuacán	Huehuetenango	Guatemala	1819	747055
Jacaltenango	Huehuetenango	Guatemala	1752	746868
Jacaltenango	Huehuetenango	Guatemala	1801	763388
Jacaltenango	Huehuetenango	Guatemala	1803	747296
Jacaltenango	Huehuetenango	Guatemala	1809	747296
Jacaltenango	Huehuetenango	Guatemala	1810	747296
Jacaltenango	Huehuetenango	Guatemala	1819	747055-747056
Malacatancito	Huehuetenango	Guatemala	1751	741889
Malacatancito	Huehuetenango	Guatemala	1751	746868
Malacatancito	Huehuetenango	Guatemala	1803	747296
Malacatancito	Huehuetenango	Guatemala	1810	747296
Malacatancito	Huehuetenango	Guatemala	1813	748131
Motozintla	Huehuetenango	Guatemala		(see Chiapas)
Petatán	Huehuetenango	Guatemala	1819	747055
San Andrés Huista	Huehuetenango	Guatemala	1819	747055
San Antonio Huista	Huehuetenango	Guatemala	1749	747061
San Antonio Huista	Huehuetenango	Guatemala	1810	747296
San Antonio Huista	Huehuetenango	Guatemala	1819	747055
San Gaspar Ixchil	Huehuetenango	Guatemala	1748	746867:3
San Gaspar Ixchil	Huehuetenango	Guatemala	1819	747055
San Juan Atitán	Huehuetenango	Guatemala	1746	746829
San Juan Atitán	Huehuetenango	Guatemala	1819	747055
San Juan Ixcoy	Huehuetenango	Guatemala	1743	746829
San Juan Ixcoy	Huehuetenango	Guatemala	1819	747055
San Marcos Huista	Huehuetenango	Guatemala	1752	746868
San Marcos Huista	Huehuetenango	Guatemala	1819	747055
San Martín	Huehuetenango	Guatemala	1738	747060
San Martín	Huehuetenango	Guatemala	1738	748128
San Martín	Huehuetenango	Guatemala	1819	747055
San Mateo Ixtatán	Huehuetenango	Guatemala	1752	746868
San Mateo Ixtatán	Huehuetenango	Guatemala	1815	746827
San Mateo Ixtatán	Huehuetenango	Guatemala	1816	746827
San Mateo Ixtatán	Huehuetenango	Guatemala	1819	747056
San Migual Acatán	Huehuetenango	Guatemala	1819	747055
San Pedro Necta	Huehuetenango	Guatemala	1743	746826
San Pedro Necta	Huehuetenango	Guatemala	1752	746868
San Pedro Necta	Huehuetenango	Guatemala	1752	741889

Locality	Province	Country	Year(s)	Reference
San Pedro Necta	Huehuetenango	Guatemala	1819	747055
San Sebastián Coatán	Huehuetenango	Guatemala	1819	747055
San Sebastián[54]	Huehuetenango	Guatemala	1819	747056
Santa Ana Huista	Huehuetenango	Guatemala	1790	763386
Santa Ana Huista	Huehuetenango	Guatemala	1810	747296
Santa Ana Huista	Huehuetenango	Guatemala	1817	748130
Santa Ana Huista	Huehuetenango	Guatemala	1819	747056
Santa Bárbara	Huehuetenango	Guatemala	1748	746867
Santa Bárbara	Huehuetenango	Guatemala	1819	747055
Santa Eulalia	Huehuetenango	Guatemala	1801	747296
Santa Eulalia	Huehuetenango	Guatemala	1819	747055
Santiago[55]	Huehuetenango	Guatemala	1819	747056
Soloma	Huehuetenango	Guatemala	1752	746868
Soloma	Huehuetenango	Guatemala	1802	747296:17
Soloma	Huehuetenango	Guatemala	1813	748131
Soloma	Huehuetenango	Guatemala	1819	747055
Tectitán	Huehuetenango	Guatemala	1746	746867
Tactitán	Huehuetenango	Guatemala	1752	746871
Tactitán	Huehuetenango	Guatemala	1780	747296
Tactitán	Huehuetenango	Guatemala	1801	747296
Tectitán	Huehuetenango	Guatemala	1813	747296:24
Tectitán	Huehuetenango	Guatemala	1819	747055
	Izabel	Guatemala	1825–1846	746825:2
	Izabel	Guatemala	1833	747058:6
Izabel	Izabel	Guatemala	1833	747058
Izabel	Izabel	Guatemala	1844	746825
	Jalapa	Guatemala	1635–1762	748130:2
Jalapa	Jalapa	Guatemala	1821	748133
Jalapa	Jalapa	Guatemala	1826	746824
Mataquescuintla	Jalapa	Guatemala	1743	746829
Mataquescuintla	Jalapa	Guatemala	1748	747061
Mataquescuintla	Jalapa	Guatemala	1750	748124
Mataquescuintla	Jalapa	Guatemala	1821	748133
Mataquescuintla	Jalapa	Guatemala	1824	746821
Mataquescuintla	Jalapa	Guatemala	1825	746823
Mataquescuintla	Jalapa	Guatemala	1828	746824
Mataquescuintla	Jalapa	Guatemala	1831	747058
San Luis Jilotepeque	Jalapa	Guatemala	1750	747061
San Luis Jilotepeque	Jalapa	Guatemala	1826	746824
San Pedro Pinula	Jalapa	Guatemala	1767	746827
San Pedro Pinula	Jalapa	Guatemala	1768–1775	748128
San Pedro Pinula	Jalapa	Guatemala	1817	746830

[54] San Sebastián Huehuetenango.
[55] Santiago Chimaltenango.

Locality	Province	Country	Year(s)	Reference
San Pedro Pinula	Jalapa	Guatemala	1826	746824
	Jutiapa	Guatemala	1753–1765	748127
	Jutiapa	Guatemala	1790–1806	763386:4
	Jutiapa	Guatemala	1813	763386:6
	Jutiapa	Guatemala	1902	737251:1
Agua Blanca	Jutiapa	Guatemala	1824	746821
Agua Blanca	Jutiapa	Guatemala	1902	737251
Asunción Mita	Jutiapa	Guatemala	1902	737251
Asunción Mita	Jutiapa	Guatemala	1908	737250
Atescatempa	Jutiapa	Guatemala	1750	746870
Atescatempa	Jutiapa	Guatemala	1826	746824
Atescatempa	Jutiapa	Guatemala	1902	737251
Azulco	Jutiapa	Guatemala	1817	746830
Azulco	Jutiapa	Guatemala	1821	748133
Azulco	Jutiapa	Guatemala	1825	746823
Azulco	Jutiapa	Guatemala	1831	747058
Azulco	Jutiapa	Guatemala	1902	737251
Canoas	Jutiapa	Guatemala	1821	748133
Canoas	Jutiapa	Guatemala	1826	746824
Comapa	Jutiapa	Guatemala	1756	741869
Comapa	Jutiapa	Guatemala	1756	741890
Comapa	Jutiapa	Guatemala	1802–1815	746829
Comapa	Jutiapa	Guatemala	1813	748131
Comapa	Jutiapa	Guatemala	1817	746830
Conguaco	Jutiapa	Guatemala	1817	746830
Conguaco	Jutiapa	Guatemala	1902	737251
El Adelanto	Jutiapa	Guatemala	1902	737251
El Progreso	Jutiapa	Guatemala	1902	737251
Jalapatagua	Jutiapa	Guatemala	1902	737251
Jérez	Jutiapa	Guatemala	1890–1911	737249
Jérez	Jutiapa	Guatemala	1897	737249
Jérez	Jutiapa	Guatemala	1902	737251
Jutiapa	Jutiapa	Guatemala	1769–1775	748128
Jutiapa	Jutiapa	Guatemala	1817	748130
Jutiapa	Jutiapa	Guatemala	1826	746824
Jutiapa	Jutiapa	Guatemala	1902	737251
Moyuta	Jutiapa	Guatemala	1744	747060
Moyuta	Jutiapa	Guatemala	1756	741890
Moyuta	Jutiapa	Guatemala	1817	746830
Moyuta	Jutiapa	Guatemala	1821	748133
Moyuta	Jutiapa	Guatemala	1902	737251
Ojo de Agua	Jutiapa	Guatemala	1826	746824
Pasaco	Jutiapa	Guatemala	1817	746830
Pasaco	Jutiapa	Guatemala	1821	748133
Pasaco	Jutiapa	Guatemala	1825	746823

Locality	Province	Country	Year(s)	Reference
Pasaco	Jutiapa	Guatemala	1902	737251
Piñuelas	Jutiapa	Guatemala	1826	746824
Quequexque	Jutiapa	Guatemala	1826	746824
Quesada	Jutiapa	Guatemala	1902	737251
Santa Catarina Mita	Jutiapa	Guatemala	1817	746830
Santa Catarina Mita	Jutiapa	Guatemala	1902	737251
Sinaca Mecayo	Jutiapa	Guatemala	1745	747058
Sinaca Mecayo	Jutiapa	Guatemala	1817	746829
Yupiltepeque	Jutiapa	Guatemala	1817	746830
Yupiltepeque	Jutiapa	Guatemala	1824	746821
Yupiltepeque	Jutiapa	Guatemala	1826	746824
Yupiltepeque	Jutiapa	Guatemala	1902	737251
Zapotitlán	Jutiapa	Guatemala	1753–1756	748126:1
Zapotitlán	Jutiapa	Guatemala	1790	748130:4
Zapotitlán	Jutiapa	Guatemala	1824	746820
Zapotitlán	Jutiapa	Guatemala	1826	746824
Zapotitlán	Jutiapa	Guatemala	1902	737251
Flores	Petén	Guatemala	1744	763388
	Quezaltenango	Guatemala	1736–1738	747060:8
	Quezaltenango	Guatemala	1738	748128:5
	Quezaltenango	Guatemala	1764–1776	748128:1
Almolonga	Quezaltenango	Guatemala	1753	748128
Almolonga	Quezaltenango	Guatemala	1821	747057
Cabricán	Quezaltenango	Guatemala	1740–1741	747060
Cabricán	Quezaltenango	Guatemala	1821	747057
Cantel	Quezaltenango	Guatemala	1821	747057
Chiquirichapa	Quezaltenango	Guatemala	1819	747055
Chiquirichapa	Quezaltenango	Guatemala	1821	747057
Chuijuyub	Quezaltenango	Guatemala	1769	746827
Coatepeque	Quezaltenango	Guatemala	1813	741892
Olintepeque	Quezaltenango	Guatemala	1748	746826
Olintepeque	Quezaltenango	Guatemala	1813	748131
Olintepeque	Quezaltenango	Guatemala	1821	747057
Ostuncalco	Quezaltenango	Guatemala	1748	746829
Ostuncalco	Quezaltenango	Guatemala	1749	746829
Ostuncalco	Quezaltenango	Guatemala	1821	747057
Quezaltenango	Quezaltenango	Guatemala	1753	746868
Quezaltenango	Quezaltenango	Guatemala	1759	748127
Quezaltenango	Quezaltenango	Guatemala	1766	748128
Quezaltenango	Quezaltenango	Guatemala	1767	746827
Quezaltenango	Quezaltenango	Guatemala	1778	741739
Salcaja	Quezaltenango	Guatemala	1803	747296
Salcaja	Quezaltenango	Guatemala	1813	748131
San Carlos Sija	Quezaltenango	Guatemala	1803	747296
San Carlos Sija	Quezaltenango	Guatemala	1810	747296

Locality	Province	Country	Year(s)	Reference
San Carlos Sija	Quezaltenango	Guatemala	1825	746820
San Martín[56]	Quezaltenango	Guatemala	1821	747057
San Mateo	Quezaltenango	Guatemala	1821	747057
San Miguel Sigyila	Quezaltenango	Guatemala	1821	747057
Santa Maria de Jesús	Quezaltenango	Guatemala	1742	746826
Zuñil	Quezaltenango	Guatemala	1744	746826
Zuñil	Quezaltenango	Guatemala	1821	747057
Chajul	Quiché	Guatemala	1752	741889
Chajul	Quiché	Guatemala	1752	746868
Chajul	Quiché	Guatemala	1813	748131
Chajul	Quiché	Guatemala	1819	747056
Chichicastenango	Quiché	Guatemala	1751	748124
Chichicastenango	Quiché	Guatemala	1768	746886
Chinique	Quiché	Guatemala	1825	746873
Cunén	Quiché	Guatemala	1819	747056
Cunén	Quiché	Guatemala	1824	746873
Jocotenango[57]	Quiché	Guatemala	1792	747296
Jocotenango	Quiché	Guatemala	1751	746868
Joyabaj	Quiché	Guatemala	1768	746867
Joyabaj	Quiché	Guatemala	1813	747056
Nebaj	Quiché	Guatemala	1813	748131
Nebaj	Quiché	Guatemala	1819	747059
Sacapulas	Quiché	Guatemala	1795–1797	747296:12-13
Sacapulas	Quiché	Guatemala	1803	747296
Sacapulas	Quiché	Guatemala	1810	747296
Sacapulas	Quiché	Guatemala	1819	747056
Sacapulas	Quiché	Guatemala	1824	746873
S. Andrés Sajcabaja	Quiché	Guatemala	1767	746826
S. Antonio Ilotenango	Quiché	Guatemala	1751	748125
S. Antonio Ilotenango	Quiché	Guatemala	1768	746867
S. Antonio Ilotenango	Quiché	Guatemala	1821	763383
S. Juan Cotzal	Quiché	Guatemala	1813	748131
S. Juan Cotzal	Quiché	Guatemala	1816	748130
S. Juan Cotzal	Quiché	Guatemala	1819	747056
S. Pedro Jocopilas	Quiché	Guatemala	1768	746867
S. Pedro Jocopilas	Quiché	Guatemala	1792	747296
S. Sebastián Lemoa	Quiché	Guatemala	1751	748125
Santa Cruz del Quiché	Quiché	Guatemala	1693	748128
Santa Cruz del Quiché	Quiché	Guatemala	1768	746867
Santa Cruz del Quiché	Quiché	Guatemala	1813	747056
Santa Cruz del Quiché	Quiché	Guatemala	1816	746829
Uspantán	Quiché	Guatemala	1802	773999

[56] San Martín Sacatepéquez.
[57] The next two entries are for San Bartolomé Jocotenango.

Locality	Province	Country	Year(s)	Reference
Uspantán	Quiché	Guatemala	1813	748131
Uspantán	Quiche	Guatemala	1819	747055
Uspantán	Quiche	Guatemala	1824	746873
Zacualpa	Quiche	Guatemala	1768	746866
Zacualpa	Quiche	Guatemala	1813	747056
Retalhuleu	Retalhuleu	Guatemala	1748	747061
Retalhuleu	Retalhuleu	Guatemala	1752	748125
Retalhuleu	Retalhuleu	Guatemala	1754	748126
Retalhuleu	Retalhuleu	Guatemala	1759	746870
Retalhuleu	Retalhuleu	Guatemala	1759	748127
Retalhuleu	Retalhuleu	Guatemala	1813	748132
Retalhuleu	Retalhuleu	Guatemala	1820	748132
Retalhuleu	Retalhuleu	Guatemala	1824	746820
Retalhuleu	Retalhuleu	Guatemala	1825	746820
Retalhuleu	Retalhuleu	Guatemala	1825	746821:1
San Andrés Villa Seca	Retalhuleu	Guatemala	1748	747061
San Andrés Villa Seca	Retalhuleu	Guatemala	1756	748126
San Andrés Villa Seca	Retalhuleu	Guatemala	1759	748127
San Andrés Villa Seca	Retalhuleu	Guatemala	1791	748130
San Andrés Villa Seca	Retalhuleu	Guatemala	1821	763389
San Andrés Villa Seca	Retalhuleu	Guatemala	1825	746820
San Felipe	Retalhuleu	Guatemala	1821	763389
S. Martín Zapotitlan	Retalhuleu	Guatemala	1723	746828
S. Martín Zapotitlan	Retalhuleu	Guatemala	1748	747061
S. Martín Zapotitlan	Retalhuleu	Guatemala	1748	748126
S. Martín Zapotitlan	Retalhuleu	Guatemala	1753	748125-748126
S. Martín Zapotitlan	Retalhuleu	Guatemala	1756	748126
S. Martín Zapotitlan	Retalhuleu	Guatemala	1759	748127
S. Martín Zapotitlan	Retalhuleu	Guatemala	1791	748130
S. Sebastián	Retalhuleu	Guatemala	1754	748126
S. Sebastián	Retalhuleu	Guatemala	1759	748127
	Sacatepéquez	Guatemala	1753–1765	748127
	Sacatepéquez	Guatemala	1804	746865:10
	Sacatepéquez	Guatemala	1813	746865:12
Alotenango	Sacatepéquez	Guatemala	1679	747059
Alotenango	Sacatepéquez	Guatemala	1741	747060
Alotenango	Sacatepéquez	Guatemala	1756	741890
Alotenango	Sacatepéquez	Guatemala	1781	763388
Antigua Guatemala	Sacatepéquez	Guatemala	1817	748130
Antigua Guatemala	Sacatepéquez	Guatemala	1818	747296
Boladilla	Sacatepéquez	Guatemala	1760	748127
Boladilla	Sacatepéquez	Guatemala	1817	748130
Ciudad Vieja	Sacatepéquez	Guatemala	1752	747058:11
Ciudad Vieja	Sacatepéquez	Guatemala	1752	741889
Ciudad Vieja	Sacatepéquez	Guatemala	1752	746868

Locality	Province	Country	Year(s)	Reference
Ciudad Vieja	Sacatepéquez	Guatemala	1762	748130
Ciudad Vieja	Sacatepéquez	Guatemala	1781	747059
Ciudad Vieja	Sacatepéquez	Guatemala	1817	746829
Jocotenango	Sacatepéquez	Guatemala	1739	746825
Jocotenango	Sacatepéquez	Guatemala	1751	741889
Jocotenango	Sacatepéquez	Guatemala	1813	748132
Jocotenango	Sacatepéquez	Guatemala	1819	773996
Jocotenango	Sacatepéquez	Guatemala	1821	748132
Jocotenango	Sacatepéquez	Guatemala	1824	746872
Magd. Milpas Altas	Sacatepéquez	Guatemala	1742	747060
Magd. Milpas Altas	Sacatepéquez	Guatemala	1768	746866
Magd. Milpas Altas	Sacatepéquez	Guatemala	1777–1781	747059
Pastores	Sacatepéquez	Guatemala	1679	747059
San Andrés Ceballos	Sacatepéquez	Guatemala	1781	747059
San Andrés Ceballos	Sacatepéquez	Guatemala	1813	748132
S. Ant. Aguascalientes	Sacatepéquez	Guatemala	1722	746825
S. Ant. Aguascalientes	Sacatepéquez	Guatemala	1781	747059
S. Ant. Aguascalientes	Sacatepéquez	Guatemala	1813	748132
S. Bartolomé Becerra	Sacatepéquez	Guatemala	1739	746826
S. Cristóbal el Alto	Sacatepéquez	Guatemala	1752	748125
S. Cristóbal el Alto	Sacatepéquez	Guatemala	1760	748127
S. Gaspar Vivar	Sacatepéquez	Guatemala	1781	747059
S. Gaspar Vivar	Sacatepéquez	Guatemala	1817	748130
S. Juan del Obispo	Sacatepéquez	Guatemala	1755	741890
S. Juan del Obispo	Sacatepéquez	Guatemala	1755	746869
S. Juan del Obispo	Sacatepéquez	Guatemala	1781	747059
S. Juan Gascon	Sacatepéquez	Guatemala	1752	746868
S. Lorenzo el Tejar	Sacatepéquez	Guatemala	1817	746829
S. Lucas Sacatepéquez	Sacatepéquez	Guatemala		748134
S. Luis las Carretas	Sacatepéquez	Guatemala	1700	746827
S. Luis las Carretas	Sacatepéquez	Guatemala	1755	741890
S. Mateo Milpas Altas	Sacatepéquez	Guatemala	1752	748125
S. Mateo Milpas Altas	Sacatepéquez	Guatemala	1755	748130
S. Miguel Dueñas	Sacatepéquez	Guatemala	1761	748127
S. Miguel Dueñas	Sacatepéquez	Guatemala	1781	763388
S. Miguel Dueñas	Sacatepéquez	Guatemala	1813	748132
S. Miguel Milpas Alt.	Sacatepéquez	Guatemala	1740	747060
S. Pedro las Huertas	Sacatepéquez	Guatemala	1781	747059
S. Pedro las Huertas	Sacatepéquez	Guatemala	1788	746870
S. Pedro las Huertas	Sacatepéquez	Guatemala	1813	773999
S. Pedro las Huertas	Sacatepéquez	Guatemala	1817	746829
Santa C. Barahona	Sacatepéquez	Guatemala	1733	747059
Santa C. Barahona	Sacatepéquez	Guatemala	1813	748132
Santa María de Jesús	Sacatepéquez	Guatemala	1732	748128
Santa María de Jesús	Sacatepéquez	Guatemala	1776	763386

Locality	Province	Country	Year(s)	Reference
Santa María de Jesús	Sacatepéquez	Guatemala	1792	773996
Santa María de Jesús	Sacatepéquez	Guatemala	1813	748132
Santa María de Jesús	Sacatepéquez	Guatemala	1821	747057
Santiago Sacatepéquez	Sacatepéquez	Guatemala	1818	746830
Santiago Zamora	Sacatepéquez	Guatemala	1752	748125
Santiago Zamora	Sacatepéquez	Guatemala	1761	748127
Santiago Zamora	Sacatepéquez	Guatemala	1781	763388
Sto Domingo Xenacoj	Sacatepéquez	Guatemala	1818	746829
Sto T. Milpas Altas	Sacatepéquez	Guatemala	1753	748130
Sto T. Milpas Altas	Sacatepéquez	Guatemala	1817	746829
Sumpango	Sacatepéquez	Guatemala	1777	746827
Sumpango	Sacatepéquez	Guatemala	1818	746830
Comitancillo	San Marcos	Guatemala	1741	747060
Comitancillo	San Marcos	Guatemala	1827	747057
Malacatán	San Marcos	Guatemala	1821	747057
S. Anto. Sacatepéquez	San Marcos	Guatemala	1750	746868
S. Anto. Sacatepéquez	San Marcos	Guatemala	1821	747057
S. Cristóbal Cucho	San Marcos	Guatemala	1821	747057
S. Miguel Ixtahuacán	San Marcos	Guatemala	1742	747060
S. Miguel Ixtahuacán	San Marcos	Guatemala	1820	763386
S. Miguel Ixtahuacán	San Marcos	Guatemala	1821	747057
S. Pablo	San Marcos	Guatemala	1821	747057
S. Pablo	San Marcos	Guatemala	1824	746822
S. Pedro Sacatepéquez	San Marcos	Guatemala	1817	746830
S. Pedro Sacatepéquez	San Marcos	Guatemala	1821	747057
Sipacapa	San Marcos	Guatemala	1756	748126
Sipacapa	San Marcos	Guatemala	1779	746828
Sipacapa	San Marcos	Guatemala	1821	747057
Tacana	San Marcos	Guatemala	1821	747057
Tajumulco	San Marcos	Guatemala	1821	747057
Tejutia	San Marcos	Guatemala	1821	747057
Tutuapa	San Marcos	Guatemala	1821	747057
	Santa Rosa	Guatemala	1816–1819	746870:5
	Santa Rosa	Guatemala	1825–1826	746825:2
Casillas	Santa Rosa	Guatemala	1821	748133
Cuilapa	Santa Rosa	Guatemala	1801	748133
Cuilapa	Santa Rosa	Guatemala	1825	746823
Chiquimulilla	Santa Rosa	Guatemala	1804	746865
Chiquimulilla	Santa Rosa	Guatemala	1805	746865
Chiquimulilla	Santa Rosa	Guatemala	1813	748131
Chiquimulilla	Santa Rosa	Guatemala	1816	746870
Chiquimulilla	Santa Rosa	Guatemala	1821	748133
Chiquimulilla	Santa Rosa	Guatemala	1825	746825
Guazacapán	Santa Rosa	Guatemala	1667	747059:17
Guazacapán	Santa Rosa	Guatemala	1667	747059

Locality	Province	Country	Year(s)	Reference
Guazacapán	Santa Rosa	Guatemala	1725–1729	747060:5
Guazacapán	Santa Rosa	Guatemala	1753–1756	748126:1
Guazacapán	Santa Rosa	Guatemala	1753	748126
Guazacapán	Santa Rosa	Guatemala	1760	747058
Guazacapán	Santa Rosa	Guatemala	1816	746870
Guazacapán	Santa Rosa	Guatemala	1825	746873
Jumaytepeque	Santa Rosa	Guatemala	1744	747061
Jumaytepeque	Santa Rosa	Guatemala	1760	746826
Jumaytepeque	Santa Rosa	Guatemala	1813	748131
Jumaytepeque	Santa Rosa	Guatemala	1817	746830
Jumaytepeque	Santa Rosa	Guatemala	1825	746825
Nancinta	Santa Rosa	Guatemala	1744	747061
San Juan Tecuaco	Santa Rosa	Guatemala	1756	741890
San Juan Tecuaco	Santa Rosa	Guatemala	1817	746830
San Juan Tecuaco	Santa Rosa	Guatemala	1821	748133
Santa María Ixhuatán	Santa Rosa	Guatemala	1652	747059
Sinacantán	Santa Rosa	Guatemala	1756	746871
Sinacantán	Santa Rosa	Guatemala	1802–1815	746829
Sinacantán	Santa Rosa	Guatemala	1813	748131
Sinacantán	Santa Rosa	Guatemala	1816	741892
Sinacantán	Santa Rosa	Guatemala	1816	746828
Tacuilula	Santa Rosa	Guatemala	1721	746829
Tacuilula	Santa Rosa	Guatemala	1743	747060
Tacuilula	Santa Rosa	Guatemala	1744–1748	747061
Tacuilula	Santa Rosa	Guatemala	1748	746868
Tacuilula	Santa Rosa	Guatemala	1751	748125
Tacuilula	Santa Rosa	Guatemala	1576	746869
Taxisco	Santa Rosa	Guatemala	1753	741890
Taxisco	Santa Rosa	Guatemala	1754	746869
Taxisco	Santa Rosa	Guatemala	1756	746869
Taxisco	Santa Rosa	Guatemala	1759	746870
Taxisco	Santa Rosa	Guatemala	1760	746826
Taxisco	Santa Rosa	Guatemala	1767	773996
Taxisco	Santa Rosa	Guatemala	1813	748132
Taxisco	Santa Rosa	Guatemala	1816	763386
Taxisco	Santa Rosa	Guatemala	1821	748132
Tecuaco	Santa Rosa	Guatemala	1802–1815	746829
Tepeaco	Santa Rosa	Guatemala	1725	747060
Tepeaco	Santa Rosa	Guatemala	1743	747060
Tepeaco	Santa Rosa	Guatemala	1751	748125
Tepeaco	Santa Rosa	Guatemala	1756	746869
Tepeaco	Santa Rosa	Guatemala	1760	746866
Tepeaco	Santa Rosa	Guatemala	1760	773996
Tepeaco	Santa Rosa	Guatemala	1767	746866
	Sololá	Guatemala	1756–1791	746865:4

Locality	Province	Country	Year(s)	Reference
	Sololá	Guatemala	1767–1768	746866:2
	Sololá	Guatemala	1768	746867:1
	Sololá	Guatemala	1804	746865:9
Concepción Quechula	Sololá	Guatemala	1756	746869
Concepción Quechula	Sololá	Guatemala	1821	747056
Panajachel	Sololá	Guatemala	1813	747056
Panajachel	Sololá	Guatemala	1821	747056
Panajachel	Sololá	Guatemala	1825	746873
S. Andrés Semetabaj	Sololá	Guatemala	1751	748125
S. Andrés Semetabaj	Sololá	Guatemala	1821	747056
S. Andrés Semetabaj	Sololá	Guatemala	1825	746873
S. Antonio Palopo	Sololá	Guatemala	1751	748125
S. Antonio Palopo	Sololá	Guatemala	1825	746873
S. José Chacaya	Sololá	Guatemala	1751	748125
S. José Chacaya	Sololá	Guatemala	1821	747056
S. José Chacaya	Sololá	Guatemala	1825	746873
S. Juan la Laguna	Sololá	Guatemala	1751	748125
S. Juan la Laguna	Sololá	Guatemala	1768	746827
S. Lucas Toliman	Sololá	Guatemala	1768	746829
S. Marcos la Laguna	Sololá	Guatemala	1751	748125
S. Marcos la Laguna	Sololá	Guatemala	1767	746826
S. Marcos la Laguna	Sololá	Guatemala	1825	746873
S. Pablo la Laguna	Sololá	Guatemala	1767	746826
S. Pablo la Laguna	Sololá	Guatemala	1825	746873
S. Pedro la Laguna	Sololá	Guatemala	1751	748125
S. Pedro la Laguna	Sololá	Guatemala	1767	746866
S. Pedro la Laguna	Sololá	Guatemala	1813	747056
S. Pedro la Laguna	Sololá	Guatemala	1825	746873
Santa Catarina Palopo	Sololá	Guatemala	1768	746827
Santa Catarina Palopo	Sololá	Guatemala	1821	747056
Santa Catarina Palopo	Sololá	Guatemala	1825	746873
Santa Clara la Laguna	Sololá	Guatemala	1767	746866
Santa Clara la Laguna	Sololá	Guatemala	1821	747056
Santa Crus la Laguna	Sololá	Guatemala	1751	741889
Santa Crus la Laguna	Sololá	Guatemala	1751	746868
Santa Crus la Laguna	Sololá	Guatemala	1751	748125
Santa Lucia Utatlán	Sololá	Guatemala	1821	747056
Santa M. Visitación	Sololá	Guatemala	1751	748125
Santa M. Visitación	Sololá	Guatemala	1767	746826
Santiago Atitlán	Sololá	Guatemala	1734	748128
Santiago Atitlán	Sololá	Guatemala	1751	748125
Santiago Atitlán	Sololá	Guatemala	1768	746826
Sololá	Sololá	Guatemala	1767	746866
Sololá	Sololá	Guatemala	1887	747294
	Suchitepéquez	Guatemala	1768	746828:1

Locality	Province	Country	Year(s)	Reference
	Suchitepéquez	Guatemala	1776	748128:3
	Suchitepéquez	Guatemala	1815	746865:2
	Suchitepéquez	Guatemala	1824–1825	746820:4
Carranza	Suchitepéquez	Guatemala	1759	748127
Cuytenango	Suchitepéquez	Guatemala	1740	746826
Cuytenango	Suchitepéquez	Guatemala	1748	747061
Cuytenango	Suchitepéquez	Guatemala	1759	748127
Cuytenango	Suchitepéquez	Guatemala	1791	748386
Cuytenango	Suchitepéquez	Guatemala	1791	773996
Cuytenango	Suchitepéquez	Guatemala	1821	763389
Mazatenango	Suchitepéquez	Guatemala	1749	748124
Mazatenango	Suchitepéquez	Guatemala	1753	748125
Mazatenango	Suchitepéquez	Guatemala	1756	748126
Mazatenango	Suchitepéquez	Guatemala	1759	748127
Mazatenango	Suchitepéquez	Guatemala	1777	741739
Mazatenango	Suchitepéquez	Guatemala	1777	741891
Mazatenango	Suchitepéquez	Guatemala	1813	748132
Patulul	Suchitepéquez	Guatemala	1751	748124
Patulul	Suchitepéquez	Guatemala	1813	747056
Patulul	Suchitepéquez	Guatemala	1821	747056
Patulul	Suchitepéquez	Guatemala	1825	746873
Samayac	Suchitepéquez	Guatemala	1726	746828
Samayac	Suchitepéquez	Guatemala	1752	748125
Samayac	Suchitepéquez	Guatemala	1759	748127
Samayac	Suchitepéquez	Guatemala	1778	746828
Samayac	Suchitepéquez	Guatemala	1813	748132
Samayac	Suchitepéquez	Guatemala	1825	746820
San Antonio	Suchitepéquez	Guatemala	1752–1753	748125:3
S. A. Suchitepéquez	Suchitepéquez	Guatemala	1752	748125
S. A. Suchitepéquez	Suchitepéquez	Guatemala	1759	748127
S. A. Suchitepéquez	Suchitepéquez	Guatemala	1768	746866
S. A. Suchitepéquez	Suchitepéquez	Guatemala	1813	748132
S. A. Suchitepéquez	Suchitepéquez	Guatemala	1821	748133
S. Bernardino	Suchitepéquez	Guatemala	1752	748125
S. Bernardino	Suchitepéquez	Guatemala	1756	748126
S. Bernardino	Suchitepéquez	Guatemala	1759	748127
S. Bernardino	Suchitepéquez	Guatemala	1821	748133
S. Francisco Zapotitlán	Suchitepéquez	Guatemala	1759	748127
S. Francisco Zapotitlán	Suchitepéquez	Guatemala	1790	748130
S. Francisco Zapotitlán	Suchitepéquez	Guatemala	1813	748132
S. Gabriel	Suchitepéquez	Guatemala	1748	747061
S. Gabriel	Suchitepéquez	Guatemala	1756	748126

Locality	Province	Country	Year(s)	Reference
S. Gabriel	Suchitepéquez	Guatemala	1790	748130
S. Gabriel	Suchitepéquez	Guatemala	1820	748132
S. Gabriel	Suchitepéquez	Guatemala	1825	746820
S. Lorenzo	Suchitepéquez	Guatemala	1743	746871
S. Lorenzo	Suchitepéquez	Guatemala	1752	746868
S. Lorenzo	Suchitepéquez	Guatemala	1759	746870
S. Lorenzo	Suchitepéquez	Guatemala	1759	748127
S. Lorenzo	Suchitepéquez	Guatemala	1781	747296
S. Lorenzo	Suchitepéquez	Guatemala	1790	763386
S. Lorenzo	Suchitepéquez	Guatemala	1819	747055
S. Lorenzo	Suchitepéquez	Guatemala	1820	748132
S. Lorenzo	Suchitepéquez	Guatemala	1825	746820
S. Miguelito	Suchitepéquez	Guatemala	1740	741889
S. Miguelito	Suchitepéquez	Guatemala	1740	746868
S. Miguelito	Suchitepéquez	Guatemala	1752	741889
S. Miguelito	Suchitepéquez	Guatemala	1752	746868
S. Miguelito	Suchitepéquez	Guatemala	1759	748127
S. Miguelito	Suchitepéquez	Guatemala	1805	763389
S. Pablo Jocopilas	Suchitepéquez	Guatemala	1748	747061
S. Pablo Jocopilas	Suchitepéquez	Guatemala	1752	746868
S. Pablo Jocopilas	Suchitepéquez	Guatemala	1753	748125
S. Pablo Jocopilas	Suchitepéquez	Guatemala	1759	748127
S. Pablo Jocopilas	Suchitepéquez	Guatemala	1768	746867
S. Pablo Jocopilas	Suchitepéquez	Guatemala	1813	748132
S. Pablo Jocopilas	Suchitepéquez	Guatemala	1824	746873
Santa Bárbara	Suchitepéquez	Guatemala	1751	746865
Santa Bárbara	Suchitepéquez	Guatemala	1821	747056
Santa Bárbara	Suchitepéquez	Guatemala	1825	746873
	Totonicapán	Guatemala	1796	746865:1
	Totonicapán	Guatemala	1804	746865:6
	Totonicapán	Guatemala	1810	747296:20
	Totonicapán	Guatemala	1818–1819	747055
	Totonicapán	Guatemala	1819	747056:1
Momostenango	Totonicapán	Guatemala	1803	747296
Momostenango	Totonicapán	Guatemala	1810	747296
Momostenango	Totonicapán	Guatemala	1813	748131
Momostenango	Totonicapán	Guatemala	1818	747055
Momostenango	Totonicapán	Guatemala	1824	746820
S. Andrés Xecul	Totonicapán	Guatemala	1813	748131
S. Andrés Xecul	Totonicapán	Guatemala	1818	747055
S. Bartolo	Totonicapán	Guatemala	1758	748126
S. Bartolo	Totonicapán	Guatemala	1819	747056
S. C. Totonicapán	Totonicapán	Guatemala	1803	747296
S. C. Totonicapán	Totonicapán	Guatemala	1810	747296
S. C. Totonicapán	Totonicapán	Guatemala	1813	748131

Locality	Province	Country	Year(s)	Reference
S. C. Totonicapán	Totonicapán	Guatemala	1819	747056
S. Francisco el Alto	Totonicapán	Guatemala	1749	746829
S. Francisco el Alto	Totonicapán	Guatemala	1812	747296
S. Francisco el Alto	Totonicapán	Guatemala	1815	748130
S. Francisco el Alto	Totonicapán	Guatemala	1818	746830
Santa M. Chiquimula	Totonicapán	Guatemala	1749	748124
Santa M. Chiquimula	Totonicapán	Guatemala	1818	746830
Santa M. Chiquimula	Totonicapán	Guatemala	1818	748130
Totonicapán	Totonicapán	Guatemala	1749	748124
Totonicapán	Totonicapán	Guatemala	1760	746870
Totonicapán	Totonicapán	Guatemala	1803	747296
Totonicapán	Totonicapán	Guatemala	1810	747296
Totonicapán	Totonicapán	Guatemala	1813	747296
Totonicapán	Totonicapán	Guatemala	1825	746820
Cabañas	Zacapa	Guatemala	1817	746829
Cabañas	Zacapa	Guatemala	1825	746823
Cabañas	Zacapa	Guatemala	1826	746824
Estanzuela	Zacapa	Guatemala	1826	746823
Gualán	Zacapa	Guatemala	1760	748127
Gualán	Zacapa	Guatemala	1797	747296
Gualán	Zacapa	Guatemala	1799	747296:14
Gualán	Zacapa	Guatemala	1817	746830
Gualán	Zacapa	Guatemala	1821	748133:1
Gualán	Zacapa	Guatemala	1824	746822
Gualán	Zacapa	Guatemala	1839	747058
Gualán	Zacapa	Guatemala	1839–1841	747058:7-8
Río Hondo	Zacapa	Guatemala	1826	746823
S. Pablo	Zacapa	Guatemala	1752	748124
S. Pablo	Zacapa	Guatemala	1756	748126
S. Pablo	Zacapa	Guatemala	1817	748130
Santa Lucía	Zacapa	Guatemala	1756	746869
Usumatlán	Zacapa	Guatemala	1742	747060
Usumatlán	Zacapa	Guatemala	1750	748124
Usumatlán	Zacapa	Guatemala	1758	748126
Usumatlán	Zacapa	Guatemala	1826	746823
Zacapa	Zacapa	Guatemala	1750	748124
Zacapa	Zacapa	Guatemala	1756	748126
Zacapa	Zacapa	Guatemala	1817	746829
Zacapa	Zacapa	Guatemala	1821	748130:1
Zacapa	Zacapa	Guatemala	1824	746822
Zacapa	Zacapa	Guatemala	1825	746823

HONDURAS

Locality	Province	Country	Year(s)	Reference
		Honduras	1796	*UNESCO 28
		Honduras	1800	UNESCO 32-33
		Honduras	1817	UNESCO 40
		Honduras	1818	UNESCO 41
		Honduras	1819	UNESCO 44-46
		Honduras	1881	AN
		Honduras	1887	AN
Aguanqueterique		Honduras	1796	UNESCO 29
Aguanqueterique partido		Honduras	1749	UNESCO 50
Aguanqueterique partido		Honduras	1752	UNESCO 51
Aguanqueterique partido		Honduras	1789	UNESCO 53
Aguanqueterique partido		Honduras	1747	UNESCO 50
Aramecina		Honduras	1801	UNESCO 34
Candelaria		Honduras	1782	744866
Comayagua		Honduras	1741–1806	744866
Comayagyela		Honduras	1797	UNESCO 29
Danlí		Honduras	1817	UNESCO 41
Ermita de Río Hondo		Honduras	1820	UNESCO 37
Goascorán		Honduras	1798	UNESCO 29
Gracía a Dios		Honduras	1797	UNESCO 29
Gracía a Dios partido		Honduras	1797	UNESCO 29
Gualcince		Honduras	1821	747059
Laboríos		Honduras	1797	UNESCO 29
Lauterique		Honduras	1796	UNESCO 29
Lepaterique		Honduras	1801	UNESCO 34
Ojojona		Honduras	1796	UNESCO 28
Ojojona		Honduras	1797	UNESCO 29
Omoa		Honduras	1777	741739
Omoa		Honduras	1777	741891
Omoa		Honduras	1777	744866
Omoa		Honduras	1825	746825
Orica		Honduras	1796	UNESCO 28
Pespire		Honduras	1819	UNESCO 44
Petoa		Honduras	1703	763390
Reitoca		Honduras	1750	746868

*The UNESCO reference refers to microfilm produced by UNESCO and available at large depository libraries.

.

Locality	Province	Country	Year(s)	Reference
Río Abajo		Honduras	1820	UNESCO 46
S. Antonio		Honduras	1765	UNESCO 50
S. Juan (Valle de)		Honduras	1819	UNESCO 44
S. Mateo		Honduras	1818	UNESCO 41
Santa Lucía (mineral)		Honduras	1820	UNESCO 37
Talanga		Honduras	1795	UNESCO 28
Tamara		Honduras	1801	UNESCO 31
Tamara		Honduras	1818	UNESCO 41
Tamarindo		Honduras	1819	UNESCO 44
Tegucigalpa		Honduras	1777	741891
Tegucigalpa		Honduras	1777	744866
Tegucigalpa		Honduras	1796	UNESCO 28
Tegucigalpa		Honduras	1810	UNESCO 36
Tegucigalpa		Honduras	1821	AHG 56:51-52
Tegucigalpa partido		Honduras	1679	UNESCO 50
Texiguat		Honduras	1819	UNESCO 43
Texiguat		Honduras	1695	UNESCO 49
Tiscagua		Honduras	1801	UNESCO 30
Tiscagua		Honduras	1789	UNESCO 26
Valle Alto		Honduras	1819	UNESCO 44
Yuscarán jurisdiction		Honduras	1820	UNESCO 45

LOUISIANA

Locality	Province	Country	Year(s)	Reference
	Arkansas	Louisiana	1777	AGI, Cuba
	Arkansas	Louisiana	1791	AGI, Cuba
	Arkansas	Louisiana	1793	LGR 27:367-368
	Arkansas	Louisiana	1794	LGR 27:367-368
	Arkansas	Louisiana	1795	LGR 27:367-368
	Arkansas	Louisiana	1796	LGR 27:367-368
	Arkansas	Louisiana	1798	AGI, Cuba
	Illinois	Louisiana	1795	LGR 27:367-368
	Illinois	Louisiana	1796	LGR 27:367-368
Allemands		Louisiana	1776	AGI, Cuba
Allemands		Louisiana	1784	AGI, Cuba
Allemands		Louisiana	1789	AGI, Cuba
Allemands		Louisiana	1795	AGI, Cuba
Allemands		Louisiana	1799	AGI, Cuba
Acadians		Louisiana	1769	AGI, Cuba
Acadians		Louisiana	1770	AGI, Cuba
Ascensión parish		Louisiana	1770	LGR 27:367-368
Ascensión parish		Louisiana	1777	LGR 27:367-368
Attakapas		Louisiana	1770	AGI, Cuba
Attakapas		Louisiana	1771	AGI, Cuba
Attakapas		Louisiana	1774	AGI, Cuba
Attakapas		Louisiana	1777	LGR 27:367-368
Attakapas		Louisiana	1785	LGR 27:367-368
Attakapas		Louisiana	1795	AGI, Cuba
Attakapas		Louisiana	1799	AGI, Cuba
Attakapas		Louisiana	1803	AGI, Cuba
Avoyelles		Louisiana	1785	AGI, Cuba
Bahia Honda		Louisiana	1783	AGI, Cuba
Batón Rouge		Louisiana	1782	AGI, Cuba
Batón Rouge		Louisiana	1786	AGI, Cuba
Batón Rouge		Louisiana	1787	LGR 27:367-368
Batón Rouge		Louisiana	1795	AGI, Cuba
Batón Rouge		Louisiana	1805	AGI, Cuba
Bayou Teche		Louisiana	1803	LGR 27:367-368
Cabahannocer		Louisiana	1775	AGI, Cuba
Cabahannocer		Louisiana	1776	AGI, Cuba
Cabahannocer		Louisiana	1777	AGI, Cuba
Cabahannocer		Louisiana	1789	AGI, Cuba
Cannes Brylees		Louisiana	1795	AGI, Cuba

Locality	Province	Country	Year(s)	Reference
Cannes Brylees		Louisiana	1799	AGI, Cuba
Chapitoulas		Louisiana	1795	AGI, Cuba
Choctaw islands		Louisiana	1803	LGR 27:367-368
False River		Louisiana	1766	AGI, Cuba
False River		Louisiana	1787	LGR 27:367-368
False River		Louisiana	1790	AGI, Cuba
False River		Louisiana	1795	LGR 27:367-368
False River		Louisiana	1803	LGR 27:367-368
German coast		Louisiana	1784	LGR 27:367-368
German coast		Louisiana	1766	LGR 27:367-368
Iberville		Louisiana	1771	AGI, Cuba
Iberville		Louisiana	1772	LGR 27:367-368
Iberville		Louisiana	1777	LGR 27:367-368
Lafourche		Louisiana	1777	LGR 27:367-368
Lafourche		Louisiana	1788	LGR 27:367-368
Lafourche		Louisiana	1789	LGR 27:367-368
Lafourche		Louisiana	1791	LGR 27:367-368
Lafourche		Louisiana	1798	LGR 27:367-368
Louisiana Regiment		Louisiana	1779	LGR 27:367-368
Manchac		Louisiana	1772	LGR 27:367-368
Manchac		Louisiana	1777	LGR 27:367-368
Manchac		Louisiana	1791	AGI, Cuba
Manchac		Louisiana	1795	AGI, Cuba
Meteaire		Louisiana	1799	AGI, Cuba
Mobile		Louisiana	1780	AGI, Cuba
Mobile		Louisiana	1781	AGI, Cuba
Mobile		Louisiana	1784	LGR 27:367-368
Mobile		Louisiana	1786	AGI, Cuba
Mobile		Louisiana	1787	AGI, Cuba
Mobile		Louisiana	1788	LGR 27:367-368
Mobile		Louisiana	1789	AGI, Cuba
Mobile		Louisiana	1795	AGI, Cuba
Mobile		Louisiana	1805	LGR 27:367-368
Mobile (slaves)		Louisiana	1787	LGR 27:367-368
Nátchez		Louisiana	1784	LGR 27:367-368
Nátchez		Louisiana	1787	LGR 27:367-368
Nátchez		Louisiana	1788	LGR 27:367-368
Nátchez		Louisiana	1792	LGR 27:367-368; 899975
Nátchez		Louisiana	1793	AGI, Cuba
Nátchez		Louisiana	1794	LGR 27:367-368
Natchitoches		Louisiana	1770	AGI, Cuba
Natchitoches		Louisiana	1774	AGI, Cuba
Natchitoches		Louisiana	1786	AGI, Cuba
Natchitoches		Louisiana	1795	AGI, Cuba
Natchitoches		Louisiana	1787	LGR 27:367-368

Locality	Province	Country	Year(s)	Reference
New Bourbon		Louisiana	1797	AGI, Cuba
New Feliciana		Louisiana	1793	LGR 27:367-368
New Feliciana		Louisiana	1796	LGR 27:367-368
New Feliciana		Louisiana	1798	AGI, Cuba
New Iberia		Louisiana	1778	LGR 27:367-368
New Iberia		Louisiana	1789	AGI, Cuba
New Madrid		Louisiana	1791	AGI, Cuba
New Madrid		Louisiana	1792	LGR 27:367-368
New Madrid		Louisiana	1793	LGR 27:367-368
New Madrid		Louisiana	1794	LGR 27:367-368
New Madrid		Louisiana	1796	LGR 27:367-368
New Madrid		Louisiana	1797	AGI, Cuba
New Orleans		Louisiana	1767	LGR 27:367-368
New Orleans		Louisiana	1778	LGR 27:367-368
New Orleans (1st quarter)		Louisiana	1795	LGR 27:367-368
New Orleans (2nd quarter)		Louisiana	1795	LGR 27:367-368
New Orleans (3rd quarter)		Louisiana	1796	LGR 27:367-368
New Orleans		Louisiana	1798	AGI, Cuba
New Orleans		Louisiana	1799	AGI, Cuba
Opelousas		Louisiana	1770	AGI, Cuba
Opelousas		Louisiana	1771	AGI, Cuba
Opelousas		Louisiana	1777	LGR 27:367-368
Opelousas		Louisiana	1785	LGR 27:367-368
Opelousas		Louisiana	1788	LGR 27:367-368
Opelousas		Louisiana	1796	LGR 27:367-368
Ouachita		Louisiana	1790	AGI, Cuba
Pointe du Teiche		Louisiana	1803	AGI, Cuba
Pointe Coupée parish		Louisiana	1766	LGR 27:367-368
Pointe Coupée parish		Louisiana	1775	AGI, Cuba
Pointe Coupée parish		Louisiana	1787	LGR 27:367-368
Pointe Coupée parish		Louisiana	1790	AGI, Cuba
Pointe Coupée parish		Louisiana	1795	LGR 27:367-368
Pointe Coupée parish		Louisiana	1803	LGR 27:367-368
Prairie Aux Mouche		Louisiana	1770	LGR 27:367-368
Rapide		Louisiana	1770	AGI, Cuba
Rapide		Louisiana	1773	AGI, Cuba
Rapide		Louisiana	1789	AGI, Cuba
Rapide		Louisiana	1792	AGI, Cuba
Recruits from Canary Islands		Louisiana	1783	LGR 27:367-368
S.Genevieve		Louisiana	1770	AGI, Cuba
S.Genevieve		Louisiana	1771	AGI, Cuba

Locality	Province	Country	Year(s)	Reference
S.Genevieve		Louisiana	1773	AGI, Cuba
S.Genevieve		Louisiana	1779	LGR 27:367-368
S.James parish		Louisiana	1769	LGR 27:367-368
S.James parish		Louisiana	1777	LGR 27:367-368
S.James parish		Louisiana	1766	LGR 27:367-368
S.Louis		Louisiana	1771–1773	AGI, Cuba
S.Louis		Louisiana	1779	LGR 27:367-368
S.Louis		Louisiana	1795–1796	AGI, Cuba

MEXICO

The colonial census called the Revillagigedo Census of 1790–1793, after the title of the viceroy then in charge of the Viceroyalty of New Spain (Mexico), Juan Francisco Güemes y Orcasitas, 1st Count of Revillagigedo, is dispersed in at least ten repositories, not all of which have been used in compiling this census index.[58]

National Censuses were taken in 1895[59], 1900[60], 1910[61], 1921 and 1930; then every ten years thereafter they have been taken on a regular basis. The Family History Library has filmed the entire 1921, or fourth national census. The original is located at the Archivo General de la Nación. Reportedly the 1930 national census is also at the AGN but it has not been microfilmed.

The following study of the state of Aguascalientes will reveal what is possible eventually for all the states of Mexico. It has been included here because it has been completed and has great value for that area of the country. Similar studies will be found in subsequent editions of this book for the other states, time permitting.

AGUASCALIENTES

The 1792 *padrón* of Aguascalientes provides a name description of each of the *partidos* within the **subdelegación** of Aguascalientes. This analysis shows the probable place names included in the rest of the *padrones* listed below as well, given the fact that the locality names include not just the name indicated but all of the surrounding ranches, haciendas and places within each jurisdiction. The subdelegation in 1792 included five pueblos, twenty-nine haciendas, fifty-two independent ranches, and 133 dependent ranches.

---

[58] Hugo Castro Aranda, *1er censo de población de la Nueva España*. México City: Secretaría de Programación y Presupuesto, 1977.

[59] The First National Census of Mexico has been preserved in its original form but has not yet been preserved on microfilm. It is reportedly located at El Instituto Nacional de Estadística, Geografía e Informática in Mexico City.

[60] Actual location unknown; unknown if it still exists; at the Archivo Histórico de la Ciudad de México there is information on the Federal District for 1900, giving municipal jurisdictions, together with an alphabetical list of all place names within the district, further identified by category, municipality and population.

[61] The third national census was taken in 1910; its location has not been determined. The portions of the census pertaining to Mexico City are located at the Archivo Histórico de la Ciudad de México, in volumes 3432, 3433, 3435, 3437, 3442, 3445, 3447 and 3450. Similar studies to those described for the 1900 census are also available at the AHC for this 1910 census.

Partido of Aguascalientes

Aguascalientes City with its wards (*barrios*) as follows: Camposanto, de la Cruz, Nuestra Señora de Guadalupe, Triana (a negro ward), and Zocabón; the Indian pueblo of San Marcos.

Alonsos ranch, Alvarados ranch, Arroyo Zarco ranch, Atajo ranch, Bocas y Morciñique hacienda (belonging to Ignacio Rincón Gallardo), Calabasas ranch, Calvillo ranch, Cantera hacienda (belonging to Ignacio Rincón Gallardo), Cañada del Rodeo ranch, Cañada Honda hacienda, Carabarin ranch, Carrizal ranch, Cerrito Colorado ranch, Chicalote ranch, Chichimeco hacienda, Ciénega de Cardona hacienda, Ciénega de Laurel hacienda, Cieneguilla hacienda (belonging to the Conde de Regla), Don Diego ranch, El Alto ranch, El Chiquihuite ranch, El Muerto ranch, El Paso Blanco ranch, El Puerto ranch, El Sauz hacienda (belonging to Vicente Valenzuela), El Tepetatillo ranch, Gracias a Dios hacienda (belonging to José Gonzáles Carreón), Jaltomate hacienda, Jesús María, Juan Pascual ranch, La Barcilla ranch, La Cocina ranch, La Estancia ranch, La Laborsilla ranch, La Ordeña ranch, La Palma ranch, La Presa ranch, Las Amarillas ranch, Las Cabras ranch, Las Palmitas ranch, Lira ranch, Los Guzmanes ranch, Los Magüeyes ranch, Los Negritos ranch, Los Potrerillos ranch, Los Pozitos ranch, Los Sandovales ranch, Los Sauces ranch, Mancillas ranch, Mesquital ranch, Mesquite de Abajo, Mesquite de Arriba, Milpillas de Abajo ranch, Milpillas de Arriba ranch, Mimbres ranch, Mirandilla ranch, Montoro ranch, Ocote ranch, Ojocaliente hacienda, Ojo Zarco ranch, Paso de Mendoza ranch, Peñuelas hacienda, Peñuelas de Abajo ranch, Puentesilla ranch, Puerto de Nieto ranch, Rincón de los Ponces ranch, San Antonio ranch, San Bartolo hacienda (belonging to Ignacio Rincón Gallardo), San Dimas ranch, San Francisco ranch, San José Guadalupe hacienda (belonging to Cosme Flores Alatorre), San José de los Potreros ranch, San Lorenzo hacienda, San Nicolás de los Horcones ranch, San Nicolás Ilamasías ranch, San Rafael de los Hoyos ranch, San Rafael del Rancho Seco ranch, Santa Inés ranch, Santa María hacienda, Seco de Buenavista ranch, Soledad ranch, Soyatal hacienda (belonging to Ignacio Rincón Gallardo), Tapias hacienda, Tecongo ranch, Tepetate ranch (a dependent ranch of San Bartolo hacienda), Tepetate ranch (a dependent ranch of San José Guadalupe hacienda), Texcareño ranch, Tinaja hacienda, Venadero ranch.

Partido of San José de Gracia

Carbonera ranch, Chicalote ranch, El Cabecillo ranch, El Carrizal ranch, El Corralillo ranch, El Muerto ranch, El Paso de los Arrieros ranch, El Potrerillo ranch, El Potrero ranch, El Rincón hacienda, El Saucillo ranch, El Sauz ranch, Escalera ranch, Estancia, Garabato hacienda, Godornices ranch, Guajolotes ranch, La Boquilla ranch, La Cueva de la Loba ranch, La Peña Blanca branch, La Presa de Molinos, La Punta ranch, Las Rosas ranch, La Vívora ranch, Los Escaleras ranches, Molinos ranch, Natillas ranch, Pabellón hacienda, Palmilla ranch, Paredes hacienda, Rincón de Romos hacienda, San Jacinto hacienda, Santiago hacienda, San Vicente de la Burta ranch, Soledad ranch, and Tepetate ranch, Vívora Ravena ranch.

Partido of San José de la Isla

Buenasvista ranch, Cornetes ranch, El Capulín ranch, El Decollaso ranch, El Madroño ranch, El Salero ranch, Estancia de Delgadillo La Candelaria ranch, Laguna de Piedra ranch, La Joya ranch, La Maxada ranch, Las Reinosas ranch, Lo de Dena ranch, Los Negritos ranch, Montegrande ranch, Natillas ranch, Piedragorda ranch, Puesto del Río ranch, San Antonio del Buen Suceso ranch, San Pedro Piedragorda hacienda, San Vicente ranch, Santa Catarina ranch, Soledad de Abajo ranch, Soledad de Arriba ranch, Tierra Colorada ranch.

Partido of the Real de Asientos de Ibarra

Aguaje de Burras ranch, Aguajito ranch, Alcaparrilla ranch, Arroyo Hondo ranch, Barranca Bermeja ranch, Berrendos ranch, Bocas de Ortega hacienda, Bocas de Ortega ranch, Borrunda ranch, Burreros ranch, Caldera ranch, Candeleas ranch, Carboneras de Arriba ranch, El Charco Azul ranch, El Chiquihuite ranch, Ciénega Grande hacienda, Cieneguilla hacienda, Clavellinas ranch, Cruz de Lobato ranch, El Imbo ranch, El Polvo ranch, El Sauz Dorado ranch, El Tepetatillo ranch, El Tule de los Rangeles ranch, El Tule hacienda, El Tulillo ranch, Estancia de Molinos, Guarda Raya ranch, Hacienda Vieja, La Barranca branch, Las Animas ranch, Las Carboneras ranch, La Soledad ranch, Las Pilas hacienda, Las Viudas ranch, Los Hornos ranch, Mesquite de Abajo ranch, Mesquite de Arriba ranch, Nuestra Señora de Guadalupe ranch, Oho de Agua de Zapateros ranch, Ojo Zarco ranch, Pilotos hacienda, San Antonio del Tule ranch, San Benito ranch, San José del Río ranch, San Pedro de Alcántara ranch, San Rafael del Tule ranch, Santa Rosa ranch, Tepesalac ranch, Tepetate ranch, and Xilotepeque ranch.

AGUASCALIENTES

Locality	Province	Country	Year(s)	Reference
	Ags.	México	1649	Archivo del Parral[62]
	Ags.	México	1770	BPT Manuscript 45
	Ags.	México	1792	AGN PAD 5; 1520345:2
Aguascalientes	Ags.	México	1760	?[63]
Aguascalientes	Ags.	México	1770	BPT Manuscript 45
Aguascalientes	Ags.	México	1780	BPT Manuscript 45
Aguascalientes[64]	Ags.	México	1803	TRI 43
Aguascalientes	Ags.	México	1818	168812
Aguascalientes	Ags.	México	1819	168817
Aguascalientes	Ags.	México	1820	168821
Aguascalientes (milit.)	Ags.	México	1820	168822
Aguascalientes	Ags.	México	1821	168823-24
Asientos	Ags.	México	????	1410909:4
Asientos	Ags.	México	1820	168818
Asientos (military)	Ags.	México	1820	168822
Asientos	Ags.	México	1822	168827
Asientos	Ags.	México	1824	168833
Calvillo (Huejúcar)	Ags.	México	1817	168809
Calvillo (Huejúcar)	Ags.	México	1820	168822
Calvillo (Huejúcar)	Ags.	México	1821	168823-24
Calvillo (Huejúcar)	Ags.	México	1822	168828
Calvillo (Huejúcar)	Ags.	México	1824	168833
Calvillo (Huejúcar)	Ags.	México	1825	168836
Calvillo (Huejúcar)	Ags.	México	1826	168838
San José de Gracia	Ags.	México	1818	168813
San José de Gracia	Ags.	México	1819	168815-16
San José de Yslas	Ags.	México	1820	168822
San José de Yslas	Ags.	México	1824	168833

---

[62] Padrón de los vecinos . . . 1649.

[63] Includes 640 Indian and 5,386 non-Indian families (omitting Ciénega de Mata) for a total of 20,441 persons.

[64] Negro heads of household, called *matrícula de tributos*.

ALTA CALIFORNIA

Locality	Province	Country	Year(s)	Reference
	A.C.	México	1777–1779	AGN PI 121:2:277-374
	A.C.	México	1795–1796	AGN PI 19:2:63-91
	A.C.	México	1798	AGN CA 49:3:137-188
	A.C.	México	1836	SAC
Caducamán[65]	A.C.	México	1793	AHH
Los Angeles	A.C.	México	1790	SSC 41:181-182
Los Angeles	A.C.	México	1816	SSC 41:228-229
Los Angeles	A.C.	México	1816	SSC 43:350-351
Los Angeles	A.C.	México	1822	CAL 4:37-39
Los Angeles	A.C.	México	1844	SSC 42:360-363
Monterey	A.C.	México	1770	AGN CA 76:27
Monterey	A.C.	México	1773	AGN CA 66:397-397v
San Diego	A.C.	México	1770	AGN CA 76:27
San Diego	A.C.	México	1790	SSC 43:107-108
San Fco. de Borja	A.C.	México	1793	AHH
San Luis	A.C.	México	1811	913166:7-8
San Vicente Ferrer	A.C.	México	1793	AHH
Santa Bárbara	A.C.	México	1815	913167:1
Santa Bárbara	A.C.	México	1840	913167:2
Santa Catarina Mártir[66]	A.C.	México	1834	AHB; Bancroft Library
Santa Cruz	A.C.	México	1845	CAL 4:45-58
Santo Domingo	A.C.	México	1793	AHH[67]
Viñadaco[68]	A.C.	México	1793	AHH

---

[65] Santa Gertrudis de Caducamán.
[66] Santa Catarina de los Yumas; sometimes also Santa Catalina.
[67] Santo Domingo de la Frontera, or de la Fronteras.
[68] Nuestra Señora del Rosario de Viñadaco.

ARIZONA

Locality	Province	Country	Year(s)	Reference
Guévavi	Sonora	México	?	AHH
San Xavier del Bac	Sonora	México	1766	AHH
San Xavier del Bac	Sonora	México	1768	SBM
San Xavier del Bac	Sonora	México	1801	PA1:21-24; 811:3
Tubac	Sonora	México	1801	AF 33:705:3
Tucson	Sonora	México	1766	AHH
Tucson	Sonora	México	1797	JAH 11
Tucson	Sonora	México	1801	PA1:13-20
Tumacácori	Sonora	México	1796	Kiva 19:1-12
Tumacácori	Sonora	México	1801	PA1:7-9; 811:3

BAJA CALIFORNIA

Locality	Province	Country	Year(s)	Reference
	B.C.	México	1797–1798	AGN PI 19:1:1-62
Borja	B.C.	México	1793	AHH
Cadegomó	B.C.	México	1793	AHH
Cadudamán	B.C.	México	1793	AHH
Comondú	B.C.	México	1793	AHH
Fronteras	B.C.	México	1793	AHH
Kadakaamán	B.C.	México	1793	AHH
Loreto	B.C.	México	1726	AHH
Loreto	B.C.	México	1773	AGN CA 66:400-400v
Loreto	B.C.	México	1793	AHH
Mulegé	B.C.	México	1793	AHH
Rosario	B.C.	México	1793	AHH
San Antonio	B.C.	México	1793	AHH
San Fernando	B.C.	México	1773	AGN MI:12
San Fernando	B.C.	México	1773	AGN PI:166
San Ignacio	B.C.	México	1730	AGN HI:308:2:465-
San Ignacio	B.C.	México	1773	AGN MI:12:202-345
San Ignacio	B.C.	México	1773	AHH PI:166
San Fco. Xavier Viggé	B.C.	México	1793	AHH
San José del Cabo	B.C.	México	1793	AHH
San Vicente Ferrer	B.C.	México	1793	AHH
Santa Catalina	B.C.	México	1834	AHB
Santa Gertrudis	B.C.	México	1773	AGN PI:166
Santa Gertrudis	B.C.	México	1773	AGN MI:12:202-345
Santa María	B.C.	México	1773	AGN MI:12
Santa María	B.C.	México	1773	AGN PI:166
Santiago	B.C.	México	1793	AHH
Santo Tomás	B.C.	México	1793	AHH
Todos Santos	B.C.	México	1793	AHH
Velicatá[69]	A.C.	México	1793	AHH

---

[69] San Fernando Rey de España Velicatá.

CHIAPAS

Locality	Province	Country	Year(s)	Reference
	Chiapas	México	1798–1880	733411-733577
Acacoyagua	Chiapas	México	1765	746826
Amatenango	Chiapas	México	1752	746868
Amatenango	Chiapas	México	1780	747296
Amatenango	Chiapas	México	1819	747059
Amatenango	Chiapas	México	1825	746820
Belén	Chiapas	México	1821	763363
Chiapa de Corso	Chiapas	México	1665	747058
Chiapa de Corso	Chiapas	México	1741	747058
Las Margaritas	Chiapas	México	1886–1912	715572
Mazapa	Chiapas	México	1746	746825
Mazapa	Chiapas	México	1752	746871
Mazapa	Chiapas	México	1780	747296
Motozintla de Mendoza	Chiapas	México	1846	747061
Motozintla de Mendoza	Chiapas	México	1752	746868
Motozintla de Mendoza	Chiapas	México	1780	747296
Motozintla de Mendoza	Chiapas	México	1819	747055
Motozintla de Mendoza	Chiapas	México	1825	746820
Ocozocoautla	Chiapas	México	1721	747058
Ocozocoautla	Chiapas	México	1741	747048
Ocozocoautla	Chiapas	México	1742	747058
San Pedro Custepéques	Chiapas	México	1755	746869
Soconusco	Chiapas	México	1765	747059
Soconusco	Chiapas	México	1795–1865	744961
Tectitán	Chiapas	México	1825	746820
Tonalá	Chiapas	México	1765	744961
Tuxtla Gutiérrez	Chiapas	México	1765	744961
Tuxtla Gutiérrez	Chiapas	México	1795–1865	744961

CHIHUAHUA

In doing research in the state of Chihuahua it is also important to look under Nueva Vizcaya for the censuses that covered the entire *gobierno* which included Chihuahua.

Locality	Province	Country	Year(s)	Reference
Atotonilco	Chihuahua	México	1777	AGI Indiferente 1526
Atotonilco	Chihuahua	México	1778	AF 16:328
Atotonilco	Chihuahua	México	1779	AGI Indiferente 102
Babonoyaba	Chihuahua	México	1778	AF 16:328
Baborígame	Chihuahua	México	1779	AGI Indiferente 102
Bachíniva	Chihuahua	México	1728	Archivo del Parral
Bachíniva	Chihuahua	México	1777–1779	AGI Indiferente 102[70]
Baqueáchic	Chihuahua	México	1777–1779	AGI Indiferente 102
Batopilillas	Chihuahua	México	1777–1779	AGI Indiferente 102
Caríchic	Chihuahua	México	1777–1779	AGI Guadalajara 255
Cerocahui	Chihuahua	México	1779	AGI Indiferente 102
Chínipas (Santa Inés)	Chihuahua	México	1779	AGI Indiferente 102
Ciénega de los Olivos	Chihuahua	México	1731	Archivo del Parral
Ciénega de los Olivos	Chihuahua	México	1786	MBL 2:36
Colonia Díaz	Chihuahua	México	1897	IGHL
Colonia Dublán	Chihuahua	México	1897	IGHL
Colonia García	Chihuahua	México	1897	IGHL
Colonia Juárez	Chihuahua	México	1897	IGHL
Colonia Mariano	Chihuahua	México	1897	IGHL
Colonia Pacheco	Chihuahua	México	1897	IGHL
Colonia Palomas	Chihuahua	México	1897	IGHL
Cosihuiriáchic	Chihuahua	México	1777–1779	AGI Indiferente 102
Coyáchic	Chihuahua	México	1777–1779	AGI Indiferente 102
El Paso del Río Norte	Chihuahua	México	1680	Santa Fé[71]
El Paso del Río Norte	Chihuahua	México	1784	NMHR 1977:524
Guadalupe del Paso	Chihuahua	México	1692	UNM[72]
Guazápares	Chihuahua	México	1779	AGI Indiferente 102
Guiseguáchic[73]	Chihuahua	México	1778	AF 16:328
Huehuáchic	Chihuahua	México	1779	AGI Indiferente 102
Julimes	Chihuahua	México	1778	AF 16:328

[70] Copy of this *padrón* is found in AF 16:328.3
[71] Possibly at the Archbishop's Archives.
[72] A copy of this census is also found at the Mesa Family History Center, Mesa, Arizona.
[73] San Andrés Guiseguáchic.

Locality	Province	Country	Year(s)	Reference
Matáchic	Chihuahua	México	1777–1779	AGI Indiferente 102
Morís	Chihuahua	México	1777–1779	AGI Indiferente 102
Navogame	Chihuahua	México	1779	AGI Indiferente 102
Parral	Chihuahua	México	1768	U. of Texas, Austin
Parral	Chihuahua	México	1777	AGI Indiferente 102
Parral	Chihuahua	México	1778	AGI Indiferente 102
San Bartolomé	Chihuahua	México	1604	AGI Guadalajara 28: 78-79
San Bartolomé	Chihuahua	México	1707	Archivo del Parral
San Bartolomé	Chihuahua	México	1728	Archivo del Parral
San Gerónimo	Chihuahua	México	1778	AF 16:328
Santa Ana	Chihuahua	México	1779	AGI Indiferente 102
Santa Bárbara	Chihuahua	México	1604	AGI Guadalajara 28: 78-79
Santa Bárbara	Chihuahua	México	1649	Archivo del Parral
Santa Bárbara	Chihuahua	México	1707	Archivo del Parral
Santa Bárbara	Chihuahua	México	1731	Archivo del Parral
Santa Bárbara	Chihuahua	México	1777	AGI Indiferente 1526
Santa Bárbara	Chihuahua	México	1778	BNP FM 201: 47v-48v
Santa Isabel	Chihuahua	México	1728	Archivo del Parral
Santa Isabel	Chihuahua	México	1778	AF 16:328
Tahueáchic[74]	Chihuahua	México	1777–1779	AGI Indiferente 102
Tapacolmes	Chihuahua	México	1778	AF 16:328
Temósachic	Chihuahua	México	1777–1779	AGI Indiferente 102
Tomóchic	Chihuahua	México	1777–1779	AGI Indiferente 102
Tubares[75]	Chihuahua	México	1779	AGI Indiferente 102
Tubares[76]	Chihuahua	México	1779	AGI Indiferente 102
Tutuaca	Chihuahua	México	1777–1779	AGI Indiferente 102

---

[74] San Francisco de Borja de Tahueáchic.
[75] Concepción Tubares.
[76] San Miguel Tubares.

COAHUILA

Locality	Province	Country	Year(s)	Reference
	Coahuila	México	1676	AM Saltillo
	Coahuila	México	1684	AM Saltillo 3/1:76[77]
	Coahuila[78]	México	1702–1703	AGN PI 28:4:113-172
	Coahuila	México	1868	AGEC
Monclova	Coahuila	México	1760	AGI Guadalajara 401
Monclova	Coahuila	México	1764	AAG
Múzquiz	Coahuila	México	1737	LBN 3:56
Parras	Coahuila	México	1604	AGI Guadalajara 28:78-89
Parras	Coahuila	México	1707	Archivo del Parral
Parras	Coahuila	México	1819	AM Saltillo
Parras	Coahuila	México	1825	AGEC
Saltillo	Coahuila	México	1604	AGI Guadalajara 28:78-89
Saltillo	Coahuila	México	1676	AM Saltillo
Saltillo	Coahuila	México	1725	Archivo del Parral
Saltillo	Coahuila	México	1760	AGI Guadalajara 401
Saltillo	Coahuila	México	1777	AM Saltillo 31:2; IGHL
Saltillo	Coahuila	México	1779	AM Saltillo 32:9
Saltillo	Coahuila	México	1785	AM Saltillo 37/1:42
Saltillo	Coahuila	México	1791[79]	AM Saltillo 43:1
Saltillo	Coahuila	México	1826	AM Saltillo
Saltillo	Coahuila	México	1833	AM Saltillo
Saltillo	Coahuila	México	1881[80]	AM Saltillo 124:38
San Francisco[81]	Coahuila	México	1703	AGN PI 28:155v-157v
San Juan Bautista[82]	Coahuila	México	1755–1770	AGN PI 22:1:1-61
Torreón	Coahuila	México	1892	AGEC
Villa Unión	Coahuila	México	1749	LBN 3:56
Zaragoza	Coahuila	México	1753	LBN 3:56

---

[77] Caja 3/1, Expediente 76.

[78] Troop Lists.

[79] May be for 1793.

[80] There are also summaries of censuses for Saltillo for 1831–1833 in AM Saltillo, Caja 78, Expediente 25, Censo de Leona Vicario y Villa Longín, Saltillo (no population data); and 1848 of Saltillo (summary information only).

[81] San Francisco de Coahuila de la Nueva Tlaxcala. The Tlaxcalan settlement, which, with its mission San Miguel de Aguayo, adjoined Monclova on the north, had a *lista de vecinos* in 1703, found at the Archivo General de la Nación, Ramo de Provincias Internas, legajo 28, folios 155v–157v.

[82] Troop Lists.

COLIMA

Locality	Province	Country	Year(s)	Reference
Almoloya	Colima	México	1820	168820
Colima	Colima	México	1532	AGN HI 41
Colima	Colima	México	1820	AGN PAD 11
Colima	Colima	México	1820	168809
Colima	Colima	México	1820	168822

DISTRITO FEDERAL

The Family History Library in Salt Lake City has filmed some of the following padrones twice. The first filming appears as a 400000 series, the second filming as a 700000 series.

Locality	Province	Country	Year(s)	Reference
Acatlán	D.F.	México	1933	442119
Acatlán	D.F.	México	1778	641724
Cuyoacán	D.F.	México	1792	AGN PAD 6; CCM 9-10
Guadalupe Hidalgo	D.F.	México	1886	AAA 6816
Ixtacalco	D.F.	México	1779	442121; 708357:4
Ixtacalco	D.F.	México	1900	707310
Mexicaltzingo[83]	D.F.	México	1778	442121; 708357:3
Mexico City	D.F.	México	1689	GLC; AGN RC 55:221-75
Mexico City	D.F.	México	1753	BAG[84]
Mexico City	D.F.	México	1754	442140; 708356
Mexico City	D.F.	México	1768–1769	442103
Mexico City	D.F.	México	1769	708358:2
Mexico City	D.F.	México	1772–1776	442104
Mexico City	D.F.	México	1776	708358
Mexico City	D.F.	México	1777	442105
Mexico City	D.F.	México	1778–1780	442106
Mexico City	D.F.	México	1780	708357:5; 708358:3
Mexico City	D.F.	México	1782–1784	442107
Mexico City	D.F.	México	1785–1787	442108
Mexico City	D.F.	México	1788–1792	442109
Mexico City	D.F.	México	1790	AGN PAD 107
Mexico City	D.F.	México	1791	Madrid[85]
Mexico City	D.F.	México	1793	442110
Mexico City	D.F.	México	1794	708358:2,3
Mexico City	D.F.	México	1794	708357:5
Mexico City	D.F.	México	1797–1801	442111
Mexico City	D.F.	México	1798–1809	AGN HI 452:XI
Mexico City	D.F.	México	1800	AGN PAD 96-106
Mexico City	D.F.	México	1802–1805	442112

---

[83] San Marcos de Mexicaltzingo.

[84] Eduardo Báez Macías, "Planos y censos de la ciudad de México, 1753," *Boletín del Archivo General de la Nación* 7 (1966):407–484; 8 (1967):486–1156.

[85] Private papers of the Counts of Revillagigedo in their archive in Madrid.

Locality	Province	Country	Year(s)	Reference
Mexico City	D.F.	México	1806–1813	442113
Mexico City	D.F.	México	1807	AGN PAD 102
Mexico City	D.F.	México	1809	AGN HI 452:II
Mexico City	D.F.	México	1811–1812	AGN PAD 53-77
Mexico City	D.F.	México	1814–1815	442114
Mexico City	D.F.	México	1816–1821	442115
Mexico City	D.F.	México	1823–1825	442116
Mexico City	D.F.	México	1842	AAA 3411, 3412
Mexico City	D.F.	México	1848	AAA 3407, 3409, 3413
Mexico City	D.F.	México	1850	AAA 3406, 3417, 3419
Mexico City	D.F.	México	1863	AAA 3410
Mexico City	D.F.	México	1866	AAA 3430
Mexico City	D.F.	México	1873	AAA 3420, 3421
Mexico City	D.F.	México	1874	AAA 3422
Mexico City	D.F.	México	1875	AAA 3415, 3416
Mexico City	D.F.	México	1876	AAA 3414
Mexico City	D.F.	México	1877	AAA 3408
Mexico City	D.F.	México	1878	AAA 3414
Mexico City	D.F.	México	1879	AAA 3427
Mexico City	D.F.	México	1882	AAA[86]
Mexico City	D.F.	Méxcio	1895	1st National Census[87]
Mexico City	D.F.	México	1900	2nd National Census
Mexico City	D.F.	México	1910	AAA[88]
Mexico City	D.F.	México	1920	AAA[89]
Mexico City	D.F.	México	1921	4th National Census
Mexico City	D.F.	México	1930	5th National Census
Mexico City	D.F.	México	1940	6th National Census
Mexico City	D.F.	México	1950	7th National Census
Mexico City	D.F.	México	1960	8th National Census
Mexico City	D.F.	México	1970	9th National Census
Mexico City	D.F.	México	1980	10th National Census
Mexico City	D.F.	México	1990	11th National Census
Milpa Alta	D.F.	México	1797	442121; 708358:5
Montecillo	D.F.	México	1803	795140
Naucalpan	D.F.	México	1775	BNE, manuscript 3650
Sagrario	D.F.	México	1670–1673	442095
Sagrario	D.F.	México	1670–1720	036415
Sagrario	D.F.	México	1678–1741	442096

---

[86] Archivo del Antiguo Ayuntamiento, bundles 3418, 3423, 3424, 3426, 3428, 3429, and 3431.

[87] See references to the national censuses at the beginning of the Mexico section.

[88] Archivo del Antiguo Ayuntamiento, bundles 3432, 3433, 3435, 3437, 3442, 3445, 3447, and 3450. This is the 3rd National Census.

[89] Archivo del Antiguo Ayuntamiento, bundles 3434, 3436, 3438–3441, 3443, 3444, 3448, 3449, and 3451.

Locality	Province	Country	Year(s)	Reference
Sagrario	D.F.	México	1702–1721	442093
Sagrario	D.F.	México	1721–1734	036416
Sagrario	D.F.	México	1728–1733	442094
Sagrario	D.F.	México	1733–1739	442095
Sagrario	D.F.	México	1735–1750	036417
Sagrario	D.F.	México	1743–1752	442097
Sagrario	D.F.	México	1751–1757	036418
Sagrario	D.F.	México	1752–1755	442098
Sagrario	D.F.	México	1756–1760	442099
Sagrario	D.F.	México	1758–1766	036419
Sagrario	D.F.	México	1761–1765	442100
Sagrario	D.F.	México	1766–1768	442101
Sagrario	D.F.	México	1767–1769	036420
Sagrario	D.F.	México	1768–1769	442102
Sagrario	D.F.	México	1770–1773	036421
Sagrario	D.F.	México	1775–1783	036422
Sagrario	D.F.	México	1784–1787	036423
Sagrario	D.F.	México	1788–1801	036424
Sagrario	D.F.	México	1802–1806	036425
Sagrario	D.F.	México	1807–1808	036426
Sagrario	D.F.	México	1810–1813	036427
Sagrario	D.F.	México	1814–1816	036428
Sagrario	D.F.	México	1821–1824	036429
Sagrario	D.F.	México	1825–1921	036430
San Antonio[90]	D.F.	México	1776	442117; 708356
San Gabriel Arcangel	D.F.	México	1777	708351:2
San Miguel Arcangel	D.F.	México	1769	708356
San Miguel Arcangel	D.F.	México	1771–1774	206264
San Miguel Arcangel	D.F.	México	1776	442117; 708356
San Miguel Arcangel	D.F.	México	1779–1784	206265
San Miguel Arcangel	D.F.	México	1786–1795	206266
San Miguel Arcangel	D.F.	México	1793	442118
San Miguel Arcangel	D.F.	México	1794	708358
San Miguel Arcangel	D.F.	México	1797	206267
San Miguel Arcangel	D.F.	México	1802–1803	206268
San Miguel Arcangel	D.F.	México	1804–1809	206269
San Miguel Arcangel	D.F.	México	1808–1809	206270
San Miguel Arcangel	D.F.	México	1810–1814	206271
San Miguel Arcangel	D.F.	México	1815–1816	206272
San Miguel Arcangel	D.F.	México	1817–1819	206273
San Miguel Arcangel	D.F.	México	1821–1822	206274
San Pablo Apóstol	D.F.	México	1780	708357

[90] San Antonio de las Huertas.

Locality	Province	Country	Year(s)	Reference
San Pablo Apóstol	D.F.	México	1780–1794	442118
San Pablo Apóstol	D.F.	México	1794	708358
San Sebastián	D.F.	México	1779	037614
San Sebastián	D.F.	México	1806–1810	037614
San Sebastián	D.F.	México	1817–1819	037614
San Sebastián	D.F.	México	1824	037614
Santa Catarina	D.F.	México	1775–1780	036139
Santa Catarina	D.F.	México	1781–1786	036140
Santa Catarina	D.F.	México	1787–1788	036141
Santa Cruz Acalpixca	D.F.	México	1797–1934	708358:6
Santa Cruz Acalpixca	D.F.	México	1933–1934	708359
Santa Cruz y Soledad	D.F.	México	1793	442118; 708358:1
Santa Fé de los Altos	D.F.	México	1797	442119; 708358:4
Santa Ma. la Redonda	D.F.	México	1777	442119; 708357:1
Santa Veracruz	D.F.	México	1768	442119; 708356
Santa Veracruz	D.F.	México	1713–1811	284860
Santa Veracruz	D.F.	México	1721–1762	035975
Santa Veracruz	D.F.	México	1726–1766	035977
Santa Veracruz	D.F.	México	1768	035976
Santa Veracruz	D.F.	México	1782–1808	035978
Tacuba	D.F.	México	1777	442119; 708357
Tacuba	D.F.	México	1792	AGN PAD 6; CCM 9-10
Xochimilco	D.F.	México	1778	AGN HI 72:71-75v
Xochimilco	D.F.	México	1783	AGN PAD 29:4
Xochimilco	D.F.	México	1792	AGN PAD 29; CCM 6-7
Xochimilco	D.F.	México	1797	442121; 708358

GUANAJUATO

Locality	Province	Country	Year(s)	Reference
Acámbaro	Guanajuato	México	1746	768901
Acámbaro	Guanajuato	México	1747	768920
Acámbaro	Guanajuato	México	1758	769986-769989
Acámbaro	Guanajuato	México	1759	772017-772020
Acámbaro	Guanajuato	México	1763	774202
Acámbaro	Guanajuato	México	1763	774211-774116
Acámbaro	Guanajuato	México	1768	774114-774116
Acámbaro	Guanajuato	México	1770	774144
Acámbaro	Guanajuato	México	1772	761550
Acámbaro	Guanajuato	México	1780	762635
Acámbaro	Guanajuato	México	1782	762635
Acámbaro	Guanajuato	México	1792	762635
Acámbaro	Guanajuato	México	1793	762635; 763127
Acámbaro	Guanajuato	México	1794	762636
Acámbaro	Guanajuato	México	1795	762636
Acámbaro	Guanajuato	México	1796	762636
Acámbaro	Guanajuato	México	1797	762637
Acámbaro	Guanajuato	México	1799	762637
Acámbaro	Guanajuato	México	1800	762637; 795136
Acámbaro	Guanajuato	México	1801	795138
Acámbaro	Guanajuato	México	1804	793816
Acámbaro	Guanajuato	México	1805	762638
Acámbaro	Guanajuato	México	1806	762638
Acámbaro	Guanajuato	México	1807	793879
Acámbaro	Guanajuato	México	1809	762638
Acámbaro	Guanajuato	México	1810	793882
Acámbaro	Guanajuato	México	1841	793884
Amoles[91]	Guanajuato	México	1746	768900-768902
Amoles	Guanajuato	México	1758	769986-769989
Amoles	Guanajuato	México	1760	763271-763272
Amoles	Guanajuato	México	1770	762931
Amoles	Guanajuato	México	1772	761553
Apaseo	Guanajuato	México	1747	768916-768918

[91] San Francisco Sichú (Xichú) de los Amues, a mining camp in the provincia of San Luis de la Paz, lying to the east of that city, and northeast of San Miguel el Grande. See also Sichú.

Locality	Province	Country	Year(s)	Reference
Apaseo	Guanajuato	México	1747	768921
Apaseo	Guanajuato	México	1758	769986-769989
Apaseo	Guanajuato	México	1759	772017-772020
Apaseo	Guanajuato	México	1770	774144
Apaseo	Guanajuato	México	1772	761553
Apaseo	Guanajuato	México	1776	776745-776746
Apaseo	Guanajuato	México	1778	776888
Arroyo Zarco	Guanajuato	México	1787	AGN PI 202:2:225-230
Arroyo Zarco	Guanajuato	México	1790	AGN PI 202:2:225-230
Arroyo Zarco	Guanajuato	México	1808	AGN PI 202:1:12
Cacalote	Guanajuato	México	1801	795138
Celaya	Guanajuato	México	1747	768916-768918
Celaya	Guanajuato	México	1747	768921
Celaya	Guanajuato	México	1758	769986-769989
Celaya	Guanajuato	México	1759	772017-772020
Celaya	Guanajuato	México	1760	763271
Celaya	Guanajuato	México	1763	774212-774213
Celaya	Guanajuato	México	1768	774114-774116
Celaya	Guanajuato	México	1770	774142-774143
Celaya	Guanajuato	México	1772	761553
Celaya	Guanajuato	México	1792	AGN HI 72:168-175v
Celaya	Guanajuato	México	1793	763127
Celaya	Guanajuato	México	1800	795135-795136
Celaya	Guanajuato	México	1801	795137
Celaya	Guanajuato	México	1802	AGN PAD 23, 26
Celaya	Guanajuato	México	1803	795140
Celaya	Guanajuato	México	1804	795143
Celaya	Guanajuato	México	1805	793876
Celaya	Guanajuato	México	1806	793878
Celaya	Guanajuato	México	1807	793879
Celaya	Guanajuato	México	1808	793880
Chamacuero	Guanajuato	México	1758	769986-769989
Chamacuero	Guanajuato	México	1763	774211-774213
Chamacuero	Guanajuato	México	1768	774103-774104
Chamacuero	Guanajuato	México	1770	774142-774143
Chamacuero	Guanajuato	México	1772	761553
Chamacuero	Guanajuato	México	1776	776736-776738
Chamacuero	Guanajuato	México	1809	793881
Coroneo	Guanajuato	México	1746	768900
Coroneo	Guanajuato	México	1759	772017-772020
Coroneo	Guanajuato	México	1763	774211-774213
Coroneo	Guanajuato	México	1768	774114-774116
Coroneo	Guanajuato	México	1770	774142-774143
Coroneo	Guanajuato	México	1800	795136
Coroneo	Guanajuato	México	1801	795138

Locality	Province	Country	Year(s)	Reference
Coroneo	Guanajuato	México	1804	793876
Coroneo	Guanajuato	México	1807	793879
Corral de Piedra	Guanajuato	México	1790	AGN PI 202:2:225-230
Corral de Piedra	Guanajuato	México	1808	AGN PI 202:1:12
Emenguaro	Guanajuato	México	1747	768916-768918
Emenguaro	Guanajuato	México	1747	768921
Guanajuato (Sta. Ana)	Guanajuato	México	1668	765591
Guanajuato	Guanajuato	México	1746	768901-768902
Guanajuato (Sta. Ana)	Guanajuato	México	1746	768900
Guanajuato	Guanajuato	México	1747	768916-768918
Guanajuato	Guanajuato	México	1747	768921
Guanajuato	Guanajuato	México	1758	762639
Guanajuato	Guanajuato	México	1759	772017-772020
Guanajuato	Guanajuato	México	1763	774202
Guanajuato	Guanajuato	México	1770	774144
Guanajuato	Guanajuato	México	1772	761550
Guanajuato	Guanajuato	México	1800	795135
Guanajuato	Guanajuato	México	1801	795138
Guanajuato	Guanajuato	México	1803	795140
Guanajuato	Guanajuato	México	1804	795142
Guanajuato	Guanajuato	México	1805	793876-793877
Guanajuato	Guanajuato	México	1808	793880
Guanajuato	Guanajuato	México	1809	793881
Iramuco`	Guanajuato	México	1759	772017
Iramuco	Guanajuato	México	1800	795136
Iramuco	Guanajuato	México	1801	795138
Iramuco	Guanajuato	México	1804	793876
Iramuco	Guanajuato	México	1807	793879
Iramuco	Guanajuato	México	1810	799882
Irapuato	Guanajuato	México	1703–1796	773538
Irapuato	Guanajuato	México	1758	769986-769989
Irapuato	Guanajuato	México	1759	772017-772020
Irapuato	Guanajuato	México	1760	785447
Irapuato	Guanajuato	México	1763	774211-774213
Irapuato	Guanajuato	México	1770	774142-774143
Irapuato	Guanajuato	México	1770	776752
Irapuato	Guanajuato	México	1772	61443
Irapuato	Guanajuato	México	1790	AGN PAD 37
Irapuato	Guanajuato	México	1804	793884
Jerécuaro	Guanajuato	México	1758	769987-769989
Jerécuaro	Guanajuato	México	1759	772017-772020
Jerécuaro	Guanajuato	México	1763	774213
Jerécuaro	Guanajuato	México	1768	774114-774116
Jerécuaro	Guanajuato	México	1770	774144
Jerécuaro	Guanajuato	México	1782	762942

Locality	Province	Country	Year(s)	Reference
León	Guanajuato	México	1746	768900-768902
León	Guanajuato	México	1747	768916-768918
León	Guanajuato	México	1747	768921
León	Guanajuato	México	1758	769986-769989
León	Guanajuato	México	1759	772017-772020
León	Guanajuato	México	1760	763271-763272
León	Guanajuato	México	1763	774211-774213
León	Guanajuato	México	1768	774103-774104
León	Guanajuato	México	1770	774142-774143
León	Guanajuato	México	1772	761553
León	Guanajuato	México	1776	776745-776746
León	Guanajuato	México	1793	763127
Marfil	Guanajuato	México	1747	768916-768918
Marfil	Guanajuato	México	1747	768921
Marfil	Guanajuato	México	1758	769986-769989
Marfil	Guanajuato	México	1759	772017-772020
Marfil	Guanajuato	México	1760	785447
Marfil	Guanajuato	México	1763	774211-774213
Marfil	Guanajuato	México	1768	774103-774104
Marfil	Guanajuato	México	1770	774154-774155
Marfil	Guanajuato	México	1772	761550
Marfil	Guanajuato	México	1776	795134
Nuestra Sra. de Gpe.	Guanajuato	México	1787	AGN PI 202:3:233-235
Neutla	Guanajuato	México	1760	763271
Neutla	Guanajuato	México	1772	761550
Octopán	Guanajuato	México	1758	768986-768989
Octopán	Guanajuato	México	1760	763271
Octopán	Guanajuato	México	1770	762931
Octopán	Guanajuato	México	1772	795134
Palmar de Vega	Guanajuato	México	1768	774114-774116
Palmar de Vega	Guanajuato	México	1777	776752
Parangueo	Guanajuato	México	1747	768916-768918
Parangueo	Guanajuato	México	1747	768921
Parangueo	Guanajuato	México	1763	774211-774213
Parangueo	Guanajuato	México	1768	782002-782003
Parangueo	Guanajuato	México	1770	774142-774143
Parangueo	Guanajuato	México	1772	761553
Parangueo	Guanajuato	México	1776	776745-776746
Pénjamo	Guanajuato	México	1758	785446
Pénjamo	Guanajuato	México	1760	772369
Pénjamo	Guanajuato	México	1768	774103-774104
Pénjamo	Guanajuato	México	1770	774144
Pénjamo	Guanajuato	México	1776	776745-776746
Pénjamo	Guanajuato	México	1778	776888
Pénjamo	Guanajuato	México	1836–1838	793884

Locality	Province	Country	Year(s)	Reference
Piedra Gorda	Guanajuato	México	1747	768916-768918
Piedra Gorda	Guanajuato	México	1747	768921
Piedra Gorda	Guanajuato	México	1758	769987-769989
Piedra Gorda	Guanajuato	México	1759	772017
Piedra Gorda	Guanajuato	México	1763	774211-774213
Piedra Gorda	Guanajuato	México	1768	774103-774014
Piedra Gorda	Guanajuato	México	1770	774144
Piedra Gorda	Guanajuato	México	1772	761550
Piedra Gorda	Guanajuato	México	1778	776888
Pinícuaro	Guanajuato	México	1763	774211-774213
Pozos	Guanajuato	México	1763	774213
Pozos	Guanajuato	México	1805	793876
Pozos	Guanajuato	México	1807	793879
Pozos	Guanajuato	México	1808	793880
Pozos	Guanajuato	México	1809	793881
Pozos	Guanajuato	México	1810	793882
Pueblo Chico	Guanajuato	México	1760	763271-763272
Pueblo Nuevo	Guanajuato	México	1746	768900-768902
Pueblo Nuevo	Guanajuato	México	1793	1163510
Purísima	Guanajuato	México	1768	774103-774104
Rincón de León	Guanajuato	México	1747	768916
Salamanca	Guanajuato	México	1668	765271
Salamanca	Guanajuato	México	1747	768916-768918
Salamanca	Guanajuato	México	1747	768921
Salamanca	Guanajuato	México	1758	769986-769989
Salamanca	Guanajuato	México	1759	772017-772020
Salamanca	Guanajuato	México	1760	785447
Salamanca	Guanajuato	México	1763	774211-774213
Salamanca	Guanajuato	México	1768	782002-782003
Salvatierra	Guanajuato	México	1747	768916-768918
Salvatierra	Guanajuato	México	1747	768921
Salvatierra	Guanajuato	México	1758	769986-769989
Salvatierra	Guanajuato	México	1759	772017-772020
Salvatierra	Guanajuato	México	1763	774211-774213
Salvatierra	Guanajuato	México	1768	774114-774116
Salvatierra	Guanajuato	México	1770	774154-774155
Salvatierra	Guanajuato	México	1772	761553
Salvatierra	Guanajuato	México	1790	AGN PAD 45
San Fco. del Rincón	Guanajuato	México	1660	765609
San Fco. del Rincón	Guanajuato	México	1746	768900-768902
San Fco. del Rincón	Guanajuato	México	1763	774211-774213
San Fco. del Rincón	Guanajuato	México	1768	774103-774104
San Fco. del Rincón	Guanajuato	México	1770	774154-774155
San Fco. del Rincón	Guanajuato	México	1772	761553
San Fco. del Rincón	Guanajuato	México	1776	776736-776738

Locality	Province	Country	Year(s)	Reference
San Fco. del Rincón	Guanajuato	México	1776	776745-776746
San José de Linares	Guanajuato	México	1790	AGN PI 202:2:225-230
San José de Linares	Guanajuato	México	1808	AGN PI 202:1:12
San Juan de la Vega	Guanajuato	México	1768	774114-774116
San Juan de la Vega	Guanajuato	México	1770	762931
San Juan de la Vega	Guanajuato	México	1772	761550
San Juan de la Vega	Guanajuato	México	1776	776736-776738
San Luis de la Paz	Guanajuato	México	1703–1796	773538
San Luis de la Paz	Guanajuato	México	1743	AGN HI 522:9:96-99v
San Luis de la Paz	Guanajuato	México	1747	768916-768918
San Luis de la Paz	Guanajuato	México	1747	774921
San Luis de la Paz	Guanajuato	México	1759	772017-772020
San Luis de la Paz	Guanajuato	México	1760	785447
San Luis de la Paz	Guanajuato	México	1763	774211-774213
San Luis de la Paz	Guanajuato	México	1768	774114-774116
San Luis de la Paz	Guanajuato	México	1770	774144
San Luis de la Paz	Guanajuato	México	1776	776745-776746
San Luis de la Paz	Guanajuato	México	1793	763127
San Luis de la Paz	Guanajuato	México	1809	793881
San Miguel el Grande	Guanajuato	México	1703–1796	773538
San Miguel el Grande	Guanajuato	México	1746	768900-768902
San Miguel el Grande	Guanajuato	México	1747	768920
San Miguel el Grande	Guanajuato	México	1792	AGN PAD 24, 34, 36
Santa Fé Real	Guanajuato	México	1747	768916-768918
Santa Fé Real	Guanajuato	México	1747	768921
Santa Fé Real	Guanajuato	México	1772	761550
Santa Fé Real	Guanajuato	México	1776	776736-776738
Santa Fé Real	Guanajuato	México	1804	795142-795143
Santa Rosa	Guanajuato	México	1772	761550
Santa Rosa	Guanajuato	México	1787	AGN PI 202:3:244
Santa Rosa	Guanajuato	México	1801	795138
Santa Rosa	Guanajuato	México	1803	795140
Santa Rosa	Guanajuato	México	1804	795142
Santa Rosa	Guanajuato	México	1805	793877
Santa Rosa	Guanajuato	México	1806	793878
Santa Rosa	Guanajuato	México	1807	793879
Santa Rosa	Guanajuato	México	1808	793880
Santa Rosa	Guanajuato	México	1809	793881
Santa Rosa	Guanajuato	México	1810	793882
Sichú[92]	Guanajuato	México	1743	AGN HI 522:8:96-97
Sichú	Guanajuato	México	1787	AGN PI 202:2:225-230
Silao	Guanajuato	México	1668	765591

---

[92] See also Amoles.

Locality	Province	Country	Year(s)	Reference
Silao	Guanajuato	México	1756	768901-768902
Silao	Guanajuato	México	1747	768916
Silao	Guanajuato	México	1758	769986-769989
Silao	Guanajuato	México	1759	772017-772020
Silao	Guanajuato	México	1760	763271-763272
Silao	Guanajuato	México	1763	774211-774213
Silao	Guanajuato	México	1768	774114-774116
Silao	Guanajuato	México	1770	774144
Silao	Guanajuato	México	1772	768917-768918
Silao	Guanajuato	México	1772	768921
Silao	Guanajuato	México	1776	776736-776738
Silao	Guanajuato	México	1790	AGN PAD 42
Tarandácuaro	Guanajuato	México	1758	769986-769989
Tarandácuaro	Guanajuato	México	1800	795136
Tarandácuaro	Guanajuato	México	1801	795138
Tarandácuaro	Guanajuato	México	1804	793876
Tarandácuaro	Guanajuato	México	1807	793879
Tarandácuaro	Guanajuato	México	1810	793882
Tarimoro	Guanajuato	México	1883	793884
Tierrablanca	Guanajuato	México	1797	641732
Tierrablanca	Guanajuato	México	1821	1158755
Uriangato	Guanajuato	México	1747	768916-768918
Uriangato	Guanajuato	México	1747	768921
Valle de Santiago	Guanajuato	México	1747	768916-768918
Valle de Santiago	Guanajuato	México	1747	768921
Valle de Santiago	Guanajuato	México	1758	769986-769989
Valle de Santiago	Guanajuato	México	1759	772017-772020
Valle de Santiago	Guanajuato	México	1763	774211-774213
Valle de Santiago	Guanajuato	México	1768	774114-774116
Valle de Santiago	Guanajuato	México	1770	774144
Valle de Santiago	Guanajuato	México	1793	763127
Yurirapúndaro	Guanajuato	México	1747	768916-768918
Yurirapúndaro	Guanajuato	México	1747	768921
Yurirapúndaro	Guanajuato	México	1758	769986-769989
Yurirapúndaro	Guanajuato	México	1759	772017-772020
Yurirapúndaro	Guanajuato	México	1763	774211-774213
Yurirapúndaro	Guanajuato	México	1768	774114-774116
Yurirapúndaro	Guanajuato	México	1770	774154-774155
Yurirapúndaro	Guanajuato	México	1772	761550
Yurirapúndaro	Guanajuato	México	1776	776736

GUERRERO

Locality	Province	Country	Year(s)	Reference
Acapetlahuaya	Guerrero	México	1778	442121:6
Acapetlahuaya	Guerrero	México	1778	641724:2
Acapetlahuaya	Guerrero	México	1790	AGN PAD 4
Acapulco	Guerrero	México	1792	AGN PAD 16:213-430
Alahuistlán	Guerrero	México	1790	AGN PAD 9
Alcozauca	Guerrero	México	1777	AGI México 2578-2581
Apastla	Guerrero	México	1790	AGN PAD 10
Atenango del Río	Guerrero	México	1797	442122:5
Atenango del Río	Guerrero	México	1797	641724:6
Atenango del Río	Guerrero	México	1831–1840	1222604:4
Atlamaxacingo	Guerrero	México	1777	AGI México 2578-2581
Atlistaca	Guerrero	México	1777	AGI México 2578-2581
Atoyac	Guerrero	México	1747	768920
Atoyac	Guerrero	México	1758	769986-769989
Atoyac	Guerrero	México	1759	772017-772020
Atoyac	Guerrero	México	1763	774202
Atoyac	Guerrero	México	1768	774103-774104
Atoyac	Guerrero	México	1770	774142-774143
Atoyac	Guerrero	México	1776	776736-776738
Axuchitlán	Guerrero	México	1668	765271
Axuchitlán	Guerrero	México	1746	768900-768902
Axuchitlán	Guerrero	México	1759	772017-772020
Axuchitlán	Guerrero	México	1763	774202
Axuchitlán	Guerrero	México	1768	782002-782003
Axuchitlán	Guerrero	México	1770	774154-774155
Axuchitlán	Guerrero	México	1772	761550
Ciudad Guerrero	Guerrero	México	1760	763271
Ciudad Guerrero	Guerrero	México	1763	774213
Ciudad Guerrero	Guerrero	México	1772	761550
Coahuayutla	Guerrero	México	1758	769986-769989
Coahuayutla	Guerrero	México	1759	772017-772020
Coahuayutla	Guerrero	México	1770	774154-774155
Coahuayutla	Guerrero	México	1776	776736-776738
Coahuayutla	Guerrero	México	1800	795135-795136
Coahuayutla	Guerrero	México	1803	795140
Coatepec	Guerrero	México	1790	AGN PAD 10
Coxcatlán	Guerrero	México	1760	785447
Coyuca de Benítez	Guerrero	México	1743	AGI, Indiferentes 107
Coyuca de Benítez	Guerrero	México	1747	768916

Locality	Province	Country	Year(s)	Reference
Coyuca de Benítez	Guerrero	México	1760	763271
Coyuca de Benítez	Guerrero	México	1763	774213
Coyuca de Benítez	Guerrero	México	1772	761550
Curingueas	Guerrero	México	1782	762942
Cutzamalá de Pinzón	Guerrero	México	1746	768900-768902
Cutzamalá de Pinzón	Guerrero	México	1770	774142-774143
Cutzamalá de Pinzón	Guerrero	México	1772	761553
Cutzamalá de Pinzón	Guerrero	México	1776	776736-776738
Cutzamalá de Pinzón	Guerrero	México	1777	776752
Cutzamalá de Pinzón	Guerrero	México	1778	776888
Cutzamalá de Pinzón	Guerrero	México	1793	763127
Cutzamalá de Pinzón	Guerrero	México	1800	795135
Cutzamalá de Pinzón	Guerrero	México	1893	1164184:7
Guamuchtitlán	Guerrero	México	1777	AGI México 2578-2581
Igualapan	Guerrero	México	1743	AGI Indiferentes 107:2:1-98
Igualapan	Guerrero	México	1791	AGN PAD 18:209-306
Ixcateopan	Guerrero	México	1800	AGN PAD 9
Ixcateopan	Guerrero	México	1777	AGI México 2578-2581
Metlatono	Guerrero	México	1777	AGI México 2578-2581
Petatlán	Guerrero	México	1746	768900-768902
Petatlán	Guerrero	México	1747	768920
Petatlán	Guerrero	México	1759	772017-772020
Petatlán	Guerrero	México	1768	774114-774116
Petatlán	Guerrero	México	1770	774154-774155
Petatlán	Guerrero	México	1776	776736-776738
Petatlán	Guerrero	México	1800	795135
Pilcaya	Guerrero	México	1797	442127:2-3; 641728:3
Poliutla	Guerrero	México	1747	768920
Pungarabato	Guerrero	México	1743	AGI, Indiferentes 107
Pungarabato	Guerrero	México	1760	763271
Sochihuehuetlán	Guerrero	México	1777	AGI México 2578-2581
Soyatlán	Guerrero	México	1777	AGI México 2578-2581
Taxco de Alarcón	Guerrero	México	1797	442133:1; 641730:4
Tecpán	Guerrero	México	1758	769986-769989
Tecpán	Guerrero	México	1759	772017-772020
Tecpán	Guerrero	México	1772	761553
Tecpán	Guerrero	México	1810	793882
Teloloapan	Guerrero	México	1790	AGN PAD 15
Tetela del Río	Guerrero	México	1743	AGI Indiferente 108
Tistla	Guerrero	México	1790	AGN PAD 17
Tlalcozautitlán	Guerrero	México	1777	AGI México 2578, 2580
Tlapa	Guerrero	México	1791	AGN PAD 21
Tlapehuala	Guerrero	México	1763	774213
Zacatula	Guerrero	México	1758	769986-769989

Locality	Province	Country	Year(s)	Reference
Zacatula	Guerrero	México	1763	774202
Zirándaro	Guerrero	México	1760	763271-763272
Zitlala	Guerrero	México	1777	AGI México 2578, 2580

HIDALGO

The state of Hidalgo has received special attention in this study in order to show the extended type of information that is available for each state in the Revillagigedo census of 1790–1794. Eventually this kind of listing needs to be done for all of the states included in that census.

Locality	Province	Country	Year(s)	Reference
Acatlán	Hidalgo	México	1756–1843	267110
Acatlán	Hidalgo	México	1778	442121; 641724:1
Acatlán	Hidalgo	México	1790	AGN PAD 1:137-138
Acaxochitlán	Hidalgo	México	1790	AGN PAD 1:157-161
Acosa	Hidalgo	México	1790	AGN PAD 2:151
Actopán	Hidalgo	México	1777	442122; 641724
Actopán	Hidalgo	México	1791	AGN PAD 3:26-29v
Aguascalientes	Hidalgo	México	1790	AGN PAD 1:221-223
Alcholoya	Hidalgo	México	1790	AGN PAD 1:97
Altica	Hidalgo	México	1790	AGN PAD 2:151
Amaxaque	Hidalgo	México	1790	AGN PAD 1:213-216
Apán	Hidalgo	México	1792	AGN PAD 5:315-317v
Apapaxtla	Hidalgo	México	1790	AGN PAD 1:162
Apetlalpa	Hidalgo	México	1790	AGN PAD 1:123
Atalpa	Hidalgo	México	1790	AGN PAD 2:328
Atotonilco el Chico	Hidalgo	México	1768	774114-774116
Atotonilco el Chico	Hidalgo	México	1770	774142-774143
Atotonilco el Chico	Hidalgo	México	1776	776745-776746
Atotonilco el Chico	Hidalgo	México	1790	AGN PAD 2:190-202
Atotonilco el Chico	Hidalgo	México	1790	AGN PAD 1:173-189
Atotonilco el Chico	Hidalgo	México	1793	763127
Azuchiclán	Hidalgo	México	1790	AGN PAD 2:60-61
Baños de Atotonilco	Hidalgo	México	1790	AGN PAD 1:231
Barranca de S. Seb.	Hidalgo	México	1790	AGN PAD 2:249-251
Bolsa	Hidalgo	México	1790	AGN PAD 1S:98-99
Cadena	Hidalgo	México	1790	AGN PAD 2:141
Calera	Hidalgo	México	1790	AGN PAD 1:97
Canadá	Hidalgo	México	1790	AGN PAD 2:144
Capulín	Hidalgo	México	1790	AGN PAD 1:115
Cardonal	Hidalgo	México	1790	AGN PAD 2: 36-50; 50
Carmen	Hidalgo	México	1790	AGN PAD 2:53-54
Carmen	Hidalgo	México	1790	AGN PAD 2:186-187
Casas Viejas	Hidalgo	México	1790	AGN PAD 1:231

Locality	Province	Country	Year(s)	Reference
Cempoala	Hidalgo	México	1791	AGN PAD 20:1-4v
Cerro Colorado	Hidalgo	México	1790	AGN PAD 1:216-217
Cerro Gordo	Hidalgo	México	1790	AGN PAD 2:147
Chacalapa	Hidalgo	México	1790	AGN PAD 1:163
Chapultepec	Hidalgo	México	1790	AGN PAD 1:110
Chavarría	Hidalgo	México	1790	AGN PAD 2:142
Chilcuautla	Hidalgo	México	1778	641725
Chilcuautla	Hidalgo	México	1790	AGN PAD 2:56-65
Chilcuautla	Hidalgo	México	1797	641725
Chilcuautla	Hidalgo	México	1797–1798	641725
Chimalguacán	Hidalgo	México	1790	AGN PAD 1:121
Conial	Hidalgo	México	1790	AGN PAD 2:146
Coyado	Hidalgo	México	1790	AGN PAD 2:147
Cruz Santorum	Hidalgo	México	1790	AGN PAD 1:220-221
Cuesco	Hidalgo	México	1790	AGN PAD 2:139
Deca	Hidalgo	México	1790	AGN PAD 2:64-65
Deminyo	Hidalgo	México	1790	AGN PAD 2:61-63
Detentla	Hidalgo	México	1603	AGN HI 522:1:1-7
Devodee	Hidalgo	México	1790	AGN PAD 2:35
Epazoyucán	Hidalgo	México	1768–1836	267065
Exquitlán	Hidalgo	México	1790	AGN PAD 1:126-128
Florida	Hidalgo	México	1790	AGN PAD 2:50-51
Guadalupe	Hidalgo	México	1790	AGN PAD 1:254-257
Guadalupe	Hidalgo	México	1790	AGN PAD 2:54
Guapacalco	Hidalgo	México	1790	AGN PAD 1:130-131
Guasca Saloya	Hidalgo	México	1790	AGN PAD 1:241-249
Guatengo	Hidalgo	México	1790	AGN PAD 1:117
Guatongo	Hidalgo	México	1790	AGN PAD 2:145
Guayapán	Hidalgo	México	1790	AGN PAD 1:100-103
Guerrero	Hidalgo	México	1790	AGN PAD 2:179
Guitepec	Hidalgo	México	1790	AGN PAD 2:143
Huasca	Hidalgo	México	1748–1777	266891
Huasca	Hidalgo	México	1779–1820	266892
Huasca	Hidalgo	México	1848–1864	266893
Huasca	Hidalgo	México	1790	AGN PAD 1:241-249
Huasca Soloya	Hidalgo	México	1790	AGN PAD 1:241-249
Huautla Hidalgo	Hidalgo	México	1797	442126; 641726
Huehuetlan	Hidalgo	México	1777	AGI México 2581
Huejutla	Hidalgo	México	1790	AGN PAD 3
Huichicapan	Hidalgo	México	1722[93]	638445
Huichicapan	Hidalgo	México	1768[94]	638444

[93] This film contains many censuses or padrones for Huichicapan, including the following years: 1722, 1768, 1773, 1777, 1779, 1780, 1781, 1785, 1792, 1795, 1798, 1803, 1818, 1819, 1820, 1822, 1823, 1826, 1846, and 1847.
[94] This film contains padrones for the years 1768, 1773, and 1776.

Locality	Province	Country	Year(s)	Reference
Ilucán	Hidalgo	México	1603	AGN HI 522:1:1-7
Istengo	Hidalgo	México	1790	AGN PAD 1:129-130
Ixcateopan	Hidalgo	México	1790	AGN PAD 15
Ixmiquilpán	Hidalgo	México	1791	AGN PAD 2:4-55; 44
Jesús	Hidalgo	México	1790	AGN PAD 2:202
La Joya	Hidalgo	México	1790	AGN PAD 1:155
Los Reyes	Hidalgo	México	1790	AGN PAD 1:162
Los Reyes	Hidalgo	México	1790	AGN PAD 1:223-230
Mesa	Hidalgo	México	1790	AGN PAD 2:51
Metepec	Hidalgo	México	1790	AGN PAD 1:126
Meztitlán	Hidalgo	México	1809	AHH, Ms 397-2
Mineral del Chico	Hidalgo	México	1820[95]	639811
Nueva	Hidalgo	México	1790	AGN PAD 2:188
Ocotlán	Hidalgo	México	1790	AGN PAD 2:55
Ojo de Agua	Hidalgo	México	1790	AGN PAD 1:110
Omitlán	Hidalgo	México	1790	AGN PAD 2:180-184
Omitlán	Hidalgo	México	1814	267027
Ornillo	Hidalgo	México	1790	AGN PAD 1:230
Pachuca	Hidalgo	México	1790	AGN PAD 2:95-142
Pachuquilla	Hidalgo	México	1790	AGN PAD 2:142
Palmar	Hidalgo	México	1790	AGN PAD 2:140
Paredones	Hidalgo	México	1790	AGN PAD 1:136
Paso	Hidalgo	México	1790	AGN PAD 2:147
Pedregal	Hidalgo	México	1790	AGN PAD 1:124
Peña Fiel	Hidalgo	México	1790	AGN PAD 2:185-186
Peñuela	Hidalgo	México	1790	AGN PAD 1:98-99
Pichiscastla[96]	Hidalgo	México	1790	AGN PAD 1:129-130
Pipilihuasco	Hidalgo	México	1790	AGN PAD 1:209-213
Pirajallas	Hidalgo	México	1790	AGN PAD 2:141
Pozuelos	Hidalgo	México	1790	AGN PAD 2:51
Puerto de Quesada	Hidalgo	México	1790	AGN PAD 2:147
Quaxochapan	Hidalgo	México	1603	AGN HI 522:1:1-7
Real del Monte	Hidalgo	México	1768	442127; 641723
Real del Monte	Hidalgo	México	1790	AGN PAD 2:158-179
Regla (N.S. de)	Hidalgo	México	1790	AGN PAD 1:258-261
Reyes	Hidalgo	México	1790	AGN PAD 1:221-223
Río Grande	Hidalgo	México	1790	AGN PAD 1:207-209
Río Hondo	Hidalgo	México	1790	AGN PAD 1:187-188
Sabina	Hidalgo	México	1790	AGN PAD 2:65
Sabinos	Hidalgo	México	1790	AGN PAD 1:204-207
Saloya	Hidalgo	México	1790	AGN PAD 1:113

---

[95] This film contains padrones for the following years: 1820, 1822, 1836, 1837, 1838, 1839, and 1840.

[96] San Cristóbal de Pichicastla.

Locality	Province	Country	Year(s)	Reference
San Alexo	Hidalgo	México	1790	AGN PAD 1:113
San Andrés	Hidalgo	México	1790	AGN PAD 1:120
San Andrés	Hidalgo	México	1790	AGN PAD 1:123
San Antonio	Hidalgo	México	1790	AGN PAD 1:123
San Antonio	Hidalgo	México	1790	AGN PAD 1:163-165
San Antonio	Hidalgo	México	1790	AGN PAD 1:251-252
San Antonio	Hidalgo	México	1790	AGN PAD 2:53-54
San Antonio	Hidalgo	México	1790	AGN PAD 1:139
San Anto. Buenavista	Hidalgo	México	1790	AGN PAD 1:147
San Anto. Buenavista	Hidalgo	México	1790	AGN PAD 2:63
San Anto. Cabrera	Hidalgo	México	1790	AGN PAD 2:139
San Anto. Guatepec	Hidalgo	México	1790	AGN PAD 1:131-133
San Anto. Tenanco	Hidalgo	México	1790	AGN PAD 1:166-170
San Anto. Xinguilucán	Hidalgo	México	1790	AGN PAD 1:140-143
San Anto. la Estancia	Hidalgo	México	1790	AGN PAD 1:153
S. Anto. Agueguetes	Hidalgo	México	1790	AGN PAD 1:126-128
San Bartolomé	Hidalgo	México	1790	AGN PAD 2:140
San Cayetano	Hidalgo	México	1790	AGN PAD 1:233-234
Sánchez	Hidalgo	México	1790	AGN PAD 2:184-185
San Diego Apulco	Hidalgo	México	1790	AGN PAD 1:128-129
San Diego Caltengo	Hidalgo	México	1790	AGN PAD 1:111-112
San Francisco	Hidalgo	México	1790	AGN PAD 1:149-150
San Francisco	Hidalgo	México	1790	AGN PAD 1:114-115
San Francisco	Hidalgo	México	1790	AGN PAD 2:301
San Francisco	Hidalgo	México	1790	AGN PAD 2:144
S. Fco. Xaltepec	Hidalgo	México	1790	AGN PAD 1:123
San Gerónimo	Hidalgo	México	1790	AGN PAD 1:254-257
San Isidro	Hidalgo	México	1790	AGN PAD 1:236-240
San Isidro Guajomulco	Hidalgo	México	1790	AGN PAD 1:106-107
San Isidro Xocopa	Hidalgo	México	1790	AGN PAD 1:115
San José (el Zéliz)[97]	Hidalgo	México	1790	AGN PAD 2:263-264
San José	Hidalgo	México	1790	AGN PAD 2:52
San José	Hidalgo	México	1790	AGN PAD 2:201
San José Cuyamaloya	Hidalgo	México	1790	AGN PAD 1:144-146
San José Tecanecapa	Hidalgo	México	1790	AGN PAD 1:148-149
San José Tepenacasco	Hidalgo	México	1790	AGN PAD 1:122-123
San Juan	Hidalgo	México	1790	AGN PAD 1:232
San Juan	Hidalgo	México	1790	AGN PAD 1:252-253
San Marcos	Hidalgo	México	1790	AGN PAD 1:163
San Mateo Huichapan	Hidalgo	México	1768–1846	638448
San Miguel	Hidalgo	México	1790	AGN PAD 1:261-263
San Miguel	Hidalgo	México	1790	AGN PAD 2:55-54
San Miguel	Hidalgo	México	1790	AGN PAD 2:144

---

[97] See also Zeliz.

Locality	Province	Country	Year(s)	Reference
San Miguel Escalticia	Hidalgo	México	1790	AGN PAD 1:155
San Miguel Guatengo	Hidalgo	México	1790	AGN PAD 1:108
San Miguel Ocozoa	Hidalgo	México	1790	AGN PAD 2:36-50
San Miguel Terrones	Hidalgo	México	1790	AGN PAD 1:234-236
San Nicolás	Hidalgo	México	1790	AGN PAD 1:119
San Nicolás Acotengo	Hidalgo	México	1790	AGN PAD 1:257-258
San Nicolás Laminilla	Hidalgo	México	1790	AGN PAD 1:154
San Nicolás Tecuaro	Hidalgo	México	1790	AGN PAD 1:150-151
San Nicolás Xalapilla	Hidalgo	México	1790	AGN PAD 1:150-151
San Nicolás Xalatlalco	Hidalgo	México	1790	AGN PAD 1:112-113
San Nicolás el Chico	Hidalgo	México	1790	AGN PAD 1:107
San Pablo	Hidalgo	México	1790	AGN PAD 1:232
San Pasqual	Hidalgo	México	1790	AGN PAD 2:199-200
San Pedro	Hidalgo	México	1790	AGN PAD 1:223-230
San Salvador	Hidalgo	México	1790	AGN PAD 2:153-157
San Sebastián Zopillán	Hidalgo	México	1790	AGN PAD 1:116-117
San Xavier	Hidalgo	México	1790	AGN PAD 2:145
Santa Ana	Hidalgo	México	1790	AGN PAD 1:217-220
Santa Ana Chichicuautla	Hidalgo	México	1790	AGN PAD 1:146-147
Santa Clara	Hidalgo	México	1790	AGN PAD 1:121
Santa Gertrudis	Hidalgo	México	1790	AGN PAD 2:52
Santiago	Hidalgo	México	1790	AGN PAD 1:156
Santiago Tongo	Hidalgo	México	1790	AGN PAD 1:108-109
Santiago del Molino	Hidalgo	México	1790	AGN PAD 1:133-135
Santo Cristo de Zereso	Hidalgo	México	1790	AGN PAD 2:139
Santo Domingo	Hidalgo	México	1790	AGN PAD 2:52
Santo Tomás	Hidalgo	México	1797	442136
Saucillo	Hidalgo	México	1790	AGN PAD 2:140
Suchitepec	Hidalgo	México	1790	AGN PAD 1:154
Tasquillo	Hidalgo	México	1900	707310
Teacalco	Hidalgo	México	1603	AGN HI 522:1:1-7
Tecocomulco	Hidalgo	México	1790	AGN PAD 1:104
Temacaque	Hidalgo	México	1790	AGN PAD 1:152
Tenango	Hidalgo	México	1777	AGI México 2581
Tenango	Hidalgo	México	1790	AGN PAD 1:103
Tepantitla	Hidalgo	México	1790	AGN PAD 1:106-107
Tepeapulco	Hidalgo	México	1779	641732
Tepeapulco	Hidalgo	México	1790	AGN PAD 5
Tepepi del Río	Hidalgo	México	1797	442125
Tepetongo	Hidalgo	México	1790	AGN PAD 1:151
Tesontepec	Hidalgo	México	1790	AGN PAD 2:147-151
Tesontepec	Hidalgo	México	1790	AGN PAD 2:147-157
Tesontepec	Hidalgo	México	1797	641732
Tetepango	Hidalgo	México	1790	AGN PAD 18

Locality	Province	Country	Year(s)	Reference
Tetepango	Hidalgo	México	1900	641752
Teusitlán	Hidalgo	México	1790	AGN PAD 2:265-328
Tezoquipa	Hidalgo	México	1790	AGN PAD 1:99
Tlacapoali	Hidalgo	México	1603	AGN HI 522:1:1-7
Tlanalapán	Hidalgo	México	1779	641732
Tlalistacapa	Hidalgo	México	1603	AGN HI 522:1:1-7
Torcayuca	Hidalgo	México	1790	AGN PAD 2:143-147
Torje Vieja	Hidalgo	México	1790	AGN PAD 1:154
Toro	Hidalgo	México	1790	AGN PAD 2:327
Totoapa el Chico	Hidalgo	México	1790	AGN PAD 1:104-106
Totoapa el Grande	Hidalgo	México	1790	AGN PAD 1:139
Tula	Hidalgo	México	1720[98]	635369
Tula	Hidalgo	México	1720[99]	635370
Tula	Hidalgo	México	1791	AGN PAD 7
Tulancingo	Hidalgo	México	1792	AGN PAD 1:28-89[100]; 46
Tulancingo	Hidalgo	México	1794	266392
Tuni	Hidalgo	México	1790	AGN PAD 2:65
Tutotepec	Hidalgo	México	1790	AGN PAD 1:170-172
Velasco	Hidalgo	México	1790	AGN PAD 2:189
Ventorrillo	Hidalgo	México	1790	AGN PAD 1:118-119
Xagüey de Arriba	Hidalgo	México	1790	AGN PAD 2:152
Xaltepec	Hidalgo	México	1790	AGN PAD 2:146
Zacualoya	Hidalgo	México	1790	AGN PAD 2:64-65
Zacatepec	Hidalgo	México	1790	AGN PAD 1:90-97
Zéliz[101]	Hidalgo	México	1790	AGN PAD 2:263-264
Zimapán	Hidalgo	México	1768	442092; 641723
Zimapán	Hidalgo	México	1770	641734
Zimapán	Hidalgo	México	1771	641734
Zimapán	Hidalgo	México	1779	AGN HI 72:70; 641735
Zimapán	Hidalgo	México	1797	641735
Zirándaro	Hidalgo	México	1760	763271
Zopillán (S. Sebastián)	Hidalgo	México	1790	AGN PAD 1:116-117
Zoquital	Hidalgo	México	1790	AGN PAD 1:190-203

---

[98] This film contains a number of censuses or padrones for Tula including the years 1720, 1727, 1739–1752, 1768, 1769, 1778, and 1792.

[99] This film contains a number of censuses or padrones for Tula including the years 1779, 1780, 1792, 1802, 1804, and 1805.

[100] The entire province is included in pages 21–376.

[101] See also San José el Zeliz.

JALISCO

The microfilm series 168803-168849 contains hundreds of entries for the 1600s through the 1800s for the state of Jalisco. It has not been studied thoroughly, but what has been identified is noted here.

Locality	Province	Country	Year(s)	Reference
	Jalisco	México	1649	Archivo del Parral[102]
	Jalisco	México	1777	AGI Guadalajara 103:3:26
Acatic in Sayula	Jalisco	México	1817	168808
Acatlán	Jalisco	México	1831	168848
Adares	Jalisco	México	1820	168820
Adobe	Jalisco	México	1831	168848
Agostadero	Jalisco	México	1820	168818
Agostadero	Jalisco	México	1822	168827
Agua Gorda	Jalisco	México	1820	168818
Aguatlán	Jalisco	México	1817	168811
Ahuiscalco	Jalisco	México	1817	168811
Ajojúcar	Jalisco	México	1817	168811
Ajojúcar	Jalisco	México	1819	168815
Alospaquillo	Jalisco	México	1819	168817
Amacueca	Jalisco	México	1760	168805
Amacueca	Jalisco	México	1818	168812
Amacueca	Jalisco	México	1819	168816
Amacueca	Jalisco	México	1820	168822
Amacueca	Jalisco	México	1822	168827
Amacueca	Jalisco	México	1824	168831
Amacueca	Jalisco	México	1830	168841
Amatitán	Jalisco	México	1817	168811
Amatitán	Jalisco	México	1819	168816
Amatitlán	Jalisco	México	1817	168811
Amatitlán	Jalisco	México	1822	168825
Amazatlán	Jalisco	México	1822	168828
Ameca	Jalisco	México	1819	168817
Ameca	Jalisco	México	1820	168819
Ameca	Jalisco	México	1822	168827
Ameca	Jalisco	México	1824	168831
Ameca	Jalisco	México	1825	168835

---

[102] Padrón de los vecinos . . . 1649.

Locality	Province	Country	Year(s)	Reference
Ameca	Jalisco	México	1831	168846
Amo	Jalisco	México	1831	168848
Amula	Jalisco	México	1801	AGN Tributos 43[103]
Amula	Jalisco	México	1825	168835
Amula	Jalisco	México	1828	168839
Analco	Jalisco	México	1819	168817
Analco	Jalisco	México	1820	168818
Analco	Jalisco	México	1824	168831
Analco	Jalisco	México	1830	168842
Apango	Jalisco	México	1817	168810
Arandas	Jalisco	México	1821	168823
Arandas	Jalisco	México	1825	168835
Arandas	Jalisco	México	1826	168807
Arandas	Jalisco	México	1828	168839
Arandas	Jalisco	México	1830	168841
Arandas	Jalisco	México	1831	168848
Arangüés	Jalisco	México	1820	168819
Atemajac	Jalisco	México	1817	168810
Atemajac	Jalisco	México	1819	168816
Atemánica	Jalisco	México	1818	168812
Atemánica	Jalisco	México	1819	168816
Atemánica	Jalisco	México	1820	168822
Atemánica	Jalisco	México	1821	168823
Atemánica	Jalisco	México	1823	AAG
Atemánica	Jalisco	México	1824	168831
Atemánica	Jalisco	México	1825	168835
Atemánica	Jalisco	México	1828	168839
Atengo	Jalisco	México	1818	168812
Atiquiza	Jalisco	México	1820	168822
Atiquiza	Jalisco	México	1821	168823
Atiquiza	Jalisco	México	1822	168828
Atolinga	Jalisco	México	1822	168825
Atotonilco	Jalisco	México	1772	761550
Atotonilco	Jalisco	México	1817	168808
Atotonilco	Jalisco	México	1822	168828
Atotonilco	Jalisco	México	1824	168831
Atotonilco	Jalisco	México	1830	168841
Atotonilco	Jalisco	México	1831	168848
Atoyac	Jalisco	México	1760	168805
Atoyac	Jalisco	México	1820	168819
Atoyac	Jalisco	México	1824	168831
Atoyac	Jalisco	México	1830	168841

[103] The census for Amula is found in the last *expediente* of bundle 43.

Locality	Province	Country	Year(s)	Reference
Autlán	Jalisco	México	1760	AGI Guadalajara 401:47, 76, 77
Autlán	Jalisco	México	1817	168809
Autlán	Jalisco	México	1830	168841
Axixic	Jalisco	México	1820	168821
Ayo el Chico	Jalisco	México	1818	168812
Ayo el Chico	Jalisco	México	1819	168816
Ayo el Chico	Jalisco	México	1820	168818
Ayo el Chico	Jalisco	México	1821	168824
Ayo el Chico	Jalisco	México	1822	168828
Ayo el Chico	Jalisco	México	1824	168831
Ayo el Chico	Jalisco	México	1825	168835
Ayo el Chico	Jalisco	México	1831	168848
Ayutla	Jalisco	México	1817	168809
Ayutla	Jalisco	México	1819	168817
Ayutla	Jalisco	México	1820	168822
Ayutla	Jalisco	México	1821	168824
Ayutla	Jalisco	México	1822	168828
Ayutla	Jalisco	México	1824	168831
Ayutla	Jalisco	México	1825	168835
Bandras	Jalisco	México	1830	168843
Barranca[104]	Jalisco	México	1817	168811
Barranca	Jalisco	México	1820	168818; 168821
Barranca	Jalisco	México	1821	168824
Barranca	Jalisco	México	1822	168825; 168828
Barranca	Jalisco	México	1823	AAG[105]
Barranca	Jalisco	México	1831	168845
Belén del Refugio	Jalisco	México	1819	168815
Bentilla	Jalisco	México	?	168803
Bolaños	Jalisco	México	1623	AF 11:173
Bolaños	Jalisco	México	1770	AAG
Bolaños	Jalisco	México	1817	168809
Bolaños	Jalisco	México	1818	168812
Bolaños	Jalisco	México	1820	168820
Bolaños	Jalisco	México	1822	168830
Bolaños	Jalisco	México	1831	168849
Cacaluta	Jalisco	México	1817	168809
Cacaluta	Jalisco	México	1818	168813
Cacaluta	Jalisco	México	1820	168820
Cacaluta	Jalisco	México	1822	168830
Cacaluta	Jalisco	México	1831	168849
Camotlán	Jalisco	México	1824	168831

---

[104] San Cristóbal de la Barranca.
[105] Padrón de los feligreses havitantes en la Parroquia de San Cristoval de la Barranca.

Locality	Province	Country	Year(s)	Reference
Cañada	Jalisco	México	1819	168815
Carrizal	Jalisco	México	1856	793884
Castillo en Tonalá	Jalisco	México	1824	168834
Caverna	Jalisco	México	1830	168842
Chacala	Jalisco	México	1817	168811
Chapala	Jalisco	México	1819	168816
Chapala	Jalisco	México	1820	168822
Chapala	Jalisco	México	1831	168846
Chamacuero	Jalisco	México	1760	785447
Chamacuero	Jalisco	México	1763	774213
Chimaltitán	Jalisco	México	1689	AAG
Chimaltitán	Jalisco	México	1820	168818
Chiquilistlán	Jalisco	México	1817	168810
Ciénega del Rincón	Jalisco	México	1823	168829
Ciénega del Rincón	Jalisco	México	1824	168833
Ciénega del Rincón	Jalisco	México	1825	168836
Cocula	Jalisco	México	1818	168812
Cocula	Jalisco	México	1820	168820
Cocula	Jalisco	México	1830	168841
Cocula	Jalisco	México	1881	233002
Colotlán	Jalisco	México	1760	AGI Guadalajara 401[106]
Colotlán	Jalisco	México	1770	BPT 45
Colotlán	Jalisco	México	1817	168809
Comatitlán	Jalisco	México	1819	168816
Coyula	Jalisco	México	1817	168811
Coyula	Jalisco	México	1824	168834
Cuale	Jalisco	México	1854	1156216
Cuautitlán	Jalisco	México	1824	168831
Cuautitlán	Jalisco	México	1825	168835
Cuquío	Jalisco	México	1770	AAG
Cuquío	Jalisco	México	1820	168821
Cuquío	Jalisco	México	1825	168836
Cuquío	Jalisco	México	1830	168841
Cuyacapan en Sayula	Jalisco	México	1820	168819
Econagua	Jalisco	México	1822	168828
Econagua	Jalisco	México	1824	168831
Ejutla	Jalisco	México	1817	168809
Ejutla	Jalisco	México	1818	168812
Ejutla	Jalisco	México	1820	168820
Ejutla	Jalisco	México	1821	168824
Ejutla	Jalisco	México	1824	168831
Ejutla	Jalisco	México	1825	168835
Ejutla	Jalisco	México	1828	168839

[106] Includes *padrones* for the entire province of Colotlán.

Locality	Province	Country	Year(s)	Reference
Ejutla	Jalisco	México	1830	168842
Encarnación	Jalisco	México	1819	168816
Encarnación	Jalisco	México	1820	168820
Encarnación	Jalisco	México	1821	168826
Encarnación	Jalisco	México	1824	168834
Encarnación	Jalisco	México	1825	168837
Encarnación	Jalisco	México	1826	168838
Encarnación	Jalisco	México	1828	168840
Encarnación	Jalisco	México	1830	168843
Encarnación	Jalisco	México	1831	168845
Guachinango	Jalisco	México	1817	168809
Guachinango	Jalisco	México	1820	168820
Guachinango	Jalisco	México	1821	168824
Guachinango	Jalisco	México	1824	168831
Guachinango	Jalisco	México	1830	168842
Guadalajara	Jalisco	México	1679	168804
Guadalajara	Jalisco	México	1750	168804
Guadalajara	Jalisco	México	1768	168805
Guadalajara, Jesús	Jalisco	México	1819	168817
Guadalajara, Jesús	Jalisco	México	1820	168819
Guadalajara, Jesús	Jalisco	México	1824	168832
Guadalajara, Jesús	Jalisco	México	1828	168839
Guadalajara, Jesús	Jalisco	México	1830	168842
Guadalajara, Jesús	Jalisco	México	1831	168846
Guadalajara, Sagrario	Jalisco	México	1820	168819
Guadalajara, Sagrario	Jalisco	México	1831	168846-168847
Guanusco	Jalisco	México	1817	168811
Hostotipac	Jalisco	México	1790	AGI Guadalajara 250
Hostotipaquillo	Jalisco	México	1817	168809
Hostotipaquillo	Jalisco	México	1818	168812
Hostotipaquillo	Jalisco	México	1819	163816
Hostotipaquillo	Jalisco	México	1820	168822
Hostotipaquillo	Jalisco	México	1821	168824
Hostotipaquillo	Jalisco	México	1824	168831
Hostotipaquillo	Jalisco	México	1820	168842
Huejotitlán	Jalisco	México	1817	168811
Huejotitlán	Jalisco	México	1820	168821
Huejúcar	Jalisco	México	1820	168819
Huejúcar	Jalisco	México	1822	168828
Huejúcar	Jalisco	México	1824	168833
Huejúcar	Jalisco	México	1825	168836
Huejúcar	Jalisco	México	1826	168838
Huejuquilla	Jalisco	México	1770	AAG
Huejuquilla	Jalisco	México	1819	168817
Huejuquilla	Jalisco	México	1821	168824

Locality	Province	Country	Year(s)	Reference
Huejuquilla	Jalisco	México	1822	168828
Huejuquilla	Jalisco	México	1824	168832
Huejuquilla	Jalisco	México	1825	168835
Huejuquilla	Jalisco	México	1828	168839
Huejuquilla	Jalisco	México	1830	168842
Huentitán	Jalisco	México	1819	168817
Huentitán	Jalisco	México	1820	168818
Ixtlahuacán[107]	Jalisco	México	1760	?
Ixtlahuacán del Río	Jalisco	México	1817	168809
Ixtlahuacán del Río	Jalisco	México	1820	168818
Ixtlahuacán del Río	Jalisco	México	1821	168824
Ixtlahuacán del Río	Jalisco	México	1824	168832
Ixtlahuacán del Río	Jalisco	México	1830	168842
Ixtlahuacán Reyes	Jalisco	México	1822	168828
Ixtlahuacán Reyes	Jalisco	México	1825	168835
Ixtlahuacán Reyes	Jalisco	México	1826	168838
Ixtlahuacán Reyes	Jalisco	México	1828	168839
Izatlán	Jalisco	México	1817	168809
Izatlán	Jalisco	México	1818	168812
Izatlán	Jalisco	México	1819	168816
Izatlán	Jalisco	México	1820	168818
Izatlán	Jalisco	México	1821	168824
Izatlán	Jalisco	México	1822	168828
Izatlán	Jalisco	México	1824	168831
Izatlán	Jalisco	México	1831	168849
Jalostotitlán	Jalisco	México	1650	AAG
Jalostotitlán	Jalisco	México	1764–1765	279420
Jalostotitlán	Jalisco	México	1817	168810
Jalostotitlán	Jalisco	México	1819	168816
Jalostotitlán	Jalisco	México	1824	168832
Jalostotitlán	Jalisco	México	1831	168849
Jalpa	Jalisco	México	1760	168805
Jalpa	Jalisco	México	1762	168804
Jalpa	Jalisco	México	1817	168810
Jamay	Jalisco	México	1828	168839
Jilotlán	Jalisco	México	1830	168844
Jiquilpán	Jalisco	México	1817	168810
Jocotepec	Jalisco	México	1820	168820
Jocotepec	Jalisco	México	1820	168821
Jocotepec	Jalisco	México	1831	168846
José María	Jalisco	México	1822	168827
José María	Jalisco	México	1824	168831
Juanacatic	Jalisco	México	1817	168811

[107] Ixtlahuacán de los Membrillos.

Locality	Province	Country	Year(s)	Reference
Juanacatic	Jalisco	México	1822	168825
Juanacatlán	Jalisco	México	1817	168810
Juquilpán	Jalisco	México	1763	774213
Juquilpán	Jalisco	México	1817	797803
La Barca	Jalisco	México	17--	782018
La Barca	Jalisco	México	17--	761550
La Barca	Jalisco	México	1768	782003
La Barca	Jalisco	México	1817	168810
La Barca	Jalisco	México	1818	168813
La Barca	Jalisco	México	1820	168818
La Barca	Jalisco	México	1822	168828
La Barca	Jalisco	México	1824	168832
La Barca	Jalisco	México	1825	168835
La Barca	Jalisco	México	1828	168839
La Razón	Jalisco	México	1773	758093
Lagos	Jalisco	México	1669	AGI Guadalajara 543
Lagos	Jalisco	México	1676	AGI Guadalajara 543
Lagos	Jalisco	México	1820	168822
Lagos	Jalisco	México	1824	168833
Lagos	Jalisco	México	1831	168847-168848
Lagos de Moreno	Jalisco	México	1810	221883
Lagos de Moreno	Jalisco	México	1874	221884
Los Reyes	Jalisco	México	1820	168821
Los Reyes	Jalisco	México	1830	168842
Magdalena	Jalisco	México	1818	168813
Magdalena	Jalisco	México	1819	168816
Magdalena	Jalisco	México	1820	168820
Magdalena	Jalisco	México	1821	168824
Magdalena	Jalisco	México	1822	168828
Magdalena	Jalisco	México	1824	168832
Magdalena	Jalisco	México	1830	168842
Magdalena	Jalisco	México	1875	1389277
Mascota	Jalisco	México	1760	168805
Mascota	Jalisco	México	1762	168804
Mascota	Jalisco	México	1817	168809
Mascota	Jalisco	México	1820	168819
Mascota	Jalisco	México	1822	168828
Mascota	Jalisco	México	1824	168832
Mascota	Jalisco	México	1825	168836
Mascota	Jalisco	México	1828	168839
Mascota	Jalisco	México	1830	168842
Mascota	Jalisco	México	1831	168846-168848
Mazamitla	Jalisco	México	1821	168824
Mazamitla	Jalisco	México	1822	168828
Mazatlán	Jalisco	México	1817	168811

Locality	Province	Country	Year(s)	Reference
Mechoacanejo	Jalisco	México	1818	168813
Mechoacanejo	Jalisco	México	1819	168815
Mescala	Jalisco	México	1822	168828
Mescala	Jalisco	México	1824	168832
Mesquitán	Jalisco	México	1820	168819
Mesquitán	Jalisco	México	1824	168832
Mesquitán	Jalisco	México	1830	168842
Mesticacán	Jalisco	México	1820	168821
Mesticacán	Jalisco	México	1821	168824
Mesticacán	Jalisco	México	1822	168828
Mesticacán	Jalisco	México	1824	168833
Mesticacán	Jalisco	México	1828	168839
Mesticacán	Jalisco	México	1830	168842
Mexicalcingo	Jalisco	México	1824	168833
Mexicalcingo	Jalisco	México	1825	168835
Mexicalcingo	Jalisco	México	1831	168846
Mezquitic	Jalisco	México	1770	AAG
Mezquitic	Jalisco	México	1818	168813
Mezquitic	Jalisco	México	1820	168822
Mezquitic	Jalisco	México	1824	168833
Mistlán	Jalisco	México	1830	168842
Mitique	Jalisco	México	1794	168803
Ocotlán	Jalisco	México	1817	168811
Ocotlán	Jalisco	México	1820	168822
Ocotlán	Jalisco	México	1828	168840
Ojo de Agua	Jalisco	México	1817	168810
Ojuelos	Jalisco	México	1817	168810
Ojuelos	Jalisco	México	1818	168813
Ojuelos	Jalisco	México	1820	168818
Ojuelos	Jalisco	México	1821	168824
Ojuelos	Jalisco	México	1823	168829
Ojuelos	Jalisco	México	1824	168833
Ojuelos	Jalisco	México	1825	168835
Otuboa	Jalisco	México	1831	168848
Pihuamo	Jalisco	México	1831	168848
Poncitlán	Jalisco	México	1831	168811
Poncitlán	Jalisco	México	1817	168815
Poncitlán	Jalisco	México	1819	168819
Poncitlán	Jalisco	México	1820	168819, 168822
Poncitlán	Jalisco	México	1822	168825, 168828
Poncitlán	Jalisco	México	1824	168833
Poncitlán	Jalisco	México	1825	168836
Poncitlán	Jalisco	México	1830	168842
Poncitlán	Jalisco	México	1831	168848
Portezuelo	Jalisco	México	1817	168810

Locality	Province	Country	Year(s)	Reference
Portezuelo	Jalisco	México	1828	168839
Potrerillos	Jalisco	México	1820	168821
Purificación	Jalisco	México	1649	AAG
Purificación	Jalisco	México	1773	AGI Guadalajara 348[108]
Purificación	Jalisco	México	1817	168811
Purificación	Jalisco	México	1821	168826
Purificación	Jalisco	México	1824	168834
Quale	Jalisco	México	1820	168819
Quale	Jalisco	México	1828	168839
Quale	Jalisco	México	1830	168844
Quale	Jalisco	México	1831	168848
San Antonio	Jalisco	México	1820	168820
San Cosme	Jalisco	México	1820	168820
San Cosme	Jalisco	México	1822	168825, 168828
San Gabriel[109]	Jalisco	México	1817	168810
San Gabriel	Jalisco	México	1819	168817
San Gabriel	Jalisco	México	1820	168821
San Gabriel	Jalisco	México	1822	168825
San Gabriel	Jalisco	México	1822	168828
San Gabriel	Jalisco	México	1825	168836
San Gabriel	Jalisco	México	1830	168842
San Gaspar	Jalisco	México	1760	168805
San Gaspar	Jalisco	México	1819	168817
San Gaspar	Jalisco	México	1831	168849
San José	Jalisco	México	1817	168810
San José de Gracia	Jalisco	México	1847	168807
San Juan	Jalisco	México	1822	168828
San Juan in Tlaxomulco	Jalisco	México	1722	758093
San Juan in Tlaxomulco	Jalisco	México	1784	758093
San Luis	Jalisco	México	1820	168820
San Martín in Tonalá	Jalisco	México	1817	168811
San Martín in Tonalá	Jalisco	México	1824	168834
San Miguel	Jalisco	México	1824	168832
San Sebastián	Jalisco	México	1759–1866	1156263
San Sebastián	Jalisco	México	1819	168817
San Sebastián	Jalisco	México	1820	168821
San Sebastián	Jalisco	México	1828	168839
San Sebastián	Jalisco	México	1831	168846
Santa Ana	Jalisco	México	1821	168824
Santa María Angeles	Jalisco	México	1817	168809

[108] This *padrón* is for the entire *alcaldía mayor* of Purificación.
[109] Modern Venustiano Carranza.

Locality	Province	Country	Year(s)	Reference
Santa María de los Lagos	Jalisco	México	1874	221884
Sayula	Jalisco	México	1760	AGI, Guadalajara 401
Sayula	Jalisco	México	1770	BPT[110]
Sayula	Jalisco	México	1817	168811
Sayula	Jalisco	México	1820	168820
Sayula	Jalisco	México	1830	168844
Sayula	Jalisco	México	1831	168848
Sayula	Jalisco	México	1855	225056
Soyatlán	Jalisco	México	1822	168825
Tala	Jalisco	México	1817	168811
Tala	Jalisco	México	1820	168821
Tala	Jalisco	México	1822	168825, 168828
Tala	Jalisco	México	1830	168844
Tala	Jalisco	México	1831	168845
Talpa in Mascota	Jalisco	México	1820	168820
Talpa in Mascota	Jalisco	México	1822	168825, 168828
Talpa in Mascota	Jalisco	México	1824	168833
Talpa in Mascota	Jalisco	México	1825	168836
Talpa in Mascota	Jalisco	México	1828	168840
Talpa in Mascota	Jalisco	México	1830	168843
Talpa in Mascota	Jalisco	México	1836	1155779
Tamazula	Jalisco	México	1763	774202
Tamazula	Jalisco	México	1763	774211-774213
Tamazula	Jalisco	México	1768	774114-774116
Tamazula	Jalisco	México	1770	774114
Tamazula	Jalisco	México	1772	761553
Tamazula	Jalisco	México	1778	776888
Tamazula	Jalisco	México	1831	168848
Tamazula	Jalisco	México	1885	226131
Tapalpa	Jalisco	México	1817	168810
Tapalpa	Jalisco	México	1818	168812
Tapalpa	Jalisco	México	1819	168816
Tapalpa	Jalisco	México	1820	168822
Tapalpa	Jalisco	México	1830	168840
Techaluta	Jalisco	México	1760	168805
Techaluta	Jalisco	México	1803	234020
Techaluta	Jalisco	México	1817	168809
Techaluta	Jalisco	México	1819	168816
Techaluta	Jalisco	México	1824	168833
Techaluta	Jalisco	México	1831	168848
Tecohejes	Jalisco	México	1820	168822
Tecototlán	Jalisco	México	1830	168844

[110] Biblioteca Pública de Toledo, Spain, Colección Borbón-Lorenzana, Manuscript 45.

Locality	Province	Country	Year(s)	Reference
Teltlán	Jalisco	México	1822	168830
Temacapulín	Jalisco	México	1824	168832
Tenamastlán	Jalisco	México	1831	168845
Teocaltiche	Jalisco	México	1817	168811
Teocaltiche	Jalisco	México	1818	168813
Teocaltiche	Jalisco	México	1819	168815
Teocaltiche	Jalisco	México	1822	168825
Teocaltiche	Jalisco	México	1831	168847
Teocaltitlán	Jalisco	México	1817	168811
Teocuitas	Jalisco	México	1824	168834
Teocuitatlán	Jalisco	México	1765	168804
Teocuitatlán	Jalisco	México	1819	168816
Teocuitatlán	Jalisco	México	1820	168819
Teocuitatlán	Jalisco	México	1831	168849
Tepantla	Jalisco	México	1825	168835
Tepatitlán	Jalisco	México	1759–1834	220636, 220736
Tepatitlán	Jalisco	México	1770	AAG
Tepatitlán	Jalisco	México	1818	168813
Tepatitlán	Jalisco	México	1820	168819
Tepatitlán	Jalisco	México	1821	168824
Tepatitlán	Jalisco	México	1822	168828
Tepatitlán	Jalisco	México	1828	168840
Tepatitlán	Jalisco	México	1830	168844
Tepatitlán	Jalisco	México	1847	168807
Tepec in Amacuesca	Jalisco	México	1760	168805
Tepetate	Jalisco	México	1817	168811
Tepi	Jalisco	México	1817	168811
Tequila	Jalisco	México	1819	168816
Tequila	Jalisco	México	1822	168825, 168828
Tequila	Jalisco	México	1824	168834
Tequila	Jalisco	México	1828	168840
Tequila	Jalisco	México	1830	168844
Tesistlán	Jalisco	México	1820	168820
Tesquesquitla	Jalisco	México	1819	168815
Tetapán	Jalisco	México	1830	168843
Teuchitlán	Jalisco	México	1817	168811
Teuchitlán	Jalisco	México	1822	168828
Teul (San Andrés del)	Jalisco	México	1777	AGI Indiferentes 1526
Texapán	Jalisco	México	1822	168830
Texapán	Jalisco	México	1831	168846
Tlachichilco (military)	Jalisco	México	1822	168825
Tlajomulco	Jalisco	México	1777	AGI Guadalajara 348
Tlajomulco	Jalisco	México	1778–1813	224894
Tlajomulco	Jalisco	México	1817	168811
Tlajomulco	Jalisco	México	1818	168814

Locality	Province	Country	Year(s)	Reference
Tlajomulco	Jalisco	México	1831	168845
Tocolotlán	Jalisco	México	1822	168825
Toliman	Jalisco	México	1817	168811
Toliman	Jalisco	México	1820	168822
Toliman	Jalisco	México	1830	168843
Tololotlán	Jalisco	México	1817	168811
Toluquillo	Jalisco	México	1822	168825
Toluquillo	Jalisco	México	1831	168845
Tomatlán	Jalisco	México	1817	168811
Tomatlán	Jalisco	México	1819	168816
Tomatlán	Jalisco	México	1820	168821
Tomatlán	Jalisco	México	1822	168825, 168830
Tomatlán	Jalisco	México	1824	168834
Tomatlán	Jalisco	México	1828	168840
Tomatlán	Jalisco	México	1830	168843
Tonalá	Jalisco	México	1770	AAG
Tonalá	Jalisco	México	1817	168811
Tonalá	Jalisco	México	1819	168817
Tonalá	Jalisco	México	1822	168825, 168830
Tonalá	Jalisco	México	1824	168834
Tonaya	Jalisco	México	1817	168811
Tonaya	Jalisco	México	1822	168830
Tonila	Jalisco	México	1817	168811
Tonila	Jalisco	México	1820	168821
Tonila	Jalisco	México	1830	168844
Totalulu	Jalisco	México	1831	168846
Totatiche	Jalisco	México	1770	AAG
Totatiche	Jalisco	México	1773	758093
Totatiche	Jalisco	México	1819	168816
Totatiche	Jalisco	México	1820	168818
Totatiche	Jalisco	México	1822	168830
Totatiche	Jalisco	México	1842–1856	1164030
Totatiche	Jalisco	México	1905	1164030
Totatiche	Jalisco	México	1920	1164030
Totolotán	Jalisco	México	1822	168830
Totolotán	Jalisco	México	1824	168834
Tototlán	Jalisco	México	1820	168818, 168822
Tototlán	Jalisco	México	1822	168825, 168830
Tototlán	Jalisco	México	1824	168833
Tototlán	Jalisco	México	1825	168836
Tototlán	Jalisco	México	1826	168838
Tototlán	Jalisco	México	1828	168840
Tototlán	Jalisco	México	1830	168844
Trinidad de Sotos	Jalisco	México	1817	168811
Trinidad de Sotos	Jalisco	México	1819	168816

Locality	Province	Country	Year(s)	Reference
Trinidad de Sotos	Jalisco	México	1820	168819
Trinidad de Sotos	Jalisco	México	1821	168826
Trinidad de Sotos	Jalisco	México	1822	168830
Trinidad de Sotos	Jalisco	México	1824	168834
Trinidad de Sotos	Jalisco	México	1825	168836
Trinidad de Sotos	Jalisco	México	1831	168847
Tuito	Jalisco	México	1817	168811
Tuito	Jalisco	México	1825	168837
Tuito	Jalisco	México	1830	168844
Tula	Jalisco	México	1825	168835, 168837
Tula	Jalisco	México	1828	168839
Tuscacuesco	Jalisco	México	1747–1920	449375-449380
Tuscacuesco	Jalisco	México	1817	168811
Tuscacuesco	Jalisco	México	1819	168815
Tuscacuesco	Jalisco	México	1821	168826
Tuscacuesco	Jalisco	México	1822	168830
Tuscacuesco	Jalisco	México	1824	168834
Tuscacuesco	Jalisco	México	1825	168836
Tuscacuesco	Jalisco	México	1830	168844
Tuxpan	Jalisco	México	1822	168830
Tuxpan	Jalisco	México	1830	168844
Venustiano Carranza[111]	Jalisco	México		
Volunteers (military)	Jalisco	México	1820	168822
Xirosto	Jalisco	México	1817	168811
Xocotlán	Jalisco	México	1817	168811
Yahualica	Jalisco	México	1824	168834
Yahualica	Jalisco	México	1831	168848
Yahualica	Jalisco	México	1853	226555
Yahualica	Jalisco	México	1856	226555
Yahualica	Jalisco	México	1867	233964
Yahualica	Jalisco	México	1921	233964
Ysamitla	Jalisco	México	1830	168842
Zacoalco in Sayula	Jalisco	México	1793–1816	223964
Zacoalco in Sayula	Jalisco	México	1817	168811
Zacoalco in Sayula	Jalisco	México	1820	168821
Zacoalco in Sayula	Jalisco	México	1827–1832	223965
Zacoalco in Sayula	Jalisco	México	1831	168847
Zalatitlán	Jalisco	México	1819	168817
Zalatitlán	Jalisco	México	1820	168821
Zalatitlán	Jalisco	México	1821	168826
Zalatitlán	Jalisco	México	1822	168830
Zalatitlán	Jalisco	México	1831	168849
Zapopan	Jalisco	México	1820	168821

---

[111] See San Gabriel.

Locality	Province	Country	Year(s)	Reference
Zapotiltic	Jalisco	México	1831	168847
Zapotitlán	Jalisco	México	1817	168811
Zapotitlán	Jalisco	México	1820	168822
Zapotitlán	Jalisco	México	1821	168826
Zapotitlán	Jalisco	México	1824	168834
Zapotitlán	Jalisco	México	1825	168837
Zapotitlán	Jalisco	México	1828	168840
Zapotitlán	Jalisco	México	1830	168843
Zapotlán	Jalisco	México	1778	776888
Zapotlán del Rey	Jalisco	México	1813	168807
Zapotlán del Rey	Jalisco	México	1817	168811
Zapotlán del Rey	Jalisco	México	1819	168817
Zapotlán del Rey	Jalisco	México	1820	168820, 168822
Zapotlán del Rey	Jalisco	México	1822	168828
Zapotlán del Rey	Jalisco	México	1831	168845
Zapotlanejo	Jalisco	México	1820	168821
Zaptiltic	Jalisco	México	1817	168809
Zoquimatlán	Jalisco	México	1820	168822

MEXICO

Locality	Province	Country	Year(s)	Reference
Acambay	México	México	1900	708366
Aculco	México	México	1900	707311
Almoloya	México	México	1937	708367-708368
Amanalco de Becerra	México	México	1768	442122, 641724
Amatetec	México	México	1768	442122, 641724
Atlacomulco	México	México	1769	442122, 641724
Atlacomulco	México	México	1804	653185
Ayapango	México	México	1778	442123, 641725
Ayapango	México	México	1797	442123, 641725
Ayotla	México	México	1900	707310
Calimaya	México	México	1778	442123, 641725
Capulhuac[112]	México	México	1797	442123, 641725
Chalco	México	México	1777	442125, 641725
Coacalco	México	México	1900	707310
Coacalco	México	México	1935	442124, 708360
Coatepec Chalco	México	México	1743	AGN Tributos 43[113]
Coatepec Chalco	México	México	1791	AGN PAD 3:1-25
Coatepec Chalco	México	México	1799	AGN Tributos 43[114]
Coatepec Chalco	México	México	1900	641752
Cuautémoc	México	México	1777	641727
Cuautitlán	México	México	1790	AGN PAD 4
Ecatepec	México	México	1778	645388
Ecatepec	México	México	1792	AGN PAD 6; 47; CCM 9-10
Ecatepec	México	México	1810	645388
Guerrero	México	México	1797	641732
Guerrero	México	México	1900	641753
Huejotla	México	México	1797	442126, 641726
Hueypoxtla	México	México	1777	442126, 641726
Ictapán de la Sal	México	México	1900	641752
Ixtapaluca	México	México	1900	641752
Jesús del Monte	México	México	1747	768916
Jesús del Monte	México	México	1760	785447

---

[112] Calpuhuac de Mirafuentes.
[113] The census for Coatepec is found in the last *expediente* of bundle 43.
[114] The census for Coatepec is found in the last *expediente* of bundle 43.

Locality	Province	Country	Year(s)	Reference
Lerma	México	México	1790	AGN PAD 12
Malinalco	México	México	1797	442126, 641727
Otumba[115]	México	México	1791	AGN PAD 12:242-204
Otumba	México	México	1900	707310
Otzolotepec	México	México	1777	442127
San Cristóbal	México	México	1792	AGN PAD 6; 47; CCM 9-10
Tecamac	México	México	1778	641730
Tecamac	México	México	1778–1779	442133
Tecamac	México	México	1779	641731
Tecualoya	México	México	1790	AGE
Tecualoya	México	México	1797	442135
Temascaltepec	México	México	1790	AGN PAD 49
Teotihuacán	México	México	1724–1849	442134
Teotihuacán	México	México	1768–1769	647082
Teotihuacán	México	México	1778	641731
Teotihuacán	México	México	1790	AGN PAD 18
Teotihuacán	México	México	1803	647083
Texcoco	México	México	1790	AGN PAD 14
Toluca	México	México	1773	442136, 641732
Toluca	México	México	1778	442137
Toluca	México	México	1791	AGN PAD 21
Toluca	México	México	1934	442137, 641733
Toluca de Lerdo	México	México	1773	442136, 641732
Totoltepec (San Pedro)	México	México	1779	442137
Totoltepec (San Pedro)	México	México	1934	442137, 641733
Zacualpan de Amilpas	México	México	1777	442138, 641734
Zacualpan de Amilpas	México	México	1790	AGN PAD 15; 51
Zacualpan de Amilpas	México	México	1900	707310
Zitlaltepec (San Juan)	México	México	1918	641727
Zumpalhuacán	México	México	1797	442140, 641735
Zumpango	México	México	1786	AGN HI 72:v
Zumpango	México	México	1780	AGN PAD 43; CCM 9-10
Zumpango	México	México	1791	AGN HI 72
Zumpango	México	México	1918	641727

---

[115] Later became known as Otumba de Gómez Farias.

MICHOACAN

Locality	Province	Country	Year(s)	Reference
	Michoacán[116]	México	1804–1840	762639:3
Acachuen	Michoacán	México	1797	762942
Acuitzio	Michoacán	México	1747	768916-768918
Acuitzio	Michoacán	México	1747	768921
Acuitzio	Michoacán	México	1758	769986-769989
Amatlán	Michoacán	México	1709–1796	773438
Amatlán	Michoacán	México	1746	768901-768902
Amatlán	Michoacán	México	1746	768900
Amatlán	Michoacán	México	1747	768920
Amatlán	Michoacán	México	1758	769986-769989
Amatlán	Michoacán	México	1759	772017-772020
Amatlán	Michoacán	México	1760	763271-763272
Amatlán	Michoacán	México	1763	774202
Amatlán	Michoacán	México	1768	774103-774104
Amatlán	Michoacán	México	1772	761550
Amatlán	Michoacán	México	1776	776736-776738
Amatlán	Michoacán	México	1778	776888
Amatlán	Michoacán	México	1800	795135-7951356
Amatlán	Michoacán	México	1801	795135
Angamacutiro	Michoacán	México	1747	768916-768921
Angamacutiro	Michoacán	México	1758	769986-769989
Angamacutiro	Michoacán	México	1759	772017-772020
Angamacutiro	Michoacán	México	1763	774211-774213
Angamacutiro	Michoacán	México	1768	782002-782003
Angamacutiro	Michoacán	México	1770	774144
Angamacutiro	Michoacán	México	1778	776888
Angamacutiro	Michoacán	México	1794	795134
Angamacutiro	Michoacán	México	1796	AGN HI 430:374-374v
Angangueo	Michoacán	México	1758	769986-769989
Apatzingan	Michoacán	México	1746	768900-768902
Apatzingan	Michoacán	México	1747	768920
Apatzingan	Michoacán	México	1758	769986-769989
Apatzingan	Michoacán	México	1759	772017-772020
Apatzingan	Michoacán	México	1770	774154
Apatzingan	Michoacán	México	1772	761553
Apatzingan	Michoacán	México	1776	776888

---

[116] The location here is not specified. It may be Morelia, or Valladolid.

114

Locality	Province	Country	Year(s)	Reference
Apatzingan	Michoacán	México	1796	AHN HI 430:371-371v
Apatzingan	Michoacán	México	1800	795135-795136
Apó	Michoacán	México	1758	769986
Apó	Michoacán	México	1763	774211-774213
Aporo	Michoacán	México	1758	769986-769989
Aranza	Michoacán	México	1782	762942
Ario	Michoacán	México	1759	772017-772020
Ario	Michoacán	México	1763	774211-774213
Ario	Michoacán	México	1796	AGN HI 430:362-362v
Ario	Michoacán	México	1809	793881
Atapán	Michoacán	México	1668	793134
Atécuaro	Michoacán	México	1746	768900-768902
Cachan	Michoacán	México	1668	793134
Capácuaro	Michoacán	México	1746	768901-768902
Capácuaro	Michoacán	México	1747	768916-768918
Capácuaro	Michoacán	México	1759	772017-772020
Capácuaro	Michoacán	México	1760	785447; 768900
Capácuaro	Michoacán	México	1763	774211-774213
Capácuaro	Michoacán	México	1768	774114-774116
Capácuaro	Michoacán	México	1772	761553
Carapán	Michoacán	México	1797	762942
Caráquaro	Michoacán	México	1765	ODM 140-154
Caráquaro	Michoacán	México	1770	774144
Caráquaro	Michoacán	México	1799	795139
Charapán	Michoacán	México	1758	769986-769989
Charapán	Michoacán	México	1759	772017-772020
Charapán	Michoacán	México	1760	763271-763272
Charapán	Michoacán	México	1763	774221-774213
Charapán	Michoacán	México	1768	774114-774116
Charapán	Michoacán	México	1770	774144
Charapán	Michoacán	México	1772	761553
Charapán	Michoacán	México	1793	763127
Charapán	Michoacán	México	1809	793881
Charo	Michoacán	México	1668	795134
Charo	Michoacán	México	1758	769986-769989
Charo	Michoacán	México	1759	772017-772020
Charo	Michoacán	México	1768	782002
Charo	Michoacán	México	1770	774144
Charo	Michoacán	México	1772	761553
Charo	Michoacán	México	1776	776736-776738
Charo	Michoacán	México	1790	AGN PAD 12:34-54
Charo	Michoacán	México	1800	795135-795136
Charo	Michoacán	México	1801	795138
Charo	Michoacán	México	1803	795139-795140
Charo	Michoacán	México	1804	795141-95143

Locality	Province	Country	Year(s)	Reference
Charo	Michoacán	México	1804–1805	793876
Charo	Michoacán	México	1806	793878
Cherán	Michoacán	México	1758	769986-769989
Cherán	Michoacán	México	1770	774154-774155
Cherán	Michoacán	México	1782	762942
Chucándiro	Michoacán	México	1746	768900-768902
Chucándiro	Michoacán	México	1747	768916-768918
Chucándiro	Michoacán	México	1747	768921
Chucándiro	Michoacán	México	1758	769986-769989
Chucándiro	Michoacán	México	1759	772017-772020
Chucándiro	Michoacán	México	1763	774202
Chucándiro	Michoacán	México	1770	774154-774155
Chucándiro	Michoacán	México	1772	761550
Chucándiro	Michoacán	México	1776	776736-776738
Chucándiro	Michoacán	México	1778	776888
Churumuco	Michoacán	México	1747	768916-768918
Churumuco	Michoacán	México	1747	768921
Churumuco	Michoacán	México	1760	763271-763272
Churumuco	Michoacán	México	1763	774211-774213
Churumuco	Michoacán	México	1768	774103-774104
Churumuco	Michoacán	México	1770	774154-774155
Churumuco	Michoacán	México	1772	761550
Churumuco	Michoacán	México	1777	776752
Churumuco	Michoacán	México	1800	795135
Churumuco	Michoacán	México	1803	795140
Coahuayana	Michoacán	México	1800	795135
Coahuayana	Michoacán	México	1800	776752
Coahuayana	Michoacán	México	1803	795104
Coeneo	Michoacán	México	1778	776888
Coire	Michoacán	México	1763	774211-774213
Coire	Michoacán	México	1800	795135
Cojumatlán	Michoacán	México	1668	795134
Conguripo	Michoacán	México	1743	AGI, Indiferentes 107
Contepec	Michoacán	México	1746	768900-768902
Contepec	Michoacán	México	1747	768920
Contepec	Michoacán	México	1759	772017-772020
Contepec	Michoacán	México	1760	785447
Contepec	Michoacán	México	1763	774211-774213
Contepec	Michoacán	México	1768	774114-774116
Contepec	Michoacán	México	1800	795136
Contepec	Michoacán	México	1801	795138
Copándaro	Michoacán	México	1746	768900-68902
Copándaro	Michoacán	México	1747	768220
Copándaro	Michoacán	México	1763	774211-774213
Copándaro	Michoacán	México	1768	774114-774116

Locality	Province	Country	Year(s)	Reference
Copándaro	Michoacán	México	1770	774144
Copándaro	Michoacán	México	1776	776736-776738
Copándaro	Michoacán	México	1790	AGN PAD 16
Copándaro	Michoacán	México	1809	793881
Copándaro	Michoacán	México	1810	793882
Cualcomán	Michoacán	México	1759	772017-772020
Cualcomán	Michoacán	México	1760	763271-763272
Cualcomán	Michoacán	México	1763	774211-774213
Cualcomán	Michoacán	México	1768	774114-774116
Cualcomán	Michoacán	México	1770	774144
Cualcomán	Michoacán	México	1772	761553
Cualcomán	Michoacán	México	1776	776736-776738
Cuitzeo[117]	Michoacán	México	1660	765609
Cuitzeo	Michoacán	México	1743	AGI, Indiferentes 107
Cuitzeo	Michoacán	México	1746	768900-768902
Cuitzeo	Michoacán	México	1747	768902
Cuitzeo	Michoacán	México	1758	769986-769989
Cuitzeo	Michoacán	México	1759	772017-772020
Cuitzeo	Michoacán	México	1760	763271-763272
Cuitzeo	Michoacán	México	1763	774211-774213
Cuitzeo	Michoacán	México	1768	774114-774116
Cuitzeo	Michoacán	México	1770	774144
Cuitzeo	Michoacán	México	1772	761550
Cuitzeo	Michoacán	México	1776	776736
Cuitzeo	Michoacán	México	1777	776752
Cuitzeo	Michoacán	México	1791	AGN PAD 16
Cuitzeo	Michoacán	México	1801	795138
Cuitzeo	Michoacán	México	1803	795140
Cuitzeo	Michoacán	México	1804	795143
Cuitzeo	Michoacán	México	1805	793876
Cuitzeo	Michoacán	México	1807	793879
Cuitzeo	Michoacán	México	1808	793880
Cuitzeo	Michoacán	México	1810	793882
Cuitzeo	Michoacán	México	1880	795135
Ecuandureo	Michoacán	México	1759	772017-772020
Ecuandureo	Michoacán	México	1763	774202
Ecuandureo	Michoacán	México	1768	774103-774104
Ecuandureo	Michoacán	México	1772	761550
Ecuandureo	Michoacán	México	1776	776745-776746
Ecuandureo	Michoacán	México	1784	643819:4
Ecuandureo	Michoacán	México	1800	795136
Ecuandureo	Michoacán	México	1801	795137
Ecuandureo	Michoacán	México	1803	795141

[117] Cuiseo de la Laguna.

Locality	Province	Country	Year(s)	Reference
Ecuandureo	Michoacán	México	1804	795142
Ecuandureo	Michoacán	México	1805	793876
Ecuandureo	Michoacán	México	1807	793879
Ecuandureo	Michoacán	México	1808	793880
Ecuandureo	Michoacán	México	1868	643809:5
Erongaríquaro	Michoacán	México	1747	768916-768918
Erongaríquaro	Michoacán	México	1747	768921
Erongaríquaro	Michoacán	México	1758	769986-769989
Erongaríquaro	Michoacán	México	1759	772017-772020
Erongaríquaro	Michoacán	México	1760	785447
Erongaríquaro	Michoacán	México	1763	772211-772213
Erongaríquaro	Michoacán	México	1768	774114-774116
Erongaríquaro	Michoacán	México	1770	774144
Erongaríquaro	Michoacán	México	1772	761553
Erongaríquaro	Michoacán	México	1776	776745-776746
Erongaríquaro	Michoacán	México	1796	AGN HI 430:336v-337
Guagua	Michoacán	México	1668	795134
Guaymeo	Michoacán	México	1743	AGI, Indiferentes 107
Huacao	Michoacán	México	1803	795140
Huacao	Michoacán	México	1808	793880
Huacao	Michoacán	México	1810	793882
Huandacareo	Michoacán	México	1747	768916-768918
Huandacareo	Michoacán	México	1747	768921
Huandacareo	Michoacán	México	1758	769986-769989
Huandacareo	Michoacán	México	1759	772017-772020
Huandacareo	Michoacán	México	1760	763271
Huandacareo	Michoacán	México	1763	774211-774213
Huandacareo	Michoacán	México	1768	774103-774104
Huandacareo	Michoacán	México	1770	774154-774155
Huandacareo	Michoacán	México	1772	761553
Huandacareo	Michoacán	México	1776	776736-776738
Huandacareo	Michoacán	México	1800	795135
Huandacareo	Michoacán	México	1801	795138
Huandacareo	Michoacán	México	1803	795140
Huandacareo	Michoacán	México	1804	795143
Huango	Michoacán	México	1796	AGN HI 430:341v-342
Huaniqueo	Michoacán	México	1746	768900-768902
Huaniqueo	Michoacán	México	1747	768916-768918
Huaniqueo	Michoacán	México	1747	768921
Huaniqueo	Michoacán	México	1758	769986-769989
Huaniqueo	Michoacán	México	1759	772017-772020
Huaniqueo	Michoacán	México	1763	774211-774213
Huaniqueo	Michoacán	México	1768	774103-774104
Huaniqueo	Michoacán	México	1770	774144
Huaniqueo	Michoacán	México	1772	761550

Locality	Province	Country	Year(s)	Reference
Huaniqueo	Michoacán	México	1776	776736-776738
Huaniqueo	Michoacán	México	1796	AGN HI 430:372-372v
Huaniqueo	Michoacán	México	1804	793881
Huétamo	Michoacán	México	1743	AGI, Indiferentes 107
Indaparapeo	Michoacán	México	1746	768900-768902
Indaparapeo	Michoacán	México	1758	769986-769989
Indaparapeo	Michoacán	México	1759	772017-772020
Indaparapeo	Michoacán	México	1760	763271-763272
Indaparapeo	Michoacán	México	1763	774211-774213
Indaparapeo	Michoacán	México	1772	761553
Indaparapeo	Michoacán	México	1776	776745-776746
Indaparapeo	Michoacán	México	1777	785446
Irimbo	Michoacán	México	1747	768916-768918
Irimbo	Michoacán	México	1747	768921
Irimbo	Michoacán	México	1759	772017-772020
Irimbo	Michoacán	México	1760	763271-763272
Irimbo	Michoacán	México	1763	774211-774213
Irimbo	Michoacán	México	1770	774144
Irimbo	Michoacán	México	1772	761553
Irimbo	Michoacán	México	1776	776736-776738
Jacona	Michoacán	México	1746	768900-768902
Jacona	Michoacán	México	1746	768900-768902
Jacona	Michoacán	México	1747	763920
Jacona	Michoacán	México	1758	769986-769989
Jacona	Michoacán	México	1759	772017-772020
Jacona	Michoacán	México	1760	763271-763272
Jacona	Michoacán	México	1763	774211-774213
Jacona	Michoacán	México	1768	774103-774104
Jacona	Michoacán	México	1772	761553
Jacona	Michoacán	México	1777	776752
Jiquilpán	Michoacán	México	1746	768900-768902
Jiquilpán	Michoacán	México	1758	769986-769989
Jiquilpán	Michoacán	México	1763	774211-774213
Jiquilpán	Michoacán	México	1770	774154-774155
La Huacana	Michoacán	México	1759	772017-772020
La Huacana	Michoacán	México	1768	774103-774104
La Huacana	Michoacán	México	1772	761550
La Huacana	Michoacán	México	1777	776752
La Piedad	Michoacán	México	1758	769986-769989
La Piedad	Michoacán	México	1759	772017-772020
La Piedad	Michoacán	México	1760	763271-763272
La Piedad	Michoacán	México	1763	774213
La Piedad	Michoacán	México	1768	774114-774116
La Piedad	Michoacán	México	1770	774142-774143
La Piedad	Michoacán	México	1772	761550

Locality	Province	Country	Year(s)	Reference
La Piedad	Michoacán	México	1778	785446
La Piedad	Michoacán	México	1801	795137-795138
La Piedad	Michoacán	México	1803	795140
La Piedad	Michoacán	México	1804	795142
La Piedad	Michoacán	México	1805	793877
La Piedad	Michoacán	México	1806	793878
La Piedad	Michoacán	México	1808	793880
La Piedad	Michoacán	México	1810	793882
Maravatio	Michoacán	México	1668	762941
Maravatio	Michoacán	México	1746	768900-768902
Maravatio	Michoacán	México	1747	768916-768921
Maravatio	Michoacán	México	1758	769986-769989
Maravatio	Michoacán	México	1759	772017-772020
Maravatio	Michoacán	México	1763	774211-774213
Maravatio	Michoacán	México	1770	774154-774155
Maravatio	Michoacán	México	1809	793881
Nahuatzén	Michoacán	México	1746	768900-768902
Nahuatzén	Michoacán	México	1760	785447
Nahuatzén	Michoacán	México	1763	774211-774213
Nahuatzén	Michoacán	México	1768	782002-782003
Nahuatzén	Michoacán	México	1776	776736-776738
Nahuatzén	Michoacán	México	1809	793881
Nurio	Michoacán	México	1782	762942
Opopeo	Michoacán	México	1763	774211-774213
Pajacuarán	Michoacán	México	1668	795134
Pajacuarán	Michoacán	México	1800	795135
Pajacuarán	Michoacán	México	1801	795138
Pajacuarán	Michoacán	México	1803	795143
Pajacuarán	Michoacán	México	1804	795143
Pajacuarán	Michoacán	México	1805–1806	793876
Pajacuarán	Michoacán	México	1808	793880
Pajacuarán	Michoacán	México	1809	793881
Pajacuarán	Michoacán	México	1810–1819	793882
Panindícuaro	Michoacán	México	1743	768900-768902
Paracho	Michoacán	México	1746	768900-768902
Paracho	Michoacán	México	1747	768916-768918
Paracho	Michoacán	México	1760	763271-763272
Paracho	Michoacán	México	1763	774211-774213
Paracho	Michoacán	México	1768	774114-774116
Paracho	Michoacán	México	1770	774154-774155
Paracho	Michoacán	México	1772	761550
Paracho	Michoacán	México	1782	762942
Paracho	Michoacán	México	1785	785446
Paracho	Michoacán	México	1793	763127
Paracho	Michoacán	México	1809	793881

Locality	Province	Country	Year(s)	Reference
Parangaricutiro	Michoacán	México	1746	768901-768902
Parangaricutiro	Michoacán	México	1747	768916-768918
Parangaricutiro	Michoacán	México	1747	768921
Parangaricutiro	Michoacán	México	1758	769986-7689982
Parangaricutiro	Michoacán	México	1759	772017-772019
Parangaricutiro	Michoacán	México	1760	785447
Parangaricutiro	Michoacán	México	1760	768900
Parangaricutiro	Michoacán	México	1772	761553
Patambán	Michoacán	México	1747	768920
Patambán	Michoacán	México	1759	772017-772020
Patambán	Michoacán	México	1763	774211-774213
Patambán	Michoacán	México	1770	774154-774155
Patambán	Michoacán	México	1783	785446
Pátzcuaro	Michoacán	México	1746	768900-768902
Pátzcuaro	Michoacán	México	1747	768916-768918
Pátzcuaro	Michoacán	México	1747	768920-768921
Pátzcuaro	Michoacán	México	1758	769986-769989
Pátzcuaro	Michoacán	México	1759	772017-772020
Pátzcuaro	Michoacán	México	1768	774103-774104
Pátzcuaro	Michoacán	México	1768	774144-774116
Pátzcuaro	Michoacán	México	1770	774154-774155
Pátzcuaro	Michoacán	México	1772	761550
Pátzcuaro	Michoacán	México	1778	776888
Pátzcuaro	Michoacán	México	1794	795135
Pátzcuaro	Michoacán	México	1796	AGN HI 430:372
Pátzcuaro: S. Fco.	Michoacán	México	1763	774211-774213
Pátzcuaro: Santa Cat.	Michoacán	México	1763	774211-774213
Penjamillo	Michoacán	México	1740–1742	643819:7
Penjamillo	Michoacán	México	1758	769986-769989
Penjamillo	Michoacán	México	1759	772017-772020
Penjamillo	Michoacán	México	1763	774202
Penjamillo	Michoacán	México	1772	761550
Penjamillo	Michoacán	México	1800	795136
Penjamillo	Michoacán	México	1801	795137
Penjamillo	Michoacán	México	1802	795141
Penjamillo	Michoacán	México	1808	793880
Peribán	Michoacán	México	1746	768900-768902
Peribán	Michoacán	México	1747	768920
Peribán	Michoacán	México	1758	769986-769989
Peribán	Michoacán	México	1759	772017-772020
Peribán	Michoacán	México	1763	774202
Peribán	Michoacán	México	1768	782002-782003
Peribán	Michoacán	México	1770	774154-774155
Peribán	Michoacán	México	1772	761553
Pichátaro	Michoacán	México	1746	768900

Locality	Province	Country	Year(s)	Reference
Pichátaro	Michoacán	México	1747	768920
Pichátaro	Michoacán	México	1758	769986-769989
Pichátaro	Michoacán	México	1760	785447
Pichátaro	Michoacán	México	1763	774211-774213
Pichátaro	Michoacán	México	1768	774103
Pichátaro	Michoacán	México	1770	774144
Pichátaro	Michoacán	México	1770	776752
Pichátaro	Michoacán	México	1776	776736-776738
Pichátaro	Michoacán	México	1783	795134
Pichátaro	Michoacán	México	1800	795135
Pichátaro	Michoacán	México	1801	795138
Pichátaro	Michoacán	México	1803	795139-995141
Pichátaro	Michoacán	México	1804	795142-795143
Pomacuarán	Michoacán	México	1763	774213
Pomacuarán	Michoacán	México	1782	762942
Pómaro	Michoacán	México	1660	765609
Pómaro	Michoacán	México	1668	795134
Pómaro	Michoacán	México	1703–1776	773538
Pómaro	Michoacán	México	1758	769986-769989
Pómaro	Michoacán	México	1759	772017-772020
Pómaro	Michoacán	México	1760	795447
Pómaro	Michoacán	México	1763	774211-774213
Pómaro	Michoacán	México	1768	782002-782003
Pómaro	Michoacán	México	1770	774144
Pómaro	Michoacán	México	1776	776736-776738
Pómaro	Michoacán	México	1800	795135-795136
Pómaro	Michoacán	México	1801	795138
Purépero de Echáiz	Michoacán	México	1784	643819:9
Puruándiro	Michoacán	México	1682	765610
Puruándiro	Michoacán	México	1743	AGI, Indiferentes 107
Puruándiro	Michoacán	México	1746	768901-768902
Puruándiro	Michoacán	México	1747	768916-768918
Puruándiro	Michoacán	México	1747	768921
Puruándiro	Michoacán	México	1758	769986-769989
Puruándiro	Michoacán	México	1759	772017-772020
Puruándiro	Michoacán	México	1763	774211-774213
Puruándiro	Michoacán	México	1768	774114-774116
Puruándiro	Michoacán	México	1770	774142-774143
Puruándiro	Michoacán	México	1772	761553
Puruándiro	Michoacán	México	1794	795134
Puruándiro	Michoacán	México	1796	AGN HI 430:336-336v
Puruándiro	Michoacán	México	1800	795135-95136
Puruándiro	Michoacán	México	1801	795137
Puruándiro	Michoacán	México	1803	795140-795141
Puruándiro	Michoacán	México	1804	795141

Locality	Province	Country	Year(s)	Reference
Purechucho	Michoacán	México	1743	AGI, Indiferentes 107
Sahuayo	Michoacán	México	1668	795134
Sahuayo	Michoacán	México	1759	772017
Sahuayo	Michoacán	México	1763	774211-774213
Sahuayo	Michoacán	México	1768	774114-774116
Sahuayo	Michoacán	México	1770	774154-774155
Sahuayo	Michoacán	México	1772	761553
Sahuayo	Michoacán	México	1777	776652
Sahuayo	Michoacán	México	1793	763127
Sahuayo	Michoacán	México	1809	793881
San Felipe	Michoacán	México	1746	768900-768902
San Felipe	Michoacán	México	1747	768916-768918
San Felipe	Michoacán	México	1747	768921
San Felipe	Michoacán	México	1759	772017-772020
San Felipe	Michoacán	México	1760	795447
San Felipe	Michoacán	México	1763	774211-774213
San Felipe	Michoacán	México	1768	774114-774116
San Felipe	Michoacán	México	1772	761553
San Juan de los Llanos	Michoacán	México	1790	AGN PAD 7
San Sebastián	Michoacán	México	1760	763271
Santa Ana Maya	Michoacán	México	1747	768916-768921
Santa Ana Maya	Michoacán	México	1758	769986-769989
Santa Ana Maya	Michoacán	México	1759	772017-772020
Santa Ana Maya	Michoacán	México	1760	785447
Santa Ana Maya	Michoacán	México	1763	764292
Santa Ana Maya	Michoacán	México	1768	774103-774104
Santa Ana Maya	Michoacán	México	1770	774142-774143
Santa Ana Maya	Michoacán	México	1772	761553
Santa Ana Maya	Michoacán	México	1800	795135
Santa Ana Maya	Michoacán	México	1801	795138
Santa Ana Maya	Michoacán	México	1803	795140
Santa Ana Maya	Michoacán	México	1804	795143
Santa Ana Maya	Michoacán	México	1807	793879
Santa Ana Maya	Michoacán	México	1809	793881
Santa Ana Maya	Michoacán	México	1810–1819	793882
Santa Clara[118]	Michoacán	México	1747	768916-768918
Santa Clara	Michoacán	México	1747	768921
Santa Clara	Michoacán	México	1758	769986-769989
Santa Clara	Michoacán	México	1759	772017-772020
Santa Clara	Michoacán	México	1763	774211-774213
Santa Clara	Michoacán	México	1768	774114-774116
Santa Clara	Michoacán	México	1770	774142-774143

---

[118] Santa Clara de los Cobres.

Locality	Province	Country	Year(s)	Reference
Santa Clara	Michoacán	México	1772	761550
Santa Clara	Michoacán	México	1776	776745-776746
Santa Clara	Michoacán	México	1794	795134
Santa Clara	Michoacán	México	1809	793881
Santa Fé de la Laguna	Michoacán	México	1668	765271
Santa Fé de la Laguna	Michoacán	México	1758	769986-769989
Santa Fé de la Laguna	Michoacán	México	1760	?
Santa Fé de la Laguna	Michoacán	México	1763	774211-774213
Santa Fé de la Laguna	Michoacán	México	1768	774103-774105
Santa Fé de la Laguna	Michoacán	México	1770	774144
Santa Fé de la Laguna	Michoacán	México	1772	761553
Santa Fé de la Laguna	Michoacán	México	1778	776888
Santa Fé de la Laguna	Michoacán	México	1809	793881
Santa Fé del Río	Michoacán	México	1747	768916-768918
Santa Fé del Río	Michoacán	México	1747	768921
Santa Fé del Río	Michoacán	México	1758	769986-769989
Santa Fé del Río	Michoacán	México	1759	772017-772020
Santa Fé del Río	Michoacán	México	1763	774211-774213
Santa Fé del Río	Michoacán	México	1768	782002-782003
Santa Fé del Río	Michoacán	México	1770	774142-774143
Santa Fé del Río	Michoacán	México	1772	761553
Santa Fé del Río	Michoacán	México	1809	793881
Siquilpán	Michoacán	México	1796	AGN HI 430:369v-371
Siríndaro	Michoacán	México	1743	AGI, Indiferentes 107
Siríndaro	Michoacán	México	1759	772017-772020
Siríndaro	Michoacán	México	1763	774211-774213
Siríndaro	Michoacán	México	1768	782002-782003
Tacámbaro	Michoacán	México	1746	768900-768902
Tacámbaro	Michoacán	México	1747	768916-768921
Tacámbaro	Michoacán	México	1758	769986-769989
Tacámbaro	Michoacán	México	1759	772017-772020
Tacámbaro	Michoacán	México	1763	774211-774213
Tacámbaro	Michoacán	México	1768	792002-782003
Tacámbaro	Michoacán	México	1770	774154-774155
Tacámbaro	Michoacán	México	1772	761550
Tacámbaro	Michoacán	México	1778	776888
Tacámbaro	Michoacán	México	1794	795134
Tacásquaro	Michoacán	México	1768	774103-774104
Tanaco	Michoacán	México	1763	774211-774213
Tanaco	Michoacán	México	1782	762942
Tancítaro	Michoacán	México	1746	768900-768902
Tancítaro	Michoacán	México	1747	768920
Tancítaro	Michoacán	México	1758	769986-769989
Tancítaro	Michoacán	México	1759	772017-772020
Tancítaro	Michoacán	México	1763	774202

Locality	Province	Country	Year(s)	Reference
Tancítaro	Michoacán	México	1770	774142-774143
Tancítaro	Michoacán	México	1772	761553
Tancítaro	Michoacán	México	1776	776736-776738
Tangamandapeo	Michoacán	México	1758	769986-769989
Tangamandapeo	Michoacán	México	1777	776752
Tangamandapeo	Michoacán	México	1778	776888
Tangancíquaro	Michoacán	México	1746	768900-768902
Tangancíquaro	Michoacán	México	1759	772017-772020
Tangancíquaro	Michoacán	México	1763	774211-774213
Tangancíquaro	Michoacán	México	1768	774114-774116
Tangancíquaro	Michoacán	México	1770	774144
Tangancíquaro	Michoacán	México	1772	761553
Tangancíquaro	Michoacán	México	1778	776888
Tangancíquaro	Michoacán	México	1793	763127
Tanhuato	Michoacán	México	1804	795142
Tarecuato	Michoacán	México	1763	774211-774213
Tarecuato	Michoacán	México	1772	761550
Taretán	Michoacán	México	1747	768916-768918
Taretán	Michoacán	México	1747	768921
Taretán	Michoacán	México	1758	768986-768989
Taretán	Michoacán	México	1759	772017-772020
Taretán	Michoacán	México	1760	763271-763272
Taretán	Michoacán	México	1770	774144
Taretán	Michoacán	México	1772	761553
Taretán	Michoacán	México	1776	776736-776738
Tarímbaro	Michoacán	México	1746	768900-768902
Tarímbaro	Michoacán	México	1763	774211-774213
Tarímbaro	Michoacán	México	1770	774142-774143
Tarímbaro	Michoacán	México	1772	761550
Tarímbaro	Michoacán	México	1776	776736-776738
Tepalcatepec	Michoacán	México	1747	768920
Tepalcatepec	Michoacán	México	1759	772017-772020
Tepalcatepec	Michoacán	México	1760	763271-763272
Tepalcatepec	Michoacán	México	1763	774213
Tepalcatepec	Michoacán	México	1768	774211-774213
Tepalcatepec	Michoacán	México	1770	774103-774104
Tepalcatepec	Michoacán	México	1776	774142-774143
Teremendo	Michoacán	México	1668	762941
Teremendo	Michoacán	México	1747	768920
Teremendo	Michoacán	México	1760	785447
Teremendo	Michoacán	México	1763	774211-774213
Teremendo	Michoacán	México	1768	774103-774104
Teremendo	Michoacán	México	1770	774154-774155
Teremendo	Michoacán	México	1776	776736-776738
Teremendo	Michoacán	México	1793	763127

Locality	Province	Country	Year(s)	Reference
Tingambato	Michoacán	México	1746	768900-768902
Tingambato	Michoacán	México	1758	769986-769989
Tingambato	Michoacán	México	1759	772017-772020
Tingambato	Michoacán	México	1760	785447
Tingambato	Michoacán	México	1763	774202
Tingambato	Michoacán	México	1763	774211-774213
Tingambato	Michoacán	México	1768	762930
Tingambato	Michoacán	México	1770	774144
Tingambato	Michoacán	México	1772	761553
Tingambato	Michoacán	México	1776	776745-776746
Tingambato	Michoacán	México	1809	793881
Tingüindín	Michoacán	México	1668	795134
Tingüindín	Michoacán	México	1746	768900-768902
Tingüindín	Michoacán	México	1747	768920
Tingüindín	Michoacán	México	1758	769986-769989
Tingüindín	Michoacán	México	1759	772017-772020
Tingüindín	Michoacán	México	1768	774103-774104
Tingüindín	Michoacán	México	1770	774154-774155
Tingüindín	Michoacán	México	1772	761550
Tingüindín	Michoacán	México	1776	776736-776738
Tiquicheo	Michoacán	México	1800	795135
Tiquicheo	Michoacán	México	1801	795138
Tiquicheo	Michoacán	México	1803	795140
Tiquicheo	Michoacán	México	1804	795142-795143
Tiríndaro	Michoacán	México	1747	769916-769918
Tiríndaro	Michoacán	México	1747	769921
Tiríndaro	Michoacán	México	1758	769986-769989
Tiríndaro	Michoacán	México	1760	763271-763272
Tiríndaro	Michoacán	México	1760	763763
Tiríndaro	Michoacán	México	1763	774211-774213
Tiríndaro	Michoacán	México	1768	774114-774116
Tiríndaro	Michoacán	México	1770	774144
Tiríndaro	Michoacán	México	1772	761550
Tiríndaro	Michoacán	México	1776	776745-776746
Tiripitío	Michoacán	México	1747	769916-769918
Tiripitío	Michoacán	México	1747	769921
Tiripitío	Michoacán	México	1758	769986-769989
Tiripitío	Michoacán	México	1760	785447
Tiripitío	Michoacán	México	1763	774211-774213
Tiripitío	Michoacán	México	1768	774103-774104
Tiripitío	Michoacán	México	1770	774142-774143
Tiripitío	Michoacán	México	1772	7761550
Tiripitío	Michoacán	México	1776	7776745
Tiripitío	Michoacán	México	1776	7776736-776738
Tiripitío	Michoacán	México	1796	AGN HI 430:341v-342

Locality	Province	Country	Year(s)	Reference
Tiripitío	Michoacán	México	1800	795135
Tlalpujahua de Rayón	Michoacán	México	1746	768900-768902
Tlalpujahua de Rayón	Michoacán	México	1747	768920
Tlalpujahua de Rayón	Michoacán	México	1758	769986-769989
Tlalpujahua de Rayón	Michoacán	México	1759	772017-772020
Tlalpujahua de Rayón	Michoacán	México	1760	785447
Tlalpujahua de Rayón	Michoacán	México	1762	772304
Tlalpujahua de Rayón	Michoacán	México	1763	774202
Tlalpujahua de Rayón	Michoacán	México	1768	774114-774116
Tlalpujahua de Rayón	Michoacán	México	1770	774144
Tlasasalca	Michoacán	México	1668	765271
Tlasasalca	Michoacán	México	1743	AGI Indiferente[119]
Tlasasalca	Michoacán	México	1747	768916-768918
Tlasasalca	Michoacán	México	1747	768921
Tlasasalca	Michoacán	México	1759	768916-768918
Tlasasalca	Michoacán	México	1763	774202
Tlasasalca	Michoacán	México	1768	774103-774104
Tlasasalca	Michoacán	México	1770	774144
Tlasasalca	Michoacán	México	1772	761550
Tlasasalca	Michoacán	México	1776	776745-776746
Tlasasalca	Michoacán	México	1800	795131-795136
Tlasasalca	Michoacán	México	1801	795137
Tlasasalca	Michoacán	México	1803	795141
Tlasasalca	Michoacán	México	1804	795142
Tlasasalca	Michoacán	México	1805	793876
Tlasasalca	Michoacán	México	1807	793879
Tlasasalca	Michoacán	México	1808	793880
Tungareo	Michoacán	México	1668	762941
Tupataro	Michoacán	México	1760	785447
Turicato	Michoacán	México	1747	768916-768918
Turicato	Michoacán	México	1747	768921
Turicato	Michoacán	México	1778	776888
Turícuaro	Michoacán	México	1809	793881
Tuxpán	Michoacán	México	1746	768900-768902
Tuxpán	Michoacán	México	1747	768920
Tuxpán	Michoacán	México	1758	769986-769989
Tuxpán	Michoacán	México	1759	772017-772020
Tuxpán	Michoacán	México	1763	774211-774213
Tuxpán	Michoacán	México	1768	782002-782003
Tuxpán	Michoacán	México	1770	774142-774143
Tuxpán	Michoacán	México	1772	761553
Tuxpán	Michoacán	México	1776	776745-776746

---

[119] Archivo General de Indias, Sección Indiferentes, bundle 108, part iv, folios 13–85v; contains a *padrón* of the entire province of Tlazazalca.

Locality	Province	Country	Year(s)	Reference
Tuzantla	Michoacán	México	1747	768920
Tuzantla	Michoacán	México	1758	769986-769989
Tuzantla	Michoacán	México	1759	772017-772020
Tuzantla	Michoacán	México	1763	774211-77413
Tuzantla	Michoacán	México	1768	782002-782003
Tuzantla	Michoacán	México	1770	774154-774155
Tuzantla	Michoacán	México	1772	761550
Tzentzénquaro	Michoacán	México	1703–1796	773538
Tzentzénquaro	Michoacán	México	1772	761553
Tzintzuntzán	Michoacán	México	1747	768920
Tzintzuntzán	Michoacán	México	1758	769986-769989
Tzintzuntzán	Michoacán	México	1760	763271-763272
Tzintzuntzán	Michoacán	México	1763	774211-774213
Tzintzuntzán	Michoacán	México	1768	774114-774116
Tzintzuntzán	Michoacán	México	1770	774142-774143
Tzintzuntzán	Michoacán	México	1772	761550
Tzintzuntzán	Michoacán	México	1776	776736-776738
Ucareo	Michoacán	México	1703–1796	773538
Ucareo	Michoacán	México	1763	774211-774213
Ucareo	Michoacán	México	1768	774114-774116
Ucareo	Michoacán	México	1772	761553
Ucareo	Michoacán	México	1782	762942
Undameo	Michoacán	México	1746	768901-768902
Undameo	Michoacán	México	1747	768916-768921
Undameo	Michoacán	México	1758	785446
Undameo	Michoacán	México	1760	772369
Undameo	Michoacán	México	1763	774211-774213
Undameo	Michoacán	México	1763	768900
Undameo	Michoacán	México	1768	774103-774104
Undameo	Michoacán	México	1770	774154-774155
Undameo	Michoacán	México	1776	776736-776738
Undameo	Michoacán	México	1801	795138
Urecho	Michoacán	México	1760	763271
Urecho	Michoacán	México	1763	774213
Uren	Michoacán	México	1797	762942
Uruapán	Michoacán	México	1746	768900-768902
Uruapán	Michoacán	México	1747	768920
Uruapán	Michoacán	México	1758	769986-769989
Uruapán	Michoacán	México	1759	772017-772020
Uruapán	Michoacán	México	1760	763271-763272
Uruapán	Michoacán	México	1763	774213
Uruapán	Michoacán	México	1770	774154-774155
Uruapán	Michoacán	México	1772	761550
Uruapán	Michoacán	México	1776	776736-776738
Uruapán	Michoacán	México	1776	776888

Locality	Province	Country	Year(s)	Reference
Uruapán	Michoacán	México	1784	643819:10
Uruapán	Michoacán	México	1794	774211-774212
Uruapán	Michoacán	México	1794	795134
Uruapán	Michoacán	México	1796	AGN HI 430:374v
Uruapán	Michoacán	México	1810	793882
Valladolid	Michoacán	México	1757	769976
Valladolid	Michoacán	México	1758	769986-769989
Valladolid	Michoacán	México	1759	772017-772020
Valladolid	Michoacán	México	1760	785447
Valladolid	Michoacán	México	1768	782002-782003
Valladolid	Michoacán	México	1777	776752
Valladolid	Michoacán	México	1794	795134-795135
Valladolid	Michoacán	México	1796	AGN HI 430:332-336
Valladolid	Michoacán	México	1809	AGN HI 452:viii
Xiquilpa	Michoacán	México	1778	AGN HI 73:215-229
Yuréquaro	Michoacán	México	1759	772017-772020
Yuréquaro	Michoacán	México	1768	774114-774116
Yuréquaro	Michoacán	México	1782	763942
Yuréquaro	Michoacán	México	1800	795135
Yuréquaro	Michoacán	México	1801	795137-795138
Yuréquaro	Michoacán	México	1803	795140
Yuréquaro	Michoacán	México	1804	795142
Yuréquaro	Michoacán	México	1805	793877
Yuréquaro	Michoacán	México	1806	793878
Yuréquaro	Michoacán	México	1808	793880
Yuréquaro	Michoacán	México	1809	793881
Zacán	Michoacán	México	1759	772017-772020
Zacán	Michoacán	México	1763	774211-774213
Zacán	Michoacán	México	1764–1784	795135
Zacán	Michoacán	México	1770	774154-774155
Zacán	Michoacán	México	1776	776736-776738
Zacapu	Michoacán	México	1746	768901-768902
Zacapu	Michoacán	México	1747	768920
Zacapu	Michoacán	México	1758	769986-769989
Zacapu	Michoacán	México	1759	772017-772020
Zacapu	Michoacán	México	1760	774271-774272
Zacapu	Michoacán	México	1763	774211-774213
Zacapu	Michoacán	México	1768	774114-774116
Zacapu	Michoacán	México	1770	774142-774143
Zacapu	Michoacán	México	1770	774154-774155
Zacapu	Michoacán	México	1772	761550
Zacapu	Michoacán	México	1793	768900
Zacapu	Michoacán	México	1809	793881
Zacapu	Michoacán	México	1827	793883
Zamora	Michoacán	México	1632	779046

Locality	Province	Country	Year(s)	Reference
Zamora	Michoacán	México	1746	768900-768902
Zamora	Michoacán	México	1747	768916-768908
Zamora	Michoacán	México	1747	768921
Zamora	Michoacán	México	1758	769986-768989
Zamora	Michoacán	México	1759	772017-772020
Zamora	Michoacán	México	1760	763271
Zamora	Michoacán	México	1763	774211-774213
Zamora	Michoacán	México	1768	774114-774116
Zamora	Michoacán	México	1772	761553
Zamora	Michoacán	México	1776	776736-776738
Zamora	Michoacán	México	1778	776888
Zamora	Michoacán	México	1796	AGN HI 430:373-373v
Zinaparo	Michoacán	México	1781–1789	643818:2
Zinapécuaro	Michoacán	México	1782	762639:2
Zinapécuaro	Michoacán	México	1796	AGN HI 430:362v-369v

MORELOS

Locality	Province	Country	Year(s)	Reference
Amacazac	Morelos	México	1828–1836	733735:2
Cuautla	Morelos	México	1797	641728:4
Cuautla Amilpas	Morelos	México	1790	AGN PAD 8[120]
Cuernavaca	Morelos	México	1791	AGN PAD 8
Guastepec	Morelos	México	1807	AGN HS 356:viii[121]
Hueyapan	Morelos	México	1797	641726:5
Jantetelco	Morelos	México	1768	641732:3
Jonacatepec	Morelos	México	1768	641723:4
Oaxtepec	Morelos	México	1795–1851	606345
Tepuztlán	Morelos	México	1530s	Gerhard[122]
Tepuztlán	Morelos	México	1807	AGN HS 356:viii
Tetela del Volcán	Morelos	México	1778–1779	641732:2
Tlalnepantla	Morelos	México	1795–1863	706056
Xochitepec	Morelos	México	1768	708356
Xochitepec	Morelos	México	1779	641733:3
Yautepec	Morelos	México	1807	AGN HS 356:viii
Yecapixtla	Morelos	México	1787–1850	641725:1
Yecapixtla	Morelos	México	1797	641734:1
Yecapixtla	Morelos	México	1807	AGN HS 356:viii
Zacualpan	Morelos	México	1777	442138:4
Zacualpan	Morelos	México	1900	641734:3

---

[120] A related document is found in the BNP FM.

[121] Archivo General de la Nación, Ramo Hospital de Jesús, bundle 356, *expediente* 8.

[122] Peter Gerhard in his book *A Guide to the Historical Geography of New Spain*, rev. ed. (Norman, Oklahoma, 1993), page 98, says that "probably dating from the late 1530s is a detailed census (in Náhuatl) of Tepuztlan."

NAYARIT

The microfilm series 168803-168849 contains hundreds of entries for the 1600s–1800s for Nayarit. It has not been studied in detail here.

Locality	Province	Country	Year(s)	Reference
	Nayarit	México	1649	Archivo del Parral[123]
	Nayarit	México	1824–1824	CDH[124]
Acacopeta	Nayarit	México	1760	168805
Acacopeta	Nayarit	México	1770	?
Acacopeta	Nayarit	México	1772	?
Acacopeta	Nayarit	México	1790	AGI, Guadalajara 250
Acacopeta	Nayarit	México	1817	168808
Acacopeta	Nayarit	México	1831	168846
Acatic	Nayarit	México	1819	168815
Ahuacatlán	Nayarit	México	1777	?
Ahuacatlán	Nayarit	México	1792[125]	AGN HI 523:75
Ahuacatlán	Nayarit	México	1793	AGN PAD 14:1-189
Ahuacatlán	Nayarit	México	1817	168808
Ahuacatlán	Nayarit	México	1819	168815
Ahuacatlán	Nayarit	México	1820	168819
Ahuacatlán	Nayarit	México	1821	168823
Ahuacatlán	Nayarit	México	1822	168827
Ahuacatlán	Nayarit	México	1824	168831
Ahuacatlán	Nayarit	México	1825	168835
Ahuacatlán	Nayarit	México	1832	168846
Amatlán de Cañas	Nayarit	México	1776	AGI Guadalajara 348
Amatlán de Cañas	Nayarit	México	1817	168808
Amatlán de Cañas	Nayarit	México	1818	168812
Amatlán de Cañas	Nayarit	México	1820	168822
Amatlán de Cañas	Nayarit	México	1824	168831
Amatlán de Cañas	Nayarit	México	1831	168848
Amatlán de Jora	Nayarit	México	1821	168823
Amatlán de Jora	Nayarit	México	1828	168829
Astatán	Nayarit	México	1817	168808
Camotlán	Nayarit	México	1819	168815
Chimaltitlán	Nayarit	México	1650	AAG

[123] Padrón de los vecinos . . . 1649.
[124] *Colección de documentos para la historia de Nayarit* III, pages 280–289; includes *padrones* of all the missions in Nayarit at that time.
[125] This is a *padrón* of sambos.

132

Locality	Province	Country	Year(s)	Reference
Compostela	Nayarit	México	1689	AAG
Compostela	Nayarit	México	1817	168809
Compostela	Nayarit	México	1820	168819
Compostela	Nayarit	México	1830	168842
Cuyacapán	Nayarit	México	1820	168819
Cuyutlán	Nayarit	México	1817	168809
Cuyutlán	Nayarit	México	1819	168816
Cuyutlán	Nayarit	México	1820	168818
Cuyutlán	Nayarit	México	1821	168824
Cuyutlán	Nayarit	México	1822	168828
Cuyutlán	Nayarit	México	1828	168839
Cuyutlán	Nayarit	México	1830	168842
Cuyutlán	Nayarit	México	1831	168845
Guajícori	Nayarit	México	1824	168831
Guajícori	Nayarit	México	1830	168842
Guaynamota	Nayarit	México	1817	168809
Guaynamota	Nayarit	México	1820	168818
Guaynamota	Nayarit	México	1825	168835
Ixtlán	Nayarit	México	1817	168809
Ixtlán	Nayarit	México	1818	168813
Ixtlán	Nayarit	México	1821	168824
Ixtlán	Nayarit	México	1822	168828
Ixtlán	Nayarit	México	1824	168832
Ixtlán	Nayarit	México	1825	168835
Ixtlán	Nayarit	México	1828	168839
Ixtlán	Nayarit	México	1830	168842
Ixtlán	Nayarit	México	1831	168848
Ixtlán	Nayarit	México	1851	657013:5
Jalisco	Nayarit	México	1817	168810
Jomulco	Nayarit	México	1819	168815
Mespán	Nayarit	México	1820	168819
Mespán	Nayarit	México	1824	168832
Milpillas	Nayarit	México	1824	168831
Picachos	Nayarit	México	1824	168831
Quibiquinta	Nayarit	México	1824	168831
Rosa Morada	Nayarit	México	1817	168809
Rosa Morada	Nayarit	México	1817	168809
Rosa Morada	Nayarit	México	1819	168816
Rosa Morada	Nayarit	México	1820	168818
Rosa Morada	Nayarit	México	1821	168824
Rosa Morada	Nayarit	México	1822	168828
Rosa Morada	Nayarit	México	1828	168839
Rosa Morada	Nayarit	México	1830	168842
Rosa Morada	Nayarit	México	1831	168845

Locality	Province	Country	Year(s)	Reference
San Blas	Nayarit	México	1679	AAG[126]
San Blas	Nayarit	México	1796	AGN CA 67:187-189
San Blas	Nayarit	México	1817	168810
San Blas	Nayarit	México	1820	168822
San Blas	Nayarit	México	1831	168848
San José de Gracia	Nayarit	México	1817	168808
San Pedro[127]	Nayarit	México	1689	AAG
Sayula	Nayarit	México	1817	168808
Sentipac	Nayarit	México	1819	168816
Sentipac	Nayarit	México	1831	168848
Suatlán	Nayarit	México	1819	168815
Tecuala	Nayarit	México	1817	168808
Tepic	Nayarit	México	1760	168805
Tepic	Nayarit	México	1817	168811
Tepic	Nayarit	México	1828	168840
Tequepespán	Nayarit	México	1776	AGI Guadalajara 348[128]
Tetitlán	Nayarit	México	1819	168815
Xala	Nayarit	México	1790	AGN PAD 14
Xala	Nayarit	México	1819	168815
Yesca	Nayarit	México	1820	168818
Yesca	Nayarit	México	1830	168844

---

[126] Archivo del Arzobispado de Guadalajara, Visita of 1678–1679.

[127] San Pedro de la Lagunilla, included in the *padrón* of Compostela for the same year.

[128] There are a number of *padrones* for the province of Tequepespan in this source, indicating that the pueblo and other parishes are included separately in the bundle.

NUEVA VIZCAYA

Locality	Province	Country	Year(s)	Reference
	Nueva Vizcaya	México	1604	HAH 35
	Nueva Vizcaya	México	1649	Archivo del Parral
	Nueva Vizcaya	México	1707	Archivo del Parral[129]
Atotonilco	Nueva Vizcaya	México	1778	AF 16:328
Babonoyaba[130]	Nueva Vizcaya	México	1799	MBL 2:26
Babonoyahua[131]	Nueva Vizcaya	México	1778	AF 16:328
Bachiniva	Nueva Vizcaya	México	1778	AF 16:328
Basís	Nueva Vizcaya	México	1778	AGI Indiferente 102
Basís	Nueva Vizcaya	México	1779	AGI Indiferente 102
Casco (El)	Nueva Vizcaya	México	1779	AGI Guadalajara 28
Cerro Gordo[132]	Nueva Vizcaya	México	1725	Archivo del Parral
Cuéncame	Nueva Vizcaya	México	1604	AF 11:165.1
Cuéncame	Nueva Vizcaya	México	1777	AGI Guadalajara 255
Cuéncame	Nueva Vizcaya	México	1778	AGI Indiferente 102
Durango[133]	Nueva Vizcaya	México	1777	AGI Guadalajara 103:3:26
Durango	Nueva Vizcaya	México	1778	AMH 17:121-217; 18:47-96
Durango[134]	Nueva Vizcaya	México	1777–1779	AGI[135]
Durango[136]	Nueva Vizcaya	México	1779	AGI Indiferente 102
Durango	Nueva Vizcaya	México	1820	AF 18:387
La Concepción	Nueva Vizcaya	México	1778	AF 16:328
Las Bocas	Nueva Vizcaya	México	1777	AGI Indiferente 1526
Los Remedios	Nueva Vizcaya	México	1777	AGI Guadalajara 255
Guanacevi	Nueva Vizcaya	México	1604	AGI Guadalajara 28:78-89
Guanacevi	Nueva Vizcaya	México	1778	AGI Indiferente 102
Guarisamey	Nueva Vizcaya	México	1777	AGI Indiferente 102
Mapimí	Nueva Vizcaya	México	1604	AGI Guadalajara 28
Mapimí[137]	Nueva Vizcaya	México	1724	AGI Guadalajara 37

[129] This *padrón* is of non-Indians and covers much of the *gobierno* of Nueva Vizcaya.
[130] Santiago de Babonoyaba.
[131] Santiago de Babonoyahua.
[132] This record is actually a presidial inspection with a list of soldiers in 1725.
[133] The cathedral parish of the city of Durango contained three Indian villages: Analco, Guadalupe and Santa María del Tunal, along with eight haciendas and thirty-five smaller places.
[134] The cathedral parish of the city of Durango contained three Indian villages: Analco, Guadalupe and Santa María del Tunal, along with eight haciendas and thirty-five smaller places.
[135] AGI Guadalajara 255; AGI Indiferente 102 and 1526.
[136] The cathedral parish in the city of Durango in 1820 had six wards (*cuarteles*) containing 12,437 persons.
[137] A census of Indians.

Locality	Province	Country	Year(s)	Reference
Mapimí	Nueva Vizcaya	México	1777	AGI Guadalajara 255
Mapimí	Nueva Vizcaya	México	1778	AGI Indiferente 102
Mapimí[138]	Nueva Vizcaya	México	1779	AGI Indiferente 102
Mezquital[139]	Nueva Vizcaya	México	1777	AGI Guadalajara 255
Nieves	Nueva Vizcaya	México	1777	AGI Guadalajara 255
Namiquipa	Nueva Vizcaya	México	1778	AF 16:328
Nombre de Dios[140]	Nueva Vizcaya	México	1778	AF 16:328[141]
Nombre de Dios	Nueva Vizcaya	México	1790	AGN HI 522:269
Nombre de Dios	Nueva Vizcaya	México	1806	British Museum[142]
Nombre de Dios	Nueva Vizcaya	México	1820	AF 18:387
Nonoava	Nueva Vizcaya	México	1777	AGI, Guadalajara 255
Norogáchic	Nueva Vizcaya	México	1779	AGI Indiferente 102
Papasquiaro	Nueva Vizcaya	México	1707	Archivo del Parral
Papasquiaro	Nueva Vizcaya	México	1778	AGI Indiferente 102
Pueblo Nuevo	Nueva Vizcaya	México	1779	AGI Indiferente 102
Sainapuchi	Nueva Vizcaya	México	1778	AF 16:328
San Andrés	Nueva Vizcaya	México	1778	AF 16:328
San Antonio Chuviscar	Nueva Vizcaya	México	1778	AF 16:328
San Antonio Julimes	Nueva Vizcaya	México	1778	AF 16:328
San Bernabé	Nueva Vizcaya	México	1778	AF 16:328
San Bernardino	Nueva Vizcaya	México	1778	AF 16:328
San Carlos (presidio)	Nueva Vizcaya	México	1817	MBL 2:36
San Gerónimo	Nueva Vizcaya	México	1778	AF 16:328
San Gregorio	Nueva Vizcaya	México	1777	AGI Indiferente 1526
San Gregorio	Nueva Vizcaya	México	1778	AGI Indiferente 102
San Juan Bautista[143]	Nueva Vizcaya	México	1778	AF 16:328
San Juan de Alamillo	Nueva Vizcaya	México	1778	AF 16:328
San Juan del Río	Nueva Vizcaya	México	1707	Archivo del Parral
San Pablo	Nueva Vizcaya	México	1778	AF 16:328
San Pedro del Gallo[144]	Nueva Vizcaya	México	1723	Archivo del Parral
San Pedro del Gallo	Nueva Vizcaya	México	1725	Archivo del Parral
San Pedro del Gallo	Nueva Vizcaya	México	1777	AGI Guadalajara 255
San Pedro del Gallo	Nueva Vizcaya	México	1778	AGI Indiferente 102
San Pedro del Gallo[145]	Nueva Vizcaya	México	1779	AGI Indiferente 102
Santa Ana	Nueva Vizcaya	México	1778	AF 16:328

---

[138] Sometime between 1779 and 1785 El Gallo parish (San Pedro del Gallo) was attached to Mapimí parish.

[139] San Francisco del Mezquital.

[140] Includes the village of Nombre de Dios along with eighteen haciendas and fifteen ranchos. Nombre de Dios was a province that belonged to Nueva España, not to Nueva Vizcaya, but was linked in many ways with Nueva Vizcaya, hence its placement here.

[141] Also found in AGI Indiferentes 102.

[142] British Museum, Add. Manuscript 17, 557, folios 126–130.

[143] San Juan Bautista de los Norteños.

[144] Both this and the following entries are lists of soldiers at the garrison of San Pedro.

[145] Sometime between 1779 and 1785 the parish of El Gallo was combined with Mapimí.

Locality	Province	Country	Year(s)	Reference
Santa Catarina	Nueva Vizcaya	México	1777	AGI Indiferente 1526
Santa Isabel	Nueva Vizcaya	México	1778	AF 16:328
Santa Rosalia	Nueva Vizcaya	México	1778	MBL 2:36
Satevó[146]	Nueva Vizcaya	México	1778	AF 16:328
Siánori	Nueva Vizcaya	México	1624	AGI Guadalajara 37
Siánori	Nueva Vizcaya	México	1777–1778	AGI Guadalajara 255
Tapacolmes[147]	Nueva Vizcaya	México	1778	AF 16:328
Tónachic	Nueva Vizcaya	México	1778	AGI Indiferente 102

[146] San Francisco Javier de Satevó.
[147] Santa Cruz Tapacolmes.

NUEVO LEON

Locality	Province	Country	Year(s)	Reference
	Nuevo León	México	1781	AGN PI 118:1:1-568
	Nuevo León	México	1809[148]	AGN HI 452:viii
Agualeguas	Nuevo León	México	1855	HGJ 5:108
Cadereyta	Nuevo León	México	1765	AAG
Cadereyta	Nuevo León	México	1766	AAG
Villa de Santiago	Nuevo León	México	1787–1831	TSL Rolls 475-477

---

[148] This census is of foreigners only.

NUEVO MEXICO

Locality	Province	Country	Year(s)	Reference
	New Mexico	México	1642	MBL 2:21
	New Mexico	México	c1660	Scholes[149]
	New Mexico	México	1693	AF 182:1394
	New Mexico	México	1693	AF 181:1390
	New Mexico	México	1705	AF 189:1447
	New Mexico	México	1749–1750	AF 240:1772
	New Mexico	México	1749–1750	AGN PI 36:10:501-507
	New Mexico	México	1769	AF 254:1867
	New Mexico	México	1777	AF 31:646
	New Mexico	México	1790	SMC; 581470[150]
	New Mexico	México	1803	SMC
	New Mexico	México	1845	SMC
El Paso del Río Norte	New Mexico	México	1680	Santa Fé[151]
El Paso del Río Norte	New Mexico	México	1784	NMHR 1977:524
Guadalupe del Paso[152]	New Mexico	México		
Isleta[153]	New Mexico	México	1684	AF 173:1335
Isleta	New Mexico	México	1815	1162467
Laguna (Sr. San José)	New Mexico	México	1801	913167:7
Pecuries[154]	New Mexico	México	1707	AF 206:1556
Pueblo Real	New Mexico	México	1815	1162467
San Jose (presidio)[155]	New Mexico	México	1684	AF 173:1336
S. Juan[156]	New Mexico	México	1707	AF 206:1556
Santa Cruz	New Mexico	México	1707	AF 206:1556
Santa Fé (presidio)[157]	New Mexico	México	1705	AF 189:1447
Santa Fé (presidio)	New Mexico	México	1705	AGN PI 36:6: 420-425
Santa Fé (presidio)	New Mexico	México	1706	AGN PI 36:7: 426-461
Senecú	New Mexico	México	1815	1162467
Socorro	New México	México	1815	1162467

[149] France V. Scholes, "Troublous Times in New Mexico, 1659–1670," *Historical Society of New Mexico XI* (1942): 198–223; see footnote 33 "Visita general del Nuevo México y Padrones de Todas las almas xptianas" (24 pieces).

[150] Film copy of Spanish Archives of New Mexico (22 rolls) is housed at the University of New Mexico, University of Utah and elsewhere. Roll 12 contains copies of the original 1790 census of New Mexico for various pueblos including Albuquerque.

[151] Possibly at the Archbishop's Archives.

[152] See Ciudad Juárez, Chihuahua, México.

[153] Corpus Cristi de la Isleta

[154] San Lorenzo de los Pecuries.

[155] Troop lists.

[156] San Juan de los Caballeros.

[157] The following three entries are for troop lists at the Santa Fé presidio.

OAXACA

Locality	Province	Country	Year(s)	Reference
	Oaxaca	México	1807–1809[158]	AGN HI 452:I
Achiutla	Oaxaca	México	1777	AGI México 2589-2591
Acayucan	Oaxaca	México	1777	AGI México 2590
Almoloyas	Oaxaca	México	1777	AGI México 2589-2591
Amatlán	Oaxaca	México	1777	AGI México 2589, 2591
Amusgos (Los)	Oaxaca	México	1777	AGI México 2589-2591
Apuala	Oaxaca	México	1777	AGI México 2589-2591
Ayoquesco	Oaxaca	México	1777	AGI México 2589, 2591
Atoyac	Oaxaca	México	1777	AGI México 2589-2591
Betaza	Oaxaca	México	1777	AGI México 2589-2591
Calihuala	Oaxaca	México	1835–1842	1163552:2
Chiazumba	Oaxaca	México	1777	AGI México 2578, 2581
Chicaguastla	Oaxaca	México	1777	AGI México 2589-2591
Chichicastepec	Oaxaca	México	1777	AGI México 2589-2591
Chilapa	Oaxaca	México	1777	AGI México 2589-2591
Chilapa	Oaxaca	México	1790	AGN PAD 16
Chimalapa	Oaxaca	México	?	AGN HI 522:2:8-13v
Cimatlán	Oaxaca	México	1777	AGI México 2589, 2590
Coatlán	Oaxaca	México	1777	AGI México 2589, 2591
Colotepec	Oaxaca	México	1777	AGI México 2589, 2591
Cortijos (Los)	Oaxaca	México	1777	AGI México 2589-2591
Cuilapa	Oaxaca	México	1777	AGI México 2589, 2590
Cuyotepec	Oaxaca	México	1777	AGI México 2589, 2591
Ecatepec	Oaxaca	México	1777	AGI México 2590-2591
Elotepec	Oaxaca	México	1777	AGI México 2591
Exutla	Oaxaca	México	1777	AGI México 2589, 2591
Guamelula	Oaxaca	México	1790	AGN PAD 12
Guapanapa	Oaxaca	México	1777	AGI México 2578, 2581
Guaxolotitlán	Oaxaca	México	1777	AGI México 2578, 2581
Hostoticpac[159]	Oaxaca	México	1791	AGN HI 72:xvi
Huexolotitlán	Oaxaca	México	1777	AGI México 2589
Igualtepec	Oaxaca	México	1777	AGI México 2578, 2581
Itnundujia	Oaxaca	México	1777	AGI México 2589-2591
Ixtapa	Oaxaca	México	1790	AGN PAD 9
Ixtlán	Oaxaca	México	1777	AGI México 2589, 2591

---

[158] This census is of foreigners only.
[159] This census is for *pardos* only.

Locality	Province	Country	Year(s)	Reference
Iztepexi	Oaxaca	México	1777	AGI México 2591
Lachixío	Oaxaca	México	1777	AGI México 2589, 2591
Lapaguía	Oaxaca	México	1777	AGI México 2590-2591
Loxicha	Oaxaca	México	1777	AGI México 2589, 2590
Macuilsúchil	Oaxaca	México	1777	AGI México 2590-2591
Miaguatlán	Oaxaca	México	1777	AGI México 2589, 2591
Mistepec	Oaxaca	México	1777	AGI México 2581
Mitla	Oaxaca	México	1777	AGI México 2590-2591
Mixtepec	Oaxaca	México	1777	AGI México 2589-2591
Nochistlán	Oaxaca	México	1777	AGI México 2591
Oaxaca[160]	Oaxaca	México	1777	AGI México 2589-2591
Oaxaca	Oaxaca	México	1790	AGN PAD 13
Oaxaca	Oaxaca	México	1842	PGH
Oaxaca	Oaxaca	México	1875	PCO
Ocelotepec[161]	Oaxaca	México	1777	AGI México 2589, 2591
Omotepec	Oaxaca	México	1777	AGI México 2589
Pinotepa (1)	Oaxaca	México	1777	AGI México 2589-2591
Pinotepa (2)	Oaxaca	México	1777	AGI México 2589-2591
Quezaltepec	Oaxaca	México	1777	AGI México 2589-2591
Quiatoni	Oaxaca	México	1777	AGI México 2590-2591
Sanatepec	Oaxaca	México	?	AGN HI 522:2:8-13v
Sanatepec	Oaxaca	México	1777	AGI México 2591
San Francisco de Mar	Oaxaca	México	1777	AGI México 2590
Santa Catarina Minas	Oaxaca	México	1777	AGI México 2589, 2590
Santiago Huetepeque	Oaxaca	México	?	AGN HI 522:2:8-13v
Santiago Zautla	Oaxaca	México	1787	AGN HI 72:viii
Talistaca	Oaxaca	México	1777	AGI México 2589, 2591
Tanetze	Oaxaca	México	1777	AGI México 2589-2591
Tapanatepec	Oaxaca	México	?	AGN HI 522:2:8-13v
Teotitlan del Valle	Oaxaca	México	1777	AGI México 2590-2591
Teoxomulco	Oaxaca	México	1777	AGI México 2591
Tepetotutla	Oaxaca	México	1777	AGI México 2589, 2591
Tequecistepec	Oaxaca	México	1777	AGI México 2578, 2581
Teutitlán	Oaxaca	México	1777	AGI México 2591
Tezuatlán	Oaxaca	México	1777	AGI México 2578, 2581
Tlacotepec	Oaxaca	México	1777	AGI México 2581
Tlachichilco	Oaxaca	México	1777	AGI México 2578, 2581
Tlacolula	Oaxaca	México	1777	AGI México 2590-2591
Tlacuacintepec	Oaxaca	México	1777	AGI México 2589, 2591
Tlapancingo	Oaxaca	México	1777	AGI México 2578, 2581
Tonalá	Oaxaca	México	1777	AGI México 2578, 2581
Totontepec	Oaxaca	México	1777	AGI México 2589-2591

---

[160] Called Antequera during the colonial period; became Oaxaca de Juárez in 1950.
[161] San Juan Ocelotepec.

Locality	Province	Country	Year(s)	Reference
Tututepec	Oaxaca	México	1777	AGI México 2589-2591
Xalapa	Oaxaca	México	1777	AGI México 2589, 2591
Xicayán	Oaxaca	México	1777	AGN HI 72:xv[162]
Xuquila	Oaxaca	México	1777	AGI México 2589-2591
Yaeé	Oaxaca	México	1777	AGI México 2589-2591
Yalálag	Oaxaca	México	1777	AGI México 2589-2591
Yolo	Oaxaca	México	1777	AGI, México, 2591
Yolotepec	Oaxaca	México	1777	AGI México 2589-2591
Zaachila	Oaxaca	México	1777	AGI México 2589, 2591
Zaguche	Oaxaca	México	1777	AGI México 2589, 2590
Zautla	Oaxaca	México	1777	AGI México 2589

[162] Includes the entire province.

PROVINCIAS INTERNAS

Locality	Province	Country	Year(s)	Reference
	Prov. Int.	México	1777–1804	AHA 1:56
Compañías Volantes	Prov. Int.	México	1790–1791	AGN PI 27:2:231-307

PUEBLA

In the reference AGN, Historia, legajo 523, page 42 it says that Tehuacán, Tepeaca, Guayacocotla, Chiautla, Tochimilco, Tetela de Xonotla, Totomehuacán, Atlixco, Amotoque, Chieta, Teciutlán, Guauchinango and four of the seven sub-delegations of Puebla City delivered the 1790 census returns to Mexico City. It also states that Tlaxcala, Quautla Amilpas, San Juan de los Llanos, Zacatlán, Tepexi, Cholula, Xuexozingo, Acatlán, Tecali, Yzúcar and three of the seven sub-delegations of Puebla City did not submit the 1790 census returns to Mexico City.

Locality	Province	Country	Year(s)	Reference
	Puebla	México	1809[163]	AGN HI 452:iv
Acacingo	Puebla	México	1777	AGI México 2578-2581
Acajete	Puebla	México	1777	AGI México 2578-2581
Acajete	Puebla	México	1869	784099
Acatlán	Puebla	México	1681	AGN Tributos 43[164]
Acatlán	Puebla	México	1777	AGI México 2578, 2580
Aguatelco	Puebla	México	1777	AGI México 2579-2581
Ahuacatlán	Puebla	México	1777	AGI México 2579-2581
Ahuacatlán	Puebla	México	1781	1163055:6
Ahuacatlán	Puebla	México	1866	1163055:7
Ahuacatlán	Puebla	México	1930	1163055:8
Amotoque	Puebla	México	1777	AGI México 2578
Amozoc	Puebla	México	1777	AGI México 2578
Atliquizayán	Puebla	México	1777	AGI México 2579-2581
Atzitziguacán	Puebla	México	1777	AGI México 2579, 2580
Atzompa	Puebla	México	1768	442123:1
Atlixco	Puebla	México	1777	AGI México 2578
Atrisco	Puebla	México	1790	AGN PAD 25
Calpán	Puebla	México	1559–1560	BNP FM 387
Camoguautla	Puebla	México	1777	AGI México 2579-2581
Chalchicomula	Puebla	México	1777	AGI México 2578-2581
Chiapa (San José)	Puebla	México	1777	AGI México 2578-2581
Chiapulco	Puebla	México	1777	AGI México 2578-2580
Chiautla	Puebla	México	1777	AGI México 2578
Chieta	Puebla	México	1777	AGI México 2578
Chicta	Puebla	México	1791	AGN PAD 28

---

[163] This census is of foreigners only.
[164] The last *expediente* in the bundle contains this census.

Locality	Province	Country	Year(s)	Reference
Chietla	Puebla	México	1791	AGN PAD 28:157-159
Chila	Puebla	México	1777	AGI México 2578, 2580
Chignahuapan	Puebla	México	1777	AGI México 2579-2581
Chignahuapan	Puebla	México	1818	285555
Chignahuapan	Puebla	México	1823	285555
Chiconcuautla	Puebla	México	1842	638625
Cholula	Puebla	México	1777	AGI México 2578
Cholula	Puebla	México	1790	AGN Intendentes 48:11
Coatepec	Puebla	México	1889	1162770:5
Coyomeapa	Puebla	México	1777	AGI México 2578-2580
Cuautinchan	Puebla	México	1802–1866	679539
Cuautla Amilpas	Puebla	México	1777	AGI México 2578
Cuetzalán	Puebla	México	1777	AGI México 2578-2581
Cuzcatlán	Puebla	México	1777	AGI México 2578-2580
Elosuchitlán	Puebla	México	1777	AGI México 2578-2580
Epatlán	Puebla	México	1777	AGI México 2579-2581
Guaquechula	Puebla	México	1777	AGI México 2579, 2580
Guatinchan	Puebla	México	1777	AGI México 2578
Guatlatlauca	Puebla	México	1777	AGI México 2578-2579
Guayacocotla	Puebla	México	1777	AGI México 2578
Huauchinango	Puebla	México	1777	AGI México 2578
Huauchinango	Puebla	México	1780–1786	267494
Huauchinango	Puebla	México	1790–1799	267494
Huauchinango	Puebla	México	1800–1833	267495
Huauchinango	Puebla	México	1902	267495
Huexocingo	Puebla	México	1777	AGI México 2578
Huexocingo	Puebla	México	1790	AGN PAD 27
Ixitlán	Puebla	México	1777	AGI México 2578, 2580
Iztaquimaxtitlán	Puebla	México	1777	AGI México 2578-2581
Izúcar	Puebla	México	1791	AGN PAD 28
Jolalpan	Puebla	México	1907	1106954:5
Nopaluca	Puebla	México	1777	AGI México 2578-2581
Petlalcingo	Puebla	México	1777	AGI México 2578, 2580
Piaxtla	Puebla	México	1681	AGN Tributos 43[165]
Puebla	Puebla	México	1777	AGI México 2578
Quechula	Puebla	México	1777	AGI México 2578-2581
Reyes de Juárez	Puebla	México	1798–1813	706633
Reyes de Juárez	Puebla	México	1814–1816	706634
Reyes de Juárez	Puebla	México	1814–1855	706635
S. Agustín del Palmar	Puebla	México	1777	AGI México 2578-2581
S. Anto. de la Cañada	Puebla	México	1777	AGI México 2578-2580
San Juan de los Llanos	Puebla	México	1791	AGN PAD 7

---

[165] The last *expediente* in the bundle contains this census.

Locality	Province	Country	Year(s)	Reference
Santos Reyes	Puebla	México	1777	AGI México 2578-2581
Tecali	Puebla	México	1777	AGI México 2578, 2581[166]
Tecali	Puebla	México	1792	?[167]
Tecamachalco	Puebla	México	1745–1842	240911-240919
Tecamachalco	Puebla	México	1777	AGI México 2578-2581
Teciutlán	Puebla	México	1777	AGI México 2578
Tecomatlán	Puebla	México	1777	AGI México 2578, 2580
Tehuacán	Puebla	México	1773–1822	641120-641121
Tehuacán	Puebla	México	1777	AGI México 2578
Tehuacán	Puebla	México	1792	AGN PAD 3
Tehuicingo	Puebla	México	1777	AGI México 2578, 2580
Tepango	Puebla	México	1777	AGI México 2578-2580
Tepapayeca	Puebla	México	1777	AGI México 2579-2581
Tepecintla	Puebla	México	1777	AGI México 2579-2581
Tepeyagualco	Puebla	México	1777	AGI México 2578-2581
Tepeaca	Puebla	México	1777	AGI México 2578
Tepeaca	Puebla	México	1779–1842	240517-240518
Tepeaca	Puebla	México	1790	AGN PAD 38
Tepexi	Puebla	México	1777	AGI México 2578
Tepexillo	Puebla	México	1777	AGI México 2578, 2580
Tetela de Xonotla	Puebla	México	1777	AGI México 2578
Teupantlán	Puebla	México	1777	AGI México 2579-2581
Teutlalco	Puebla	México	1777	AGI México 2580
Tlacotepec	Puebla	México	1777	AGI México 2578-2581
Tlalauquitepec	Puebla	México	1777	AGI México 2578-2581
Tlaxcuapan	Puebla	México	1745	AGN HIS 522:226-243
Tochimilco	Puebla	México	1777	AGI México 2578
Tochimilco	Puebla	México	1791	AGN PAD 12
Tochtepec	Puebla	México	1831	655164:6
Totoltepec	Puebla	México	1777	AGI México 2578, 2580
Totomeguacán	Puebla	México	1777	AGI México 2578
Tuzantla	Puebla	México	1777	AGI México 2578, 2580
Xicocingo[168]	Puebla	México	1777	AGI México 2579-2581
Xiutetelco	Puebla	México	1875	790277:12
Xochitlán	Puebla	México	1777	AGI México 2578-2581
Yagualtepec	Puebla	México	1777	AGI México 2578-2581
Yzúcar	Puebla	México	1777	AGI México 2578
Zacapala	Puebla	México	1777	AGI México 2578-2579
Zacapoaztla	Puebla	México	1777	AGI México 2578-2581
Zacatlán	Puebla	México	1777	AGI México 2578

[166] There were twenty or more *barrios* in the 1777 *padrón* of Tecali which probably correspond to the colonial *estancias* which were moved into the congregations.
[167] The reference to this *padrón* is found in AGN, Ramo de Historia, bundle 73, folios 109–110.
[168] Actually included in the parish of Aguatelco, but listed separately for purposes of research.

Locality	Province	Country	Year(s)	Reference
Zapotitlán	Puebla	México	1777	AGI México 2579-2581
Zapotlán	Puebla	México	1777	AGI México 2578-2580
Zautla	Puebla	México	1777	AGI México 2578-2581
Zoltepec	Puebla	México	1777	AGI México 2578-2581
Zoquitlán	Puebla	México	1777	AGI México 2578-2580
Zoyatitlanapa	Puebla	México	1790	AGN PAD 12:258v-259

QUERETARO

Locality	Province	Country	Year(s)	Reference
Aguacatlán	Querétaro	México	1743	AGN HI 522:6:92-92v
Cadereyta	Querétaro	México	1792	AGN Tributos 43[169]
Conca	Querétaro	México	1799	AGN HI 523:215
Huimilpán	Querétaro	México	1781	641725
Huimilpán	Querétaro	México	1784	641726
Jalpán	Querétaro	México	1777–1781	442130
Jilaco	Querétaro	México	1743	AGN HI 522:5:89-90v
La Cañada[170]	Querétaro	México	1777	442130; 651727
La Cañada	Querétaro	México	1778	442130; 651728
La Cañada[171]	Querétaro	México	1781	651728
Lobo	Querétaro	México	1743	AGN HI 522:5:89-90v
Pascual	Querétaro	México	1742–1743	AGN HI 522:4:70-81v
Pueblito (corregidora)	Querétaro	México	1781	641725
Pueblito (corregidora)	Querétaro	México	1784	641726
Querétaro	Querétaro	México	1768	442128; 641722
Querétaro[172]	Querétaro	México	1776–1779	442131
Querétaro	Querétaro	México	1777–1778	AGN PAD 12:117-141
Querétaro[173]	Querétaro	México	1777–1792	442132; 641729
Querétaro	Querétaro	México	1790	AGN PAD 12, 35, 39, 40
Querétaro	Querétaro	México	1791	1162401
San Francisco	Querétaro	México	1784	442129:1
San Francisco	Querétaro	México	1787	442129:2
San Juan del Río	Querétaro	México	?	641727
San Juan del Río	Querétaro	México	1779	442129
San Juan del Río	Querétaro	México	1790	AGN PAD 35
San Miguel	Querétaro	México	1743	AGN HI 522:7:94-94v
Santiago Xalpan	Querétaro	México	1743	AGN HI 522:10:100-101
Santo Domingo	Querétaro	México	1743	AGN HI 522:11:103-103v
Toliman	Querétaro	México	1743	AGN HI 522:3:14-61v
Visarrón	Querétaro	México	1743	AGN HI 522:12:104-104v

[169] The census for Cadereyta is found in the last *expediente* of bundle 43.
[170] Municipio del Marqués.
[171] San Pedro de la Cañada.
[172] San Sebastián parish, Querétaro.
[173] Santiago parish, Querétaro.

SAN LUIS POTOSI

Locality	Province	Country	Year(s)	Reference
	S.L.P.	México	1649	Archivo del Parral[174]
	S.L.P.	México	1809	AGN HI 452:viii
Ahualulco	S.L.P.	México	1786	168805
Ahualulco	S.L.P.	México	1824	168831
Ahualulco	S.L.P.	México	1830	168841
Armadillo	S.L.P.	México	1681	757222
Armadillo	S.L.P.	México	1747	768920
Armadillo	S.L.P.	México	1758	769986-769989
Armadillo	S.L.P.	México	1763	774211
Armadillo	S.L.P.	México	1770	774154-774155
Armadillo	S.L.P.	México	1772	761550
Armadillo	S.L.P.	México	1778	776888
Cedral	S.L.P.	México	1822	168825
Cedral	S.L.P.	México	1828	168839
Charcas	S.L.P.	México	1785	AAG
Charcas	S.L.P.	México	1794	AAG
Charcas	S.L.P.	México	1797	AAG
Charcas	S.L.P.	México	1789	AAG
Ciudad de Maís	S.L.P.	México	1880	1481731
Guadalcázar	S.L.P.	México	1758	769986-769989
Guadalcázar	S.L.P.	México	1760	763271-763272
Guadalcázar	S.L.P.	México	1763	774211-774213
Guadalcázar	S.L.P.	México	1770	774144
Guadalcázar	S.L.P.	México	1776	776736-776738
Guadalcázar	S.L.P.	México	1798	785446
Hedionda	S.L.P.	México	1820	168818
Hedionda	S.L.P.	México	1822	168825; 168828
Matehuala	S.L.P.	México	1817	168810; 307332
Mexquitic	S.L.P.	México	1793	763127
Mexquitic	S.L.P.	México	1800	795135-795136
Mexquitic	S.L.P.	México	1801	795138
Mexquitic	S.L.P.	México	1803	795140
Mexquitic	S.L.P.	México	1804	795142
Mexquitic	S.L.P.	México	1806	793878
Mexquitic	S.L.P.	México	1807	793879
Mexquitic	S.L.P.	México	1808	793880

[174] Padrón de los vecinos . . . 1649; partial census only, for the northwest part of the state of San Luis Potosí.

Locality	Province	Country	Year(s)	Reference
Mexquitic	S.L.P.	México	1810	793882
Motecillo	S.L.P.	México	1803	795140
Motecillo	S.L.P.	México	1804	795143
Motecillo	S.L.P.	México	1808	793880
Motecillo	S.L.P.	México	1809	793881
Motecillo	S.L.P.	México	1810	793882
Ojocaliente	S.L.P.	México	1797	AAG
Río Verde	S.L.P.	México	1759	772017-772020
Río Verde	S.L.P.	México	1763	774211-774213
Río Verde	S.L.P.	México	1768	774114-774116
Río Verde	S.L.P.	México	1770	774142-774143
Río Verde	S.L.P.	México	1772	761550
Río Verde	S.L.P.	México	1800	795135-795137
Río Verde	S.L.P.	México	1803	795141
Río Verde	S.L.P.	México	1804	795144
Río Verde	S.L.P.	México	1805	793876
Río Verde	S.L.P.	México	1806	793878
Río Verde	S.L.P.	México	1807	793879
Río Verde	S.L.P.	México	1808	793880
Río Verde	S.L.P.	México	1809	793881
Salinas	S.L.P.	México	1820	168818
San Luis Potosí	S.L.P.	México	1668	765591
San Luis Potosí	S.L.P.	México	1758	768986-768989
San Luis Potosí	S.L.P.	México	1759	772017
San Luis Potosí	S.L.P.	México	1763	774211-774213
San Luis Potosí	S.L.P.	México	1800	795135
San Luis Potosí	S.L.P.	México	1801	795138
San Luis Potosí	S.L.P.	México	1803	795140
San Luis Potosí	S.L.P.	México	1804	795143
San Luis Potosí	S.L.P.	México	1805	793876
San Luis Potosí	S.L.P.	México	1806	793878
San Luis Potosí	S.L.P.	México	1807	793879
San Luis Potosí	S.L.P.	México	1808	793880
San Luis Potosí	S.L.P.	México	1809	793881
San Luis Potosí	S.L.P.	México	1810	793882
San Pedro	S.L.P.	México	1747	769916-769918
San Pedro	S.L.P.	México	1747	769921
San Pedro	S.L.P.	México	1759	772017-772020
San Pedro	S.L.P.	México	1772	761550
Santa María del Río	S.L.P.	México	1747	768916-768921
Santa María del Río	S.L.P.	México	1768	774103-774104
Santa María del Río	S.L.P.	México	1770	774144
Santa María del Río	S.L.P.	México	1776	795134
Soledad	S.L.P.	México	1800	795135
Soledad	S.L.P.	México	1801	795138

Locality	Province	Country	Year(s)	Reference
Soledad	S.L.P.	México	1803	795140
Soledad	S.L.P.	México	1804	795143
Soledad	S.L.P.	México	1805	793876
Soledad	S.L.P.	México	1806	793878
Soledad	S.L.P.	México	1807	793879
Soledad	S.L.P.	México	1808	793880
Soledad	S.L.P.	México	1809	793881
Soledad	S.L.P.	México	1810	793882
Soledad	S.L.P.	México	1826	793883
Valle de San Fco.	S.L.P.	México	1746	768901-768902
Valle de San Fco.	S.L.P.	México	1747	768916-768918
Valle de San Fco.	S.L.P.	México	1758	769986
Valle de San Fco.	S.L.P.	México	1759	772017
Valle de San Fco.	S.L.P.	México	1760	763271-763272
Valle de San Fco.	S.L.P.	México	1763	774211-774213
Valle de San Fco.	S.L.P.	México	1768	774103-774104
Valle de San Fco.	S.L.P.	México	1770	774154-774155
Valle de San Fco.	S.L.P.	México	1820–1822	793883
Venado	S.L.P.	México	1817	168810
Venado	S.L.P.	México	1820	168821-168822
Villa de Arriba	S.L.P.	México	1776	795134

SINALOA

Locality	Province	Country	Year(s)	Reference
Abulla	Sinaloa	México	1778	1149545
Aguacaliente	Sinaloa	México	1624	AGI Guadalajara 37
Aguacaliente	Sinaloa	México	1778	1149545
Ahome	Sinaloa	México	1737	UT
Ajoya	Sinaloa	México	1778	1149545
Apacha	Sinaloa	México	1778	1149545
Bacubirito	Sinaloa	México	1800	811:23
Badiraguato	Sinaloa	México	1777–1778	AGI Guadalajara 1526
Bamoa	Sinaloa	México	?	AHH
Bamoa	Sinaloa	México	1820	811:24
Cabazán	Sinaloa	México	1778	1149545
Cabazán	Sinaloa	México	1780	AF 292:2153
Carrizal	Sinaloa	México	1778	1149545
Casitas	Sinaloa	México	1778	1149545
Cerritos	Sinaloa	México	1778	1149545
Charcas	Sinaloa	México	1778	1149545
Chicorato	Sinaloa	México	?	AHH
Chiribicoque	Sinaloa	México	1778	1149545
Ciénega	Sinaloa	México	1778	1149545
Cogota	Sinaloa	México	1778	1149545
Conitaca	Sinaloa	México	1778	1149545
Copala	Sinaloa	México	1604	AGI Guadalajara 28:78-89
Copala	Sinaloa	México	1777	AGI Guadalajara 255
Copala[175]	Sinaloa	México	1794	AF 35:790
Cosalá	Sinaloa	México	1777–1778	AGI Guadalajara[176]
Cosalá	Sinaloa	México	1780	1149545
Cosalá	Sinaloa	México	1796	1149545
Cosalá	Sinaloa	México	1830	168843
Cuacoyole	Sinaloa	México	1778	1149545
Culiacán	Sinaloa	México	1532	AMH 16:233-235
Culiacán	Sinaloa	México	1777	AGI, Guadalajara[177]
Culiacán	Sinaloa	México	1793	IGHL

[175] This *padrón* is for the entire province of Copala, including probably Copala, San Bartolomé, San Sebastián, Charcas, Santa Lucía, Santa Catarina, Jacob, San Francisco Cabazán, San Ignacio de Piastla, San Xavier, Guadalupe and Ajoya.

[176] The *padrones* for Cosalá for 1777 and 1778 are found in AGI Guadalajara 102, and 1526.

[177] The *padrones* for Culiacán for the years 1777 and 1778 are found in AGI Guadalajara, bundles 102; 103:3:26; and 255.

Locality	Province	Country	Year(s)	Reference
Culiacán	Sinaloa	México	1804	1149545[178]
Elota	Sinaloa	México	1778	1149545
Faizan	Sinaloa	México	1778	1149545
Ginete	Sinaloa	México	1778	1149545
Guagino	Sinaloa	México	1778	1149545
Guasavé	Sinaloa	México	?	AHH
Guasavé	Sinaloa	México	1820	811:24
Guazima	Sinaloa	México	1778	1149545
Huera	Sinaloa	México	1795	811:23
La Estancia	Sinaloa	México	1778	1149545
La Labor	Sinaloa	México	1778	1149545
Las Meses	Sinaloa	México	1778	1149545
Los Cinco Señores	Sinaloa	México	1778	1149545
Maloya	Sinaloa	México	1777	AGI Guadalajara 255
Maloya	Sinaloa	México	1778	AGI Indiferente 102
Malpica	Sinaloa	México	1778	1149545
Mazatlán	Sinaloa	México	1830	168843
Mesillas	Sinaloa	México	1778	1149545
Mochicahui	Sinaloa	México	1737	UT
Mocorito	Sinaloa	México	1684	AHH
Mocorito	Sinaloa	México	1690	AHH
Mocorito	Sinaloa	México	1777	AGI Guadalajara 255
Montiel	Sinaloa	México	1778	1149545
Nanches	Sinaloa	México	1778	1149545
Nio	Sinaloa	México	?	AHH
Nio	Sinaloa	México	1684	?
Nio	Sinaloa	México	1820	811:24
Noria	Sinaloa	México	1778	1149545
Norogachic	Sinaloa	México	1725	AHH
N. S. de los Dolores	Sinaloa	México	1778	1149545
N. S. de los Dolores	Sinaloa	México	1772	761550
Ocoroni	Sinaloa	México	?	AHH
Onapa	Sinaloa	México	1725	AHH
Oso	Sinaloa	México	1778	1149545
Palmarejo	Sinaloa	México	1778	1149545
Palmillas	Sinaloa	México	1778	1149545
Piaxtla	Sinaloa	México	1778	1149545
Piaxtla	Sinaloa	México	1777	AGI Guadalajara 255
Piaxtla	Sinaloa	México	1780	AF 292:2153
Porras	Sinaloa	México	1778	1149545
Potam	Sinaloa	México	?	AHH
Puertezuelo	Sinaloa	México	1778	1149545
Pánuco	Sinaloa	México	1778	1149545

[178] Also found at AF 36:819.6 and 37:821.

Locality	Province	Country	Year(s)	Reference
Quelital	Sinaloa	México	1778	1149545
Ramada	Sinaloa	México	1778	1149545
Rosario	Sinaloa	México	1777	AGI Indiferente 102
Rosario	Sinaloa	México	1778	AGI Indiferente 1526
Sabinos	Sinaloa	México	1778	1149545
Sacar Plata	Sinaloa	México	1778	1149545
Samudio	Sinaloa	México	1778	1149545
San Agustín	Sinaloa	México	1778	1149545
San Anto. de Arrona	Sinaloa	México	1778	1149545
San Benito	Sinaloa	México	1777	AGI Guadalajara 255
San Bartolomé	Sinaloa	México	1778	1149545
San Fermín	Sinaloa	México	1778	1149545
San Ignacio	Sinaloa	México	1780	AF 34:743.1
San José de Gracia	Sinaloa	México	1778	1149545
San Juan Bautista	Sinaloa	México	1778	1149545
San Juan Cosalá	Sinaloa	México	1820	168820, 168822
San Juan de Jacobo	Sinaloa	México	1778	1149545
San Marcos	Sinaloa	México	1778	1149545
San Rafael[179]	Sinaloa	México	1778	1149545
San Sebastián	Sinaloa	México	1778	1149545[180]
San Sebastián	Sinaloa	México	1779	AGI Indiferente 102
San Sebastián	Sinaloa	México	1780	AF 292:2153
Santa Apolonia	Sinaloa	México	1778	1149545
Santa Catarina	Sinaloa	México	1778	1149545
Santa Gertrudis	Sinaloa	México	1778	1149545
Santa María	Sinaloa	México	1795	811:23
Santa Rosa	Sinaloa	México	1778	1149545
Santísima Trinidad	Sinaloa	México	1778	1149545
Sinaloa	Sinaloa	México	?	AHH
Siqueiros	Sinaloa	México	1778	1149545
Soquititán	Sinaloa	México	1778	1149545
Tabala	Sinaloa	México	1778	1149545
Tacuichamona	Sinaloa	México	1778	1149545
Tamasula	Sinaloa	México	1624	AGI Guadalajara 37
Tamasula	Sinaloa	México	1684	AHH
Tamasula	Sinaloa	México	1777–1778	AGI Indiferente 102
Tamasula	Sinaloa	México	1820	811:24
Tayares	Sinaloa	México	1778	1149545
Tecuala	Sinaloa	México	1817	168808
Tehueco	Sinaloa	México	?	AHH
Tlacote	Sinaloa	México	1778	1149545

---

[179] San Rafael de las Juntas.
[180] Also found in AGI, Indiferente, bundle 102.

Locality	Province	Country	Year(s)	Reference
Veranos	Sinaloa	México	1778	1149545
Verde	Sinaloa	México	1778	1149545
Vinapa	Sinaloa	México	1778	1149545
Zabala	Sinaloa	México	1778	1149545

SONORA

At the Archivo General de la Nación, Ramo de Historia, legajo 523, page 54 it says: "Solo Moloya falta en Sonora para tener un padrón completo, 1 de junio 1792." It is obvious that a census was compiled for this period as the statistics are still available, but the padrón itself has yet to be found.

Locality	Province	Country	Year(s)	Reference
Aconchi	Sonora	México	1774	AGN CA 39:2:20-149
Aconchi	Sonora	México	1848	AHS 258; IGHL
Aconchi	Sonora	México	1853	AHS
Aduana	Sonora	México	1868	AHS 409
Agua Caliente	Sonora	México	1856	AHS 4-2
Alamito (hacienda)	Sonora	México	1868	AHS 409
Alamos	Sonora	México	1852	ASG, 1986
Alamos	Sonora	México	1843	AHS 647
Alamos	Sonora	México	1856	AHS 4-2
Alamos	Sonora	México	1868	AHS 409
Alamos	Sonora	México	1890	AHS 687
Alamos	Sonora	México	1895	AHS 715-716
Altar	Sonora	México	1767	1149545
Altar	Sonora	México	1775	AF 34:729.1
Altar	Sonora	México	1796	AGEM 2
Altar	Sonora	México	1852	ASG, 1986; AES 248; AHS 248
Altar	Sonora	México	1868	AHS 409
Altar	Sonora	México	1890	AHS 687
Altar	Sonora	México	1895	AHS 717
Arizpe	Sonora	México	?	811:9-18
Arizpe	Sonora	México	1843	AHS 647
Arizpe	Sonora	México	1848	AHS 258
Arizpe	Sonora	México	1852	AHS 248
Arizpe	Sonora	México	1853	AHS
Arizpe	Sonora	México	1868	AHS 409
Arizpe	Sonora	México	1890	AHS 687
Arizpe	Sonora	México	1895	AHS 716
Arivechí	Sonora	México	1796	811:2
Arivechí	Sonora	México	1852	AHS 248
Arivechí	Sonora	México	1868	AHS 409
Asituana (hacienda)	Sonora	México	1852	ASG, 1986
Atil	Sonora	México	1766	AHH

Locality	Province	Country	Year(s)	Reference
Atil	Sonora	México	1801	ASG, 1986
Atil	Sonora	México	1802	811:3
Atil	Sonora	México	1852	ASG, 1986
Babboyahuy	Sonora	México	1868	AHS 409
Bacadeguachi	Sonora	México	1849	AHS 258
Bacadeguachi	Sonora	México	?	AHH
Bacadeguachi	Sonora	México	?	AHH
Bacadeguachi	Sonora	México	1765	AHH
Bacadeguachi	Sonora	México	1868	AHS 409
Bacanora	Sonora	México	1796	811:2
Bacanora	Sonora	México	1833	AHS 4-2
Bacanora	Sonora	México	1852	AHS 249
Bacanora	Sonora	México	1868	AHS 409
Bacanuchi	Sonora	México	?	811:13
Bacanuchi	Sonora	México	1796	811:26
Bacerac	Sonora	México	1765	AHH
Bacerac	Sonora	México	1837	AHS 4-2
Bacerac	Sonora	México	1849	AHS 259
Bacoachi	Sonora	México	1788	AGN PI 76:15:395-397
Bacoachi	Sonora	México	1837	AHS 4-2
Bacoachi	Sonora	México	1848	AHS 259
Bacoachi	Sonora	México	1853	AHS
Bacum	Sonora	México	1796	AGEM 4
Bacum	Sonora	México	1805	1149545
Bacuma	Sonora	México	1856	AHS 4-2
Bado Seco	Sonora	México	1841	AHS 4-2
Bamorí	Sonora	México	1796	811:2
Bamorí	Sonora	México	1852	AHS 249
Bamorí	Sonora	México	1868	AHS 409
Banámichi	Sonora	México	?	811:9-10
Banámichi	Sonora	México	1835	AHS 4-2
Banámichi	Sonora	México	1848	AHS 258
Banámichi	Sonora	México	1853	AHS
Banámichi	Sonora	México	1868	AHS 409
Banámichi	Sonora	México	1903	811:10
Baroyeca	Sonora	México	1868	AHS 409
Baserac	Sonora	México	1868	AHS 409
Batacora	Sonora	México	1856	AHS 4-2
Batuc	Sonora	México	1690	AHH
Batuc	Sonora	México	1736	AHH
Batuc	Sonora	México	1849	AHS 258
Batuc	Sonora	México	1868	AHS 409
Batuc	Sonora	México	1895	AHS 715
Batuc	Sonora	México	?	AHH
Baviacora	Sonora	México	1848	AHS 258

Locality	Province	Country	Year(s)	Reference
Baviacora	Sonora	México	1853	AHS
Baviacora	Sonora	México	1868	AHS 409
Bavispe	Sonora	México	?	AHH
Bavispe	Sonora	México	1766	AHH
Bavispe	Sonora	México	1837	AHS 4-2
Bavispe	Sonora	México	1849	AHS 258
Bavispe	Sonora	México	1868	AHS 409
Belem[181]	Sonora	México	1796	AGEM 4
Belem	Sonora	México	1805	1149545
Caborca	Sonora	México	1852	ASG, 1986
Caborca	Sonora	México	1868	AHS 409
Caborca[182]	Sonora	México	?	AHH
Caborca	Sonora	México	1766	AHH
Caborca	Sonora	México	1801	ASG, 1986; 811:3
Caborica[183]	Sonora	México	1684	AHH
Caborica	Sonora	México	1766	AHH
Caborica	Sonora	México	1768	?
Caborica	Sonora	México	1801	811:3
Camoa	Sonora	México	1726	AHH
Camoa	Sonora	México	1856	AHS 4-2
Cangrejos	Sonora	México	1856	AHS 4-2
Cedros	Sonora	México	1856	AHS 4-2
Celaduría del Ranchito	Sonora	México	1848	AHS 258
Chimecas	Sonora	México	1856	AHS 4-2
Chinal	Sonora	México	1868	AHS 409
Chinapa	Sonora	México	?	AHH
Chinapa	Sonora	México	?	AHH
Chinapa	Sonora	México	?	811:13
Chinapa	Sonora	México	1796	811:26
Chinapa	Sonora	México	1835	AHS 4-2
Chinapa	Sonora	México	1842	AHS 4-2
Chinapa	Sonora	México	1847	AHS 258
Chino de Guerrero	Sonora	México	1868	AHS 409
Chinos	Sonora	México	1856	AHS 4-2
Cocorim	Sonora	México	1796	AGEM 4
Cocorim	Sonora	México	1805	1149545
Cocóspera	Sonora	México	?	AHH
Cocóspera	Sonora	México	1796	811:2; AGEM 1
Cocóspera	Sonora	México	1801	ASG, 1986
Cocóspera	Sonora	México	1802	811:3
Collotillo	Sonora	México	1852	AHS 249

[181] San Miguel Belém de los Pimas.
[182] This and the next two entries are for Nuestra Señora de la Concepción de Caborca.
[183] This and the next three entries are for San Ignacio de Caborica.

Locality	Province	Country	Year(s)	Reference
Comuripa	Sonora	México	1852	AHS 248
Cuchuta[184]	Sonora	México	1767	1149545
Cucuri	Sonora	México	1837	AHS 4-2
Cucurpe	Sonora	México	1684	AHH
Cucurpe	Sonora	México	1772	AGN PI 81:5:155-159
Cucurpe	Sonora	México	1796	AGEM 2-3
Cucurpe	Sonora	México	1837	AHS 4-2
Cucurpe	Sonora	México	1841	AHS 4-2
Cucurpe	Sonora	México	1852	AHS 249
Cucurpe	Sonora	México	?	AHH
Cumpas	Sonora	México	1803	811:3
Cumpas	Sonora	México	1837	AHS 4-2
Cumpas	Sonora	México	1849	AHS 258
Cumpas	Sonora	México	1868	AHS 409
Cumuripa (San Pedro)	Sonora	México	1796	811:2
Cuquiarachi	Sonora	México	1726	AHH
Cuquiarachi	Sonora	México	1767	1149545
Cuquiarachi	Sonora	México	1847	AHS 258
Curimpo	Sonora	México	1856	AHS 4-2
Echojoa	Sonora	México	1856	AHS 4-2
Fronteras	Sonora	México	1767	1149545
Fronteras	Sonora	México	1848	AHS 258
Fronteras	Sonora	México	1868	AHS 409
Gacori	Sonora	México	1803	811:3
Geroeva	Sonora	México	1868	AHS 409
Granadas	Sonora	México	1849	AHS 258
Granados	Sonora	México	1868	AHS 409
Guadalupe	Sonora	México	1814	811:4
Guadalupe	Sonora	México	1852	AHS 248
Guadalupe Trinidad	Sonora	México	1868	AHS 409
Guadunesa	Sonora	México	1849	AHS 258
Guasavas	Sonora	México	1690	AHH
Guasavas	Sonora	México	1837	AHS 4-2
Guasavas	Sonora	México	1849	AHS 258
Guasavas	Sonora	México	1868	AHS 409
Guaymas	Sonora	México	1843	AHS 647
Guaymas	Sonora	México	?	AES 355:1047
Guaymas	Sonora	México	1890	AHS 687
Guirivis	Sonora	México	1796	1149545
Guorí	Sonora	México	1849	AHS 258
Hermosillo	Sonora	México	1796	811:2; AGEM 3
Hermosillo	Sonora	México	1820	811:4
Hermosillo	Sonora	México	1843	AHS 647

---

[184] San Francisco Xavier Cuchuta.

Locality	Province	Country	Year(s)	Reference
Hermosillo	Sonora	México	1890	AHS 687
Hermosillo (military)	Sonora	México	1852	AHS 248
Horcasitas	Sonora	México	1895	AHS 715
Huepac	Sonora	México	1848	AHS 258
Huepac	Sonora	México	1868	AHS 409
Huepac (San Lorenzo)	Sonora	México	?	AHH
Huepavarachi	Sonora	México	?	811:13
Huepavarachi	Sonora	México	1796	811:26
Imuris	Sonora	México	1690	AHH
Imuris	Sonora	México	1801	ASG, 1986; 811:3
Imuris	Sonora	México	1852	AHS 249
Imuris	Sonora	México	1868	AHS 409
Jarachi	Sonora	México	1852	AHS 248
Llano Colorado	Sonora	México	1848	AHS 258
Maciaca	Sonora	México	1856	AHS 4-2
Macoyahuy	Sonora	México	1856	AHS 4-2
Magdalena	Sonora	México	1801	ASG, 1986; 811:3
Magdalena	Sonora	México	1843	AHS 647
Magdalena	Sonora	México	1867	AHS 409
Magdalena	Sonora	México	1890	AHS 687
Magdalena	Sonora	México	1895	AHS 716
Mazatán	Sonora	México	1848	AHS 258
Mazatán	Sonora	México	1852	AHS 249
Mazatán	Sonora	México	1895	AHS 715
Metape (Sr. San José)	Sonora	México	1765	AHH
Metape (Sr. San José)	Sonora	México	1673	AHH
Metape (Sr. San José)	Sonora	México	1814	811:4
Metape (Sr. San José)	Sonora	México	1852	AHS 249
Metape (Sr. San José)	Sonora	México	1895	AHS 715
Minas Nuevas	Sonora	México	1868	AHS 409
Moctezuma	Sonora	México	1837	AHS 4-2
Moctezuma	Sonora	México	1843	AHS 647
Moctezuma	Sonora	México	1849	AHS 258
Moctezuma	Sonora	México	1868	AHS 409
Moctezuma	Sonora	México	1895	AHS 716
Movas	Sonora	México	1800	811:3
Movas	Sonora	México	1856	AHS 4-2
Movas	Sonora	México	1868	AHS 409
Movas	Sonora	México	?	AHH
Moxtezuma	Sonora	México	1890	AHS 687
Mulatos	Sonora	México	1868	AHS 409
Nacámeri	Sonora	México	1726	AHH
Nacámeri	Sonora	México	1796	811:2
Nacori	Sonora	México	1868	AHS 409
Nacori Chiquito	Sonora	México	1849	AHS 258

Locality	Province	Country	Year(s)	Reference
Nacori Grande	Sonora	México	1895	AHS 715
Navojoa	Sonora	México	1856	AHS 4-2
Nogales (municipio)	Sonora	México	1886	AHS 616
Nogales (municipio)	Sonora	México	1889	AHS 616
Nucias Nuevas	Sonora	México	1856	AHS 4-2
Nuri	Sonora	México	1856	AHS 4-2
Nuri	Sonora	México	1868	AHS 409
Nuri	Sonora	México	1800	811:3
Onavas	Sonora	México	?	AHH
Onavas	Sonora	México	1848	AHS 258
Onavas	Sonora	México	1895	AHS 715
Opodepe	Sonora	México	1895	AHS 715
Oposura (San Miguel)	Sonora	México	1765	AHH
Oposura (San Miguel)	Sonora	México	1803	811:3
Oputo (San Ignacio)	Sonora	México	1868	AHS 409
Oquitoa	Sonora	México	1801	ASG, 1986
Oquitoa	Sonora	México	1852	ASG, 1986
Oquitoa	Sonora	México	1868	AHS 409
Ostimuri	Sonora	México	1742	UT[185]
Ostimuri	Sonora	México	1742	AF 37:823[186]
Pimas (San José)	Sonora	México	1796	811:2
Pitiquito	Sonora	México	1801	ASG, 1986
Pitiquito	Sonora	México	1852	ASG, 1986
Pitiquito	Sonora	México	1868	AHS 409
Pivipa (San Pedro)	Sonora	México	1803	811:3
Poneda (Pur. Conc.)	Sonora	México	1796	811:2
Potam	Sonora	México	?	AHH
Potam	Sonora	México	1805	1149545
Potrero de Esquer	Sonora	México	1868	AHS 409
Pópulo de Bisani[187]	Sonora	México	?	AHH
Pópulo de Bisani	Sonora	México	1801	811:3
Quinego	Sonora	México	1868	AHS 409
Rahum	Sonora	México	?	AHH
Rahum	Sonora	México	1684	AHH
Rahum	Sonora	México	1805	1149545
Ranchito	Sonora	México	1868	AHS 409
Rayón	Sonora	México	1848	AHS 258
Rayón	Sonora	México	1868	AHS 409

[185] This census is for the southern part of Ostimuri, comprising southeast Sonora, roughly from Río Chico south to the Río Mayo (the border of Sinaloa) and south along the Río Yaqui from Río Chico to Guaymas.

[186] This apparently incomplete *matrícula* of the pueblos of the Yaqui delta region probably includes Cocorim, Bacum, Torim, Vicam, Potam, Rahum, Belem, and Húirivis.

[187] Nuestra Señora del Pópulo de Bisani.

Locality	Province	Country	Year(s)	Reference
Rayón	Sonora	México	1895	AHS 715
Río Chico[188]	Sonora	México	1800	811:3
Río Mayo[189]	Sonora	México	?	AHH
Río Mayo	Sonora	México	1831	ASG 17:2-3
Río Tres Hermanos	Sonora	México	1868	AHS 409
Ruqui Naiado[190]	Sonora	México	1801	811:3
Sahuaripa	Sonora	México	?	AHH
Sahuaripa	Sonora	México	1843	AHS 647
Sahuaripa	Sonora	México	1852	AHS 249
Sahuaripa	Sonora	México	1868	AHS 409
Sahuaripa	Sonora	México	1890	AHS 687
Sahuaripa	Sonora	México	1895	AHS 716
Salado	Sonora	México	1868	AHS 409
Salvación	Sonora	México	1852	AHS 249
San Anto. de la Huerta	Sonora	México	1852	AHS 249
San Felipe	Sonora	México	1868	AHS 409
San Ignacio	Sonora	México	1801	ASG, 1986
San Ignacio	Sonora	México	1841	AHS 4-2
San Ignacio	Sonora	México	1852	AHS 249
San Ignacio	Sonora	México	1856	AHS 4-2
San Ignacio	Sonora	México	1867	AHS 409
San Javier	Sonora	México	1851	AHS 249
San José de Gracia	Sonora	México	1870–1872	AHS 702
S. José de los Mulatos	Sonora	México	1814	811:4
S. Juan Bautista	Sonora	México	1793	AHH
San Lorenzo	Sonora	México	1801	ASG, 1986; 811:3
San Pedro	Sonora	México	1856	AHS 4-2
San Pedro de la Cueva	Sonora	México	1849	AHS 258
San Pedro de la Cueva	Sonora	México	1895	AHS 715
San Ventura	Sonora	México	1868	AHS 409
San Vicente	Sonora	México	1856	AHS 4-2
Santa Ana	Sonora	México	1801	ASG, 1986; 811:3
Santa Ana	Sonora	México	1852	AHS 249
Santa Ana Magdalena	Sonora	México	1868	AHS 409
Santa Cruz	Sonora	México	1852	AHS 248
Santa Cruz	Sonora	México	1856	AHS 4-2
Santa Cruz	Sonora	México	1868	AHS 409
Santa Gertrudis[191]	Sonora	México		
Santa Marta	Sonora	México	1852	AHS 249
Santa Teresa	Sonora	México	1801	ASG, 1986; 811:3

---

[188] San Francisco de Asís del Río Chico.
[189] Santa Cruz del Río Mayo.
[190] San Diego de Ruqui Naiado.
[191] See Altar.

Locality	Province	Country	Year(s)	Reference
Santa Teresa	Sonora	México	1841	AHS 4-2
Saracachi	Sonora	México	1841	AHS 4-2
Saric	Sonora	México	1765	AHH
Saric	Sonora	México	1801	811:3; AGEM 29; ASG, 1986
Saric	Sonora	México	1852	ASG, 1986
Saric	Sonora	México	1868	AHS 409
Sinoquipe	Sonora	México	1848	AHS 258
Sinoquipe	Sonora	México	1853	AHS
Sinoquipe	Sonora	México	1868	AHS 409
Soamca (Santa Maríá)	Sonora	México	?	AHH
Soledad	Sonora	México	1868	AHS 409
Soyapa	Sonora	México	1848	AHS 258
Soyapa	Sonora	México	1895	AHS 715
Suaqui	Sonora	México	1766	1149545
Suaqui	Sonora	México	1796	811:2
Suaqui	Sonora	México	1849	AHS 258
Suaqui	Sonora	México	1895	AHS 715
Suviate	Sonora	México	1852	AHS 248
Tacupeto	Sonora	México	1796	811:2
Tacupeto	Sonora	México	1852	AHS 248
Tacupeto	Sonora	México	1868	AHS 409
Tarachi	Sonora	México	1835	AHS 4-2
Tarachi	Sonora	México	1868	AHS 409
Tasajera	Sonora	México	1848	AHS 258
Taupe	Sonora	México	1895	AHS 715
Tecia	Sonora	México	1856	AHS 4-2
Tecoripa	Sonora	México	1867	AHS 409
Tepachi	Sonora	México	?	AHH
Tepachi	Sonora	México	1793	811:3
Tepachi	Sonora	México	1837	AHS 4-2
Tepachi	Sonora	México	1849	AHS 258
Tepachi	Sonora	México	1868	AHS 409
Tepahuy	Sonora	México	1856	AHS 4-2
Tepehajes	Sonora	México	1868	AHS 409
Tepupa	Sonora	México	1895	AHS 715
Terrenate[192]	Sonora	México	1767	1149545
Terrenate	Sonora	México	1801	ASG, 1986; 811:3
Terrenate (Santa Cruz)	Sonora	México	1852	AES:249
Tónachi	Sonora	México	1852	AHS 249
Tónichi	Sonora	México	1895	AHS 715
Torim	Sonora	México	1796	AGEM 4
Torim	Sonora	México	1805	1149545

---

[192] San Felipe de G. Real de Terrenate.

Locality	Province	Country	Year(s)	Reference
Trigo	Sonora	México	1856	AHS 4-2
Tuape	Sonora	México	1796	AGEM 2-3
Tuape	Sonora	México	1841	AHS 4-2
Tubutama	Sonora	México	1690	AHH
Tubutama	Sonora	México	1766	AHH
Tubutama	Sonora	México	1772	AGN PI 81:13:175
Tubutama	Sonora	México	1801	ASG, 1986; 811:3
Tubutama	Sonora	México	1852	ASG, 1986
Tubutama	Sonora	México	1868	AHS 409
Ures	Sonora	México	?	AHH
Ures	Sonora	México	1690	AHH
Ures	Sonora	México	1843	AHS 647
Ures	Sonora	México	1852	AHS 249
Ures	Sonora	México	1890	AHS 687
Ures	Sonora	México	1894	AHS 715
Ures	Sonora	México	1895	AHS 716
Vicam	Sonora	México	1796	AGEM 4
Vicam	Sonora	México	1805	1149545
Villa Pesqueira	Sonora	México	1868	AHS 409
Viñatería	Sonora	México	1868	AHS 409
Visanic	Sonora	México	1801	ASG, 1986

TAMAULIPAS

Locality	Province	Country	Year(s)	Reference
	Tamaulipas[193]	México	1744	AGI México 690
	Tamaulipas	México	1746–1755	AGI[194]
	Tamaulipas	México	1750	AGN PI 172:17:309-325
	Tamaulipas[195]	México	1770–1771	AGN PI 31:1:1-531
	Tamaulipas	México	1778–1779	AGN PI 115:1:1-287
	Tamaulipas	México	1779	AGN PI 15:34:247-277
Aguayo (Santa María)	Tamaulipas	México	1749–1750	AGN PI 180:12:168-182
Altamira	Tamaulipas	México	1749–1750	AGN PI 180:9:117-138
Burgos	Tamaulipas	México	1749–1750	AGN PI 180:3:39-49
Camargo	Tamaulipas	México	1750	AGN PI 180:1:4-25; LBN 3:173-178
Cinco Señores	Tamaulipas	México[196]		
Escandón	Tamaulipas	México	1749–1750	AGN PI 180:10:139-152
Güemes	Tamaulipas	México	1749–1750	AGN PI 180:14:201-214
Horcasitas	Tamaulipas	México	1749–1750	AGN PI 180:15:215-228
Jaumave[197]	Tamaulipas	México	c.1740	AGI México 690
Jiménez	Tamaulipas	México	1750	DRV 5-24
Jiménez[198]	Tamaulipas	México	1751	DRV 30-32
Jiménez	Tamaulipas	México	1753	DRV 60-61
Jiménez	Tamaulipas	México	1754	DRV 60-61
Jiménez[199]	Tamaulipas	México	1753	DRV 33-56
Jiménez	Tamaulipas	México	1755	DRV 65-85
Jiménez	Tamaulipas	México	1757	DRV 93-111
Llera	Tamaulipas	México	1749–1750	AGN PI 180:5:64-70
Mier	Tamaulipas	México	1753	WAA 267
Mier	Tamaulipas	México	1757	WAS 268
Mier	Tamaulipas	México	1782–1870	1511692
Mier	Tamaulipas	México	1820–1826	1511692
Nuevo Santander	Tamaulipas	México[200]		
Padilla	Tamaulipas	México	1749–1750	AGN PI 180:13:183-199

[193] Contains complete *padrones* of Escandón's villages in Río Verde settlements.
[194] Archivo General de Indias, Indiferente, bundle 108; and México, bundles 690-691.
[195] This entry and the next two entries are troop lists.
[196] See Jiménez.
[197] San Lorenzo Jaumave
[198] This entry and the next two entries are censuses of the civilian population only.
[199] This entry and the following two entries are for both the civilian and military population
[200] See Jiménez.

Locality	Province	Country	Year(s)	Reference
Ocampo	Tamaulipas	México	1782	640301
Ocampo	Tamaulipas	México	1800	640301
Parras (military)	Tamaulipas	México	1807	HGJ 6:91-95
Revilla	Tamaulipas	México	1749–1750	AGN PI 180:16:229-244
Reynosa	Tamaulipas	México	1749–1750	AGN PI 180:2:24-37; LBN 4:28-31, continued
San Fernando	Tamaulipas	México	1749–1750	AGN PI 180:4:50-63
Santa Bárbara	Tamaulipas	México	1749–1750	AGN PI 180:11:153-168
Santander	Tamaulipas	México	1749–1750	AGN PI 180:8:98-116
Tancalum	Tamaulipas	México	1721	1149545

TEXAS

Locality	Province	Country	Year(s)	Reference
	Téxas	México	1705	?
	Téxas	México	1774	AGN CA 39:2:20-149
	Téxas	México	1777	BNM:
	Téxas	México	1829–1836	?
	Téxas	México	1840	?
Acuña[201]	Téxas	México	1792	ROT 1:102-104
Acuña	Téxas	México	1793	ROT 1:149-150
Acuña	Téxas	México	1798	ROT 1:296-297
Acuña	Téxas	México	1799	ROT 1:310-311
Acuña	Téxas	México	1709	ROT 2:38-39
Adaes	Téxas	México	1739	AGN PI 182:1:1-127
Atacosita	Téxas	México	1826	TEX 1:300-305
Barrio Laredo[202]	Téxas	México	1809	ROT 2:42-46
Capistrano	Téxas	México	1794	ROT 1:165-166
Capistrano	Téxas	México	1795	ROT 1:220-221
Parras[203]	Téxas	México	1807	ROT 2:1-5
El Paso del Río Norte	New Mexico	México	1680	Santa Fé[204]
El Paso del Río Norte	New Mexico	México	1784	NMHR 1977:524
Espada	Téxas	México	1793	ROT 1:147-149
Espada	Téxas	México	1794	ROT 1:164-165
Espada	Téxas	México	1796	ROT 1:222-223
Espiritu Santo	Téxas	México	1804	ROT 1:385
Galveston	Téxas	México	1789	LGR 27:367
Galveston	Téxas	México	1783	LGR 27:367
Galveston	Téxas	México	1793	LGR 27:367
Guadalupe del Paso[205]	Téxas	México		
La Bahía	Téxas	México	1780	HGJ 1:102-104
La Bahía	Téxas	México	1790	ROT 1:47-58
La Bahía	Téxas	México	1804	ROT 1:381-384
La Bahía	Téxas	México	1810	ROT 2:46-64
La Bahía	Téxas	México	1811	ROT 2:74-90
La Bahía	Téxas	México	1825	ROT 1:74-83
Laredo	Téxas	México	1757	LBN 4:27

---

[201] La Purísima Concepción de Acuña.
[202] Barrio Laredo de la Villa de San Fernando.
[203] Compañía Volante of San Carlos de Parras.
[204] Possibly at the Archbishop's Archives.
[205] See Ciudad Juárez, Chihuahua, México.

Locality	Province	Country	Year(s)	Reference
Nacagdoches	Téxas	México	1792	ROT 1:104-114
Nacagdoches	Téxas	México	1792	TSG 13:15-23
Nacagdoches	Téxas	México	1793	ROT 1:151-163
Nacagdoches	Téxas	México	1794	LBN 1:94-104
Nacagdoches	Téxas	México	1794	ROT 1:173-180
Nacagdoches	Téxas	México	1795	ROT 1:181-193
Nacagdoches	Téxas	México	1796	ROT 1:246-257
Nacagdoches	Téxas	México	1797	ROT 1:282-294
Nacagdoches	Téxas	México	1798	ROT 1:299-310
Nacagdoches	Téxas	México	1799	ROT 1:313-327
Nacagdoches	Téxas	México	1803	ROT 1:355-371
Nacagdoches	Téxas	México	1805	ROT 1:404-418; 421-423
Nacagdoches	Téxas	México	1806	ROT 1:423-435
Nacagdoches	Téxas	México	1809	ROT 2:10-35
Neve[206]	Téxas	México	1809	LBN 4:187-188
Neve	Téxas	México	1809	ROT 2:40-42
Orcoquisac	Téxas	México	1807	ROT 2:5-7
Real del Barranco[207]	Téxas	México	1844	?
Refugio	Téxas	México	1804	ROT 1:386
Rosario	Téxas	México	1804	ROT 1:385
San Antonio Valero	Téxas	México	1792	ROT 1:93-95
San Antonio Valero	Téxas	México	1795	ROT 1:215-218
San Antonio Valero	Téxas	México	1796	ROT 1:224-226
San Antonio Valero	Téxas	México	1797	ROT 1:262-265
San Antonio Valero	Téxas	México	1798	ROT 1:297-299
San Antonio Valero	Téxas	México	1804	ROT 1:378-380
San Antonio Valero	Téxas	México	1806	ROT 1:435-437
San Antonio Valero	Téxas	México	1808	ROT 2:7-8
San Antonio Béxar	Téxas	México	1784	TSL
San Antonio Béxar	Téxas	México	1790	ROT 1:58-74
San Antonio Béxar	Téxas	México	1792	TSL
San Antonio Béxar	Téxas	México	1795	LBN 1:5-13, 29-36, 49-55
San Antonio Béxar	Téxas	México	1803	LBN 2:58-66, 77-86, 112-117
San Antonio Béxar	Téxas	México	1804	ROT 1:371-377
San Antonio Béxar	Téxas	México	1805	TSL
San Antonio Béxar	Téxas	México	1817	LBN 4:73-82, continued
S. Fco. de la Espada	Téxas	México	1790	ROT 1:46
S. Fco. de la Espada	Téxas	México	1792	ROT 1:98-100
S. Fco. de la Espada	Téxas	México	1795	ROT 1:218-220
S. Fco. de la Espada	Téxas	México	1797	ROT 1:260-262
S. Fco. de la Espada	Téxas	México	1803	ROT 1:353-354

---

[206] San Marcos de Neve.
[207] Real del Barranco, Villa El Paso

Locality	Province	Country	Year(s)	Reference
S. Fco. de la Espada	Téxas	México	1804	ROT 1:386-387
S. Fern. de Austria	Téxas	México	1735	LBN 2:46
S. Fern. de Austria	Téxas	México	1762	LBN 1:23-26
S. Fern. de Austria	Téxas	México	1782	ROT 1:39-44
S. Fern. de Austria	Téxas	México	1792	ROT 1:75-92
S. Fern. de Austria	Téxas	México	1793	ROT 1:114-141
S. Fern. de Austria	Téxas	México	1795	ROT 1:193-215
S. Fern. y Presidio[208]	Téxas	México	1796	ROT 1:226-246
S. Fern. y Presidio	Téxas	México	1797	ROT 1:265-282
S. Fern. y Presidio	Téxas	México	1803	ROT 1:327-352
S. Fern. y Presidio	Téxas	México	1804	ROT 1:388-404
San José	Téxas	México	1790	ROT 1:45-46
San José	Téxas	México	1792	ROT 1:95-98
San José	Téxas	México	1793	ROT 1:141-145
San José	Téxas	México	1805	ROT 1:419-420
San José de Aguallo	Téxas	México	1794	ROT 1:170-172
San José de Aguallo	Téxas	México	1797	ROT 1:258-260
San José de Aguallo	Téxas	México	1798	ROT 1:295-296
San José de Aguallo	Téxas	México	1799	ROT 1:311-313
San Juan Bautista[209]	Téxas	México	1777	?
San Juan Capistrano	Téxas	México	1792	ROT 1:101-102
San Juan Capistrano	Téxas	México	1793	ROT 1:145-146
San Juan Capistrano	Téxas	México	1797	ROT 1:257-258
San Juan Capistrano	Téxas	México	1798	ROT 1:294
San Juan Capistrano	Téxas	México	1804	ROT 1:377-378
San Juan Capistrano	Téxas	México	1809	ROT 2:36-38
Sindic & its ranches	Téxas	México	1810	ROT 2:64-73
Terre aux Boeufs	Téxas	México	1779	LGR 27:367
Trinidad	Téxas	México	1809	ROT 2:8-9
Valenzuela	Téxas	México	1779	LGR 27:367
Valero	Téxas	México	1794	ROT 1:167-169

[208] San Fernando y Presidio de San Antonio de Béxar.
[209] San Juan Bautista del Río Grande.

TLAXCALA

Locality	Province	Country	Year(s)	Reference
	Tlaxcala	México	1790	22; 48
	Tlaxcala	México	1791	AGN PAD 12:1-33
Amatlán	Tlaxcala	México	1777	AGI México 2581
Apango	Tlaxcala	México	1777	AGI México 2578, 2581
Chicontepec	Tlaxcala	México	1777	AGI México 2579, 2581
Chilpancingo	Tlaxcala	México	1777	AGI México 2578, 2581
Cozamaloapa	Tlaxcala	México	1777	AGI México 2581
Cuapiastla	Tlaxcala	México	1777	AGI México 2578-2581
Huitziltepec	Tlaxcala	México	1777	AGI México 2578, 2581
Ilamatlán	Tlaxcala	México	1777	AGI México 2579, 2581
Ixhuatlán	Tlaxcala	México	1777	AGI México 2579, 2581
Ixtenco	Tlaxcala	México	1777	AGI México 2578-2581
Muchitán	Tlaxcala	México	1777	AGI México 2578, 2581
Naupán	Tlaxcala	México	1777	AGI México 2580-2581
Petaquillas	Tlaxcala	México	1777	AGI México 2578, 2581
San Pablo del Monte	Tlaxcala	México	1777	AGI México 2578-2581
Santa Cruz Tlaxcala	Tlaxcala	México	1777	AGI México 2578-2581
Tamiagua	Tlaxcala	México	1791	AGN PAD 18
Tetla	Tlaxcala	México	1777	AGI México 2578-2581
Tezcuco	Tlaxcala	México	1786	AGN PAD 43:5-14
Tezcuco	Tlaxcala	México	1792	AGN PAD 14:190-191v
Tistla	Tlaxcala	México	1777	AGI México 2578, 2581
Tistla	Tlaxcala	México	1792	AGN PAD 17
Tlacuiloltepec	Tlaxcala	México	1777	AGI México 2580-2581
Tlaxcala	Tlaxcala	México	1777	AGI México 2578
Tlaxcala	Tlaxcala	México	1778	AGN PAD 22
Tlaxcala	Tlaxcala	México	1792	AGN PAD 22
Tuxpán	Tlaxcala	México	1777	AGI México 2580-2581
Yauquemecan	Tlaxcala	México	1777	AGI México 2578-2581
Zompaxtepec	Tlaxcala	México	1777	AGI México 2578-2581

VERACRUZ

Locality	Province	Country	Year(s)	Reference
	Veracruz[210]	México	1809–1810	AGN HI 452:vii
Actopan	Veracruz	México	1777	AGI México 2579-2580
Alvarado	Veracruz	México	1777	AGI México 2580
Amatlán	Veracruz	México	1777	AGI México 2578, 2580
Apazapán	Veracruz	México	1777	AGI México 2580
Atzalán	Veracruz	México	1777	AGI México 2578-2581
Chicontepec	Veracruz	México	1783	AGN HI 72:xxii
Chicontepec	Veracruz	México	1790	AGN PAD 12
Guatusco	Veracruz	México	1777	AGI México 2578, 2580
Guayacocotla	Veracruz	México	1783	AGN HI 72:xxii
Ixguacán	Veracruz	México	1777	AGI México 2578-2581
Izontecomatlán	Veracruz	México	1797	442137; 641733
Medellín	Veracruz	México	1777	AGI México 2580
Mizantla	Veracruz	México	1777	AGI México 2579-2580
Naranjal	Veracruz	México	1777	AGI México 2579-2580
Necoxtla	Veracruz	México	1777	AGI México 2579-2580
Orizaba	Veracruz	México	1721–1836	772180-772184
Orizaba	Veracruz	México	1777	AGI México 2579-2580
Orizaba[211]	Veracruz	México	1790	AGN PAD 19:1-426v
Otumba	Veracruz	México	1790	AGN PAD 12
Ozuluama	Veracruz	México	1789	INA 147:299-
Pánuco	Veracruz	México	1738–1744	AGI Indiferentes 108[212]
Perote	Veracruz	México	1777	AGI México 2578-2581
San Andrés Tuxtla	Veracruz	México	1777	AGI México 2590
Tahlacum	Veracruz	México	1721	1147545
Tamiagua	Veracruz	México	1790	AGN PAD 18
Tampasquid	Veracruz	México	1721	1149545
Tanlacum	Veracruz	México	1721	1149545
Tehuipango	Veracruz	México	1777	AGI México 2579-2580
Tequila	Veracruz	México	1777	AGI México 2579-2580
Tlacotalpa	Veracruz	México	1777	AGI México 2580
Tlaliscoya	Veracruz	México	1777	AGI México 2580
Tonayan	Veracruz	México	1777	AGI México 2578-2581

[210] This census is of foreigners only.

[211] Includes the entire province of Orizaba, not just the city.

[212] AGI, Indiferentes, bundle 108, volume iv, folios 382–411v; also published in Francisco de Solano's book *Relaciónes geográficas del arzobispado de México, 1743*. 2 volumes. Madrid: Consejo Superior de Investigaciones Científicas, 1988.

Locality	Province	Country	Year(s)	Reference
Totutla	Veracruz	México	1777	AGI México 2578, 2580
Xalapa de la Feria	Veracruz	México	1777	AGI México 2578-2581
Xalapa de la Feria	Veracruz	México	1777	AGN HI 42
Xalapa de la Feria	Veracruz	México	1790	AGN PAD 20
Xilotepec	Veracruz	México	1777	AGI México 2578-2581
Zozocolco	Veracruz	México	1777	AGI México 2580

YUCATAN

Locality	Province	Country	Year(s)	Reference
Batcab	Yucatán	México	1689	AGC
Cacalchén	Yucatán	México	1688	AGI, Contaduría 920
Cacalchén	Yucatán	México	1700	AGI, México 1035
Calotmul	Yucatán	México	1688	AGI, Contaduría 920
Campeche	Yucatán	México	1688	AGI, Contaduría 920
Campeche[213]	Yucatán	México	1777	AGI, México 3018
Campechuelo	Yucatán	México	1688	AGI, Contaduría 920
Cansahcab	Yucatán	México	1700	AGI, México 1035
Champotón	Yucatán	México	1688	AGI, Contaduría 920
Champotón	Yucatán	México	1777	AGI, México 3018
Chancenote	Yucatán	México	1688	AGI, Contaduría 920
Conkal	Yucatán	México	1700	AGI, México 1035
Costa[214]	Yucatán	México	1803	?
Cozumel	Yucatán	México	1570	AGI Indiferente 1381
Espitá	Yucatán	México	1688	AGI, Contaduría 920
Espitá	Yucatán	México	1841	764185
Espitá	Yucatán	México	1848	764185
Espitá	Yucatán	México	1877	764185
Izamal	Yucatán	México	1688	AGI, Contaduría 920
Izamal	Yucatán	México	1700	AGI, México 1035
Kikil	Yucatán	México	1688	AGI, Contaduría 920
Mérida: Santiago	Yucatán	México	1688	AGI, Contaduría 920
Mocochá	Yucatán	México	1688	AGI, Contaduría 920
Mocochá	Yucatán	México	1700	AGI, México 1035
Motul	Yucatán	México	1688	AGI, Contaduría 920
Motul	Yucatán	México	1700	AGI, México 1035
Nabalam	Yucatán	México	1688	AGI, Contaduría 920
Seiba	Yucatán	México	1777	AGI, México 3018
Sierra[215]	Yucatán	México	1688	AGI, Contaduría 920
	Tabasco[216]	México	1809	AGN HI 452:viii

[213] Includes Champotón and Seiba in the province of Sahcabchén, Yucatán.

[214] This *matrícula*, the exact location of which has not been determined, may include Concal, Mocochá, Tixkokob, Izamal, Motul, Telchac, Cacalchén, Tecantó, Teyá, Zizontún, Cansahcab and Temax in the coastal province east of Mérida.

[215] The province of Sierra is south of Mérida. This *matrícula* of 1688 includes most of the Indian communities in the province possibly including, Abalá, Acanceh, Akil, Chapab, Chemeyel, Dzan, Mama, Mani, Muna, Nohcacab, Oxkutzcab, Pencuyut, Pustunich, Teabó, Tecax, Tecoh, Tekit, Telchaquillo, Ticul, Ticum, Timucuy, Tipikal, Tixcuytún, Tixmeuac, Xayá, Xul, Yotolín, and Zacalum.

[216] This census is of foreigners only.

Locality	Province	Country	Year(s)	Reference
Usumacinta	Tabasco	México	1818	746830
Tahcabo	Yucatán	México	1688	AGI, Contaduría 920
Tecantó	Yucatán	México	1688	AGI, Contaduría 920
Tecantó	Yucatán	México	1700	AGI, México 1035
Telchac	Yucatán	México	1700	AGI, México 1035
Temax	Yucatán	México	1700	AGI, México 1035
Teyá	Yucatán	México	1688	AGI, Contaduría 920
Teyá	Yucatán	México	1700	AGI, México 1035
Tixkokob	Yucatán	México	1688	AGI, Contaduría 920
Tixkokob	Yucatán	México	1700	AGI, México 1035
Tizimín	Yucatán	México	1583	AGN Civil 661
Tizimín	Yucatán	México	1688	AGI, Contaduría 920
Xcanboloná	Yucatán	México	1688	AGI, Contaduría 920
Zizantún	Yucatán	México	1688	AGI, Contaduría 920
Zizantún	Yucatán	México	1700	AGI, México 1035

ZACATECAS

The microfilm series 168803-168849 contains hundreds of entries for the 1600s through the 1800s for Zacatecas. It has not been studied in detail in this listing.

The reference Cathedral, Zacatecas in the listing below refers to the location of the records, the Cathedral of Zacatecas. Only some of these padrones have been microfilmed. All of the ones so identified have been photocopied by the Institute of Genealogy and History for Latin America.

Locality	Province	Country	Year(s)	Reference
	Zacatecas	México	1649	Archivo del Parral[217]
	Zacatecas	México	1809	AGN HI 452:v
Agua Gorda[218]	Zacatecas	México	1824	168833
Apozol	Zacatecas	México	1819	168815
Atitanac	Zacatecas	México	1819	168815
Atotonilco[219]	Zacatecas	México	1819	168815
Ceja	Zacatecas	México	1819	168815
Chalchihuites	Zacatecas	México	1777	AGI Indiferentes 102
Cuspala	Zacatecas	México	1825	1162587
Extansuela	Zacatecas	México	1828	168848
Fresnillo	Zacatecas	México	1770	AAG
Fresnillo	Zacatecas	México	1772–1773	AGI Guadalajara 348
García de la Cadena	Zacatecas	México	1819	168815
Gruñidora	Zacatecas	México	1804–1870	1164590-1164591
Gruñidora	Zacatecas	México	1819	168817
Guadalupe	Zacatecas	México	1832	168807
Huejúcar	Zacatecas	México	1817	168809
Huitzila	Zacatecas	México	1819	168815
Jalpa	Zacatecas	México	1760	168805
Jalpa	Zacatecas	México	1762	168804
Jalpa	Zacatecas	México	1817	168810
Jalpa	Zacatecas	México	1819	168816
Jalpa	Zacatecas	México	1820	168818-168819
Jalpa	Zacatecas	México	1821	168824
Jalpa	Zacatecas	México	1822	168828
Jalpa	Zacatecas	México	1824	168832
Jalpa	Zacatecas	México	1825	168835
Jalpa	Zacatecas	México	1828	168839

---

[217] Padrón de los vecinos . . . 1649.
[218] This census is of foreigners only.
[219] San Miguel de Atotonilco.

Locality	Province	Country	Year(s)	Reference
Jalpa	Zacatecas	México	1830	168842, 168844
Jérez	Zacatecas	México	1820	168818
Jérez	Zacatecas	México	1821	168824
Jérez	Zacatecas	México	1824	168832
Jérez (military)	Zacatecas	México	1820	168822
Jocotlán	Zacatecas	México	1817	168809
Juchipila	Zacatecas	México	1773	AGI Guadalajara 348
Juchipila	Zacatecas	México	1819	168815
Juchipila	Zacatecas	México	1824	168832
Juitán	Zacatecas	México	1819	168815
La Quemada	Zacatecas	México	1819	168815
La Quemada	Zacatecas	México	1820	168820
Malpaso	Zacatecas	México	1820	168820
Malpaso (Santa Rosa)	Zacatecas	México	1819	168815
Malpaso (Santiago)	Zacatecas	México	1760	168805
Mazapil	Zacatecas	México	1817	168810
Mazapil	Zacatecas	México	1820	168820
Mazapil	Zacatecas	México	1821	168824
Mazapil	Zacatecas	México	1822	168828
Mazapil	Zacatecas	México	1823	168829
Mazapil	Zacatecas	México	1824	168833
Mesquital	Zacatecas	México	1777	AGI Guadalajara 255[220]
Mesquital[221]	Zacatecas	México	1823	168829
Mesquital	Zacatecas	México	1824	168833
Mesquital	Zacatecas	México	1825	168836
Mesquital[222]	Zacatecas	México	1825	168836
Mesquital del Oro	Zacatecas	México	1817	168810
Mesquital del Oro	Zacatecas	México	1820	168820
Mesquital del Oro	Zacatecas	México	1825	168835
Mesquital del Oro	Zacatecas	México	1830	168846
Mesquituta	Zacatecas	México	1818	1162587
Mesquituta	Zacatecas	México	1825	1162587
Milpillas	Zacatecas	México	1762	168805
Monte Escobedo	Zacatecas	México	1819	168815
Moyahua	Zacatecas	México	1818–1825	1162587
Moyahua	Zacatecas	México	1822	168828
Moyahua	Zacatecas	México	1828	168840
Nieves	Zacatecas	México	1777	AGI Guadalajara 255
Nochistlán	Zacatecas	México	1817	168810
Nochistlán	Zacatecas	México	1823	168829
Nochistlán	Zacatecas	México	1846–1899	226945

[220] San Miguel del Mezquital.
[221] San Juan Bautista del Mesquital.
[222] San Miguel del Mesquital.

Locality	Province	Country	Year(s)	Reference
Ojocaliente	Zacatecas	México	1824	168833
Palomas Viejas	Zacatecas	México	1819	168805
Pánuco	Zacatecas	México	1807	1464049
Pánuco	Zacatecas	México	1840	1464049
Pánuco	Zacatecas	México	1864	1464049
Pánuco	Zacatecas	México	1878	1464049
Pánuco	Zacatecas	México	1889	1464049
Pánuco	Zacatecas	México	1922	1464049
Provincial Batallion	Zacatecas	México	1820	168822
Pueblo Viejo	Zacatecas	México	1818	1162587
Quijas	Zacatecas	México	1817	168807
Quijas	Zacatecas	México	1818	168807
Salto (S. Juan de Dios)	Zacatecas	México	1819	168815
San Buenaventura	Zacatecas	México	1820	168807
Santa Rita	Zacatecas	México	1806	168807
Sierra de Pinos	Zacatecas	México	1762	168805
Sierra de Pinos	Zacatecas	México	1766	AAG; 168805
Sierra de Pinos	Zacatecas	México	1794	168803
Sierra de Pinos	Zacatecas	México	1801	168807
Sierra de Pinos	Zacatecas	México	1803	168806
Sierra de Pinos	Zacatecas	México	1816	168807
Sierra de Pinos	Zacatecas	México	1820	168822
Sombrerete	Zacatecas	México	1777	AGI Indiferentes 1526
Sombrerete (military)	Zacatecas	México	1820	168822
Tabasco	Zacatecas	México	1822	168825
Tabasco	Zacatecas	México	1824	168834
Tabasco	Zacatecas	México	1825	168836
Tabasco	Zacatecas	México	1829	168807
Tepechitlán	Zacatecas	México	1824	168834
Tepetongo	Zacatecas	México	1824	168832
Teul	Zacatecas	México	1688	AAG
Teul	Zacatecas	México	1819	168815
Teul	Zacatecas	México	1820	168822
Teul	Zacatecas	México	1822	168825
Teul	Zacatecas	México	1824	168834
Teul	Zacatecas	México	1828	168840
Teul	Zacatecas	México	1830	168844, 168846
Tigre	Zacatecas	México	1819	168815
Tlaltenango	Zacatecas	México	1772–1777	AGI Guadalajara 348
Tlaltenango	Zacatecas	México	1819	168822
Tlaltenango	Zacatecas	México	1820	168820
Tlaltenango	Zacatecas	México	1822	168820
Valparaiso	Zacatecas	México	1819	168816
Valparaiso	Zacatecas	México	1821	168826

Locality	Province	Country	Year(s)	Reference
Valparaiso	Zacatecas	México	1822	168830
Valparaiso	Zacatecas	México	1824	168834
Valparaiso	Zacatecas	México	1825	168836
Villanueva	Zacatecas	México	1818	168814
Villanueva	Zacatecas	México	1819	168815
Villanueva	Zacatecas	México	1820	168820
Villanueva	Zacatecas	México	1821	168826
Villanueva	Zacatecas	México	1822	168830
Zacatecas	Zacatecas	México	1770	AAG
Zacatecas	Zacatecas	México	1772	AGI Guadalajara 348
Zacatecas	Zacatecas	México	1794	AAG
Zacatecas	Zacatecas	México	1819	168816; IGHL
Zacatecas	Zacatecas	México	1820	168818
Zacatecas	Zacatecas	México	1821	168826
Zacatecas	Zacatecas	México	1823	Cathedral, Zacatecas
Zacatecas	Zacatecas	México	1824	168834
Zacatecas	Zacatecas	México	1825	168837
Zacatecas	Zacatecas	México	1825	Cathedral, Zacatecas
Zacatecas	Zacatecas	México	1826	Cathedral, Zacatecas
Zacatecas	Zacatecas	México	1826	168838
Zacatecas	Zacatecas	México	1830	168843
Zacatecas	Zacatecas	México	1830	Cathedral, Zacatecas
Zacatecas	Zacatecas	México	1831	Cathedral, Zacatecas
Zacatecas	Zacatecas	México	1831	168847
Zacatecas	Zacatecas	México	1832	168807
Zacatecas	Zacatecas	México	1840	168807

NICARAGUA

Locality	Province	Country	Year(s)	Reference
Abangasca		Nicaragua	1676	763386
Boaco		Nicaragua	1701	763385
Boaco		Nicaragua	1701	773995
Boaco		Nicaragua	1718	763390
Boaco		Nicaragua	1755	763380
Boaco		Nicaragua	1815	763380
Boaco		Nicaragua	1816	763387
Candalaria		Nicaragua	1755	763380
Candalaria		Nicaragua	1772	746870
Chichigalpa		Nicaragua	1768	744866
Chichigalpa		Nicaragua	1768	747058
Chichigalpa		Nicaragua	1798	763387
Chichigalpa		Nicaragua	1817	763387
Chinandega		Nicaragua	1751	763380
Chinandega		Nicaragua	1768	747058
Chinandega		Nicaragua	1777	741739
Chinandega		Nicaragua	1798	763387
Chinandega		Nicaragua	1817	763387
Diramba		Nicaragua	1663	745817
Diramba		Nicaragua	1663	763386
Diramba		Nicaragua	1817	763387
Diriomo		Nicaragua	1817	763387
El Areo		Nicaragua	1821	763383
El Viejo		Nicaragua	1768	747058
El Viejo		Nicaragua	1777	741739
El Viejo		Nicaragua	1798	763387
El Viejo		Nicaragua	1817	763387
Espinal		Nicaragua	1824	746821
Granada		Nicaragua	1778	741759
Granada		Nicaragua	1778	741891
Jinotega		Nicaragua	1717	763390
Jinotega		Nicaragua	1816	763387
Jinotepe		Nicaragua	1817	763387
Juigalpa		Nicaragua	1755	763380
Juigalpa		Nicaragua	1816	763387
Managua		Nicaragua	1817	763387
Masatepe		Nicaragua	1817	763387
Masaya		Nicaragua	1817	763387

Locality	Province	Country	Year(s)	Reference
Matagalpa		Nicaragua	1700	763380
Matagalpa		Nicaragua	1755	763380
Matagalpa		Nicaragua	1778	741891
Matagalpa		Nicaragua	1816	763387
Matagalpa		Nicaragua	1817	763387
Mateare		Nicaragua	1816	763387
Momotombo		Nicaragua	1817	763387
Mosonte		Nicaragua	1676	745817
Mosonte		Nicaragua	1676	763386
Mosonte		Nicaragua	1741	746866
Mosonte		Nicaragua	1816	763387
Muy Muy		Nicaragua	1816	763387
Nandaime		Nicaragua	1817	763387
Nandasmo		Nicaragua	1817	763387
Nindiri		Nicaragua	1817	763387
Palacaguina		Nicaragua	1741	763380
Pelón		Nicaragua	1703	745817
Posoltega		Nicaragua	1663	745817
Posoltega		Nicaragua	1663	763386
Posoltega		Nicaragua	1676	745817
Posoltega		Nicaragua	1676	763386
Posoltega		Nicaragua	1735	763390
Posoltega		Nicaragua	1777	741739
Posoltega		Nicaragua	1816	763387
Quezalguaque		Nicaragua	1619	748128
Quezalguaque		Nicaragua	1719	763390
Quezalguaque		Nicaragua	1751	763380
Quezalguaque		Nicaragua	1816	763387
Realejo		Nicaragua	1777	741739
San Jorge		Nicaragua	1816	763387
San José		Nicaragua	1816	763387
San Ramón		Nicaragua	1816	763387
Sebaco		Nicaragua	1816	763387
Telica		Nicaragua	1751	763380
Telica		Nicaragua	1816	763387
Telpaneca		Nicaragua	1816	763387
Tepeaco		Nicaragua	1760	763390
Teustepe		Nicaragua	1718	763390
Teustepe		Nicaragua	1719	763390
Teustepe		Nicaragua	1755	763380
Teustepe		Nicaragua	1816	763387
Tola		Nicaragua	1816	763387
Totogalpa		Nicaragua	1741	746866
Totogalpa		Nicaragua	1796	763387

Locality	Province	Country	Year(s)	Reference
Totogalpa		Nicaragua	1816	763387
Trinidad		Nicaragua	1737	763385
Trinidad		Nicaragua	1737	763387
Yalaguina		Nicaragua	1816	763387

PANAMA

Locality	Province	Country	Year(s)	Reference
Natá		Panamá	1740	GHG 170
San Lucas		Panamá	1740	GHG 170
	Darién	Panamá	1787	GHG 172
	Darién	Panamá	1789	GHG 172
	Portobelo	Panamá	1777	1162417:2
	Veraguas	Panamá	1756	AGI, AP:130

PARAGUAY

Locality	Province	Country	Year(s)	Reference
Asunción	Paraguay	Paraguay	1615	HP 8-10:96-114
Asunción	Paraguay	Paraguay	1622	HP 8-10:115-127

PERU

Locality	Province	Country	Year(s)	Reference
		Perú	1772–1793	1083258-1083264[223]
		Perú	1535	AAL; GHG 243
		Perú	1569	AAL; GHG 243
General (93 bundles)		Perú	1569–1818	AAL; GHG 245; AGN
		Perú	1791	AAL; GHG 243
		Perú	1836	AAL; GHG 243
		Perú	1850	AAL; GHG 243
		Perú	1862	AAL; GHG 243
		Perú	1876	AAL; GHG 243
		Perú	1940	AAL; GHG 243
		Perú	1961	AAL; GHG 243
		Perú	1972	AAL; GHG 243
Jalca Grande	Amazonas	Perú	1849	1380319
Lonya Grande	Amazonas	Perú	1855	1389315
Acas	Ancash	Perú	1814	AAL; GHG 252
Acas	Ancash	Perú	1840	AAL; GHG 252
Acobamba	Ancash	Perú	1777	AAL; GHG 249
Apallasca	Ancash	Perú	1779	AAL; GHG 250
Aija	Ancash	Perú	1778	AAL; GHG 249
Cabana	Ancash	Perú	1777	AAL; GHG 250
Caraz (S.Ildefonso)	Ancash	Perú	1774	AAL; GHG 249
Carhuaz (indios)	Ancash	Perú	1778	AAL; GHG 251
Casma	Ancash	Perú	1778	AAL; GHG 250
Casma	Ancash	Perú	1813	AAL; GHG 251
Chacas	Ancash	Perú	1777	AAL; GHG 250
Chavin	Ancash	Perú	1814	AAL; GHG 252
Chavin de Huantar	Ancash	Perú	1777	AAL; GHG 250
Chimbote	Ancash	Perú	1813	AAL; GHG 251
Cochabamba	Ancash	Perú	1813	AAL; GHG 251
Cochas	Ancash	Perú	1778	AAL; GHG 250
Corongo	Ancash	Perú	1777	AAL; GHG 250
Corongo	Ancash	Perú	1841	AAL; GHG 253
Cotaparaco	Ancash	Perú	1778	AAL; GHG 250
Huaraz	Ancash	Perú	1774	AAL; GHG 249
Huaraz	Ancash	Perú	1778	AAL; GHG 250
Huaraz	Ancash	Perú	1813	AAL; GHG 251

---

[223] Censuses of Ecuador and Perú, microfilmed in Bogotá, Colombia by the Family History Library of Salt Lake City, Utah.

Locality	Province	Country	Year(s)	Reference
Huaraz (mestizos)	Ancash	Perú	1758	AAL; GHG 249
Huari	Ancash	Perú	1746	636941 item 4
Huari	Ancash	Perú	1777	AAL; GHG 250
Huari	Ancash	Perú	1778	AAL; GHG 250
Huari	Ancash	Perú	1813	AAL; GHG 251
Huari	Ancash	Perú	1840	AAL; GHG 252
Llapo	Ancash	Perú	1778	AAL; GHG 250
Llapo	Ancash	Perú	1840	AAL; GHG 252
Llaután	Ancash	Perú	1779	AAL; GHG 250
Llaután	Ancash	Perú	1841	AAL; GHG 253
Marca (indios)	Ancash	Perú	1778	AAL; GHG 250
Moro	Ancash	Perú	1778	AAL; GHG 250
Moro	Ancash	Perú	1813	AAL; GHG 251
Nepena	Ancash	Perú	1777	AAL; GHG 249
Nepena	Ancash	Perú	1813	AAL; GHG 251
Ocros	Ancash	Perú	1760	AAL; GHG 249
Pampas	Ancash	Perú	1777	AAL; GHG 249
Pampas	Ancash	Perú	1840	AAL; GHG 252
Pariacoto	Ancash	Perú	1813	AAL; GHG 251
Pira	Ancash	Perú	1813	AAL; GHG 252
Piscobamba	Ancash	Perú	1777	AAL; GHG 250
Pomabamba	Ancash	Perú	1777	AAL; GHG 250
Pomabamba	Ancash	Perú	1841	AAL; GHG 253
Recuay	Ancash	Perú	1778	AAL; GHG 250
Santa	Ancash	Perú	1813	AAL; GHG 251
Santa	Ancash	Perú	1841	AAL; GHG 253
Santa (S.Buenaventura)	Ancash	Perú	1813	AAL; GHG 251
Tauca	Ancash	Perú	1778	AAL; GHG 250
Ticllos	Ancash	Perú	1777	AAL; GHG 249
Uco	Ancash	Perú	1778	AAL; GHG 250
Yungay	Ancash	Perú	1777	AAL; GHG 249
Cuzco[224]	Cuzco	Perú	1560	AAL; GHG 246
Cuzco (Indios)	Cuzco	Perú	1813–1822	AAL; GHG 247
Banos	Huanuco	Perú	1808	AAL; GHG 252
Cayna	Huanuco	Perú	1777	AAL; GHG 250
Chauca	Huanuco	Perú	1813	AAL; GHG 251
Huacrachuco	Huanuco	Perú	1777	AAL; GHG 249
Huanuco	Huanuco	Perú	1760	AAL; GHG 249
Huanuco	Huanuco	Perú	1778	AAL; GHG 250
Huanuco	Huanuco	Perú	1778	AAL; GHG 251
Huanuco	Huanuco	Perú	1808	AAL; GHG 251
Huanuco	Huanuco	Perú	1813	AAL; GHG 252

[224] This census is for the Hospital de Naturales in Cuzco.

Locality	Province	Country	Year(s)	Reference
Llacta	Huanuco	Perú	1808	AAL; GHG 252
Quisqui	Huanuco	Perú	1813	AAL; GHG 251
Santa María del Valle	Huanuco	Perú	1778	AAL; GHG 250
Santa María del Valle	Huanuco	Perú	1813	AAL; GHG 252
Singa	Huanuco	Perú	1808	AAL; GHG 251
Chincha	Ica	Perú	1760	AAL; GHG 249
Chincha	Ica	Perú	1813	AAL; GHG 252
Chunchang[225]	Ica	Perú	1778	AAL; GHG 250
Humay	Ica	Perú	1777	AAL; GHG 250
Ica	Ica	Perú	1778	AAL; GHG 250
Ica	Ica	Perú	1790	AAL; GHG 251
Ica (indios)	Ica	Perú	1777	AAL; GHG 249
Ica (yanaconas)	Ica	Perú	1813	AAL; GHG 251
Luren	Ica	Perú	1759	AAL; GHG 249
Luren	Ica	Perú	1777	AAL; GHG 249
Luren	Ica	Perú	1790	AAL; GHG 251
Luren	Ica	Perú	1813	AAL; GHG 251
Nasca	Ica	Perú	1777	AAL; GHG 250
Nasca	Ica	Perú	1778	AAL; GHG 250
Nasca	Ica	Perú	1813	AAL; GHG 251
Palpa	Ica	Perú	1777	AAL; GHG 249
Palpa	Ica	Perú	1791	AAL; GHG 251
Pisco	Ica	Perú	1778	AAL; GHG 250
Pisco	Ica	Perú	1808	AAL; GHG 251
Pisco	Ica	Perú	1813	AAL; GHG 252
Apata	Junin	Perú	1778	AAL; GHG 250
Chongos	Junin	Perú	1778	AAL; GHG 251
Chupaca	Junin	Perú	1704	AAL; GHG 249
Cincos	Junin	Perú	1760	AAL; GHG 249
Cincos	Junin	Perú	1810	AAL; GHG 251
Cochangara	Junin	Perú	1778	AAL; GHG 250
Ingenio	Junin	Perú	1777	AAL; GHG 249
Ingenio	Junin	Perú	1813	AAL; GHG 252
Jauja	Junin	Perú	1777	AAL; GHG 250
Matahuasi	Junin	Perú	1831	AAL; GHG 252
Mito	Junin	Perú	1769	AAL; GHG 249
Paccha	Junin	Perú	1808	AAL; GHG 251
Sicaya	Junin	Perú	1769	AAL; GHG 249
Sicaya	Junin	Perú	17--	AAL; GHG 249
Tapu	Junin	Perú	1778	AAL; GHG 250
Tapu	Junin	Perú	1813	AAL; GHG 251
Tarma	Junin	Perú	1777	AAL; GHG 249
Tunan (S.Jerónimo)	Junin	Perú	1777	AAL; GHG 249

---

[225] San José Chunchang valley.

Locality	Province	Country	Year(s)	Reference
Yauli	Junin	Perú	1778	AAL; GHG 250
Cachen	Libertad	Perú	1788	1083264
Huamachuco	Libertad	Perú	1783	1083257
S.Lorenzo de Llama	Libertad	Perú	1788	1083264
Trujillo	Libertad	Perú	1772–1831	1083257-1083264
Ambar	Lima	Perú	1777	AAL; GHG 250
Andajes	Lima	Perú	1777	AAL; GHG 250
Andajes	Lima	Perú	1810	AAL; GHG 251
Aquicha	Lima	Perú	1814	AAL; GHG 252
Arcamfer	Lima	Perú	1814	AAL; GHG 252
Asención	Lima	Perú	1777	AAL; GHG 249
Atavillos Altos	Lima	Perú	1813	AAL; GHG 252
Atunyauyos	Lima	Perú	1814	AAL; GHG 252
Aucallama	Lima	Perú	1813	AAL; GHG 252
Aucallama	Lima	Perú	1840	AAL; GHG 253
Aucallamas	Lima	Perú	1759	AAL; GHG 249
Auco	Lima	Perú	1814	AAL; GHG 252
Ayaviri	Lima	Perú	1759	AAL; GHG 249
Ayaviri (Jesús de)	Lima	Perú	1808	AAL; GHG 251
Ayaviri (Jesús de)	Lima	Perú	1813	AAL; GHG 252
Ayaviri (Jesús de)	Lima	Perú	1840	AAL; GHG 253
Cañete	Lima	Perú	1813	AAL; GHG 252
Cajatambo	Lima	Perú	1777	AAL; GHG 250
Cajatambo	Lima	Perú	1778	AAL; GHG 250
Cajumayo	Lima	Perú	1777	AAL; GHG 250
Canta	Lima	Perú	1769	AAL; GHG 249
Canta	Lima	Perú	1813	AAL; GHG 251
Carampoma	Lima	Perú	1777	AAL; GHG 249
Chacuasi	Lima	Perú	1813	AAL; GHG 251
Chancay	Lima	Perú	1813	AAL; GHG 252
Chilla	Lima	Perú	1777	AAL; GHG 250
Chorrillo (S.José)	Lima	Perú	1813	AAL; GHG 251
Churín (Pachangara)	Lima	Perú	1777	AAL; GHG 249
Cochamarca	Lima	Perú	1813	AAL; GHG 251
Gorgor (Españoles)	Lima	Perú	1777	AAL; GHG 249
Hatún (Atunyauyos ?)	Lima	Perú	1840	AAL; GHG 252
Huanec	Lima	Perú	1836	AAL; GHG 252
Huacho	Lima	Perú	1813	AAL; GHG 252
Huamantanga	Lima	Perú	1813	AAL; GHG 251
Huanchor	Lima	Perú	1777	AAL; GHG 250
Huantán	Lima	Perú	1814	AAL; GHG 252
Huarochirí	Lima	Perú	1840	AAL; GHG 252
Huanec	Lima	Perú	1840	AAL; GHG 252
Ihuari	Lima	Perú	1759	AAL; GHG 249
Ihuari	Lima	Perú	17--	AAL; GHG 251

Locality	Province	Country	Year(s)	Reference
Lampián	Lima	Perú	1777	AAL; GHG 250
Lampián	Lima	Perú	1813	AAL; GHG 252
Laraos	Lima	Perú	1777	AAL; GHG 249
Laraos	Lima	Perú	1840	AAL; GHG 252
Lima (indios)	Lima	Perú	1613	N. D. Cook
Lima	Lima	Perú	1700	AHA 1:172
Lima, Barranca	Lima	Perú	1813	AAL; GHG 252
Lima, Chorrillos[226]	Lima	Perú	1778	AAL; GHG 250
Lima, Chorrillos	Lima	Perú	1840	AAL; GHG 252
Lima, Magdalena	Lima	Perú	1777	AAL; GHG 250
Lima, Magdalena	Lima	Perú	1813	AAL; GHG 251
Lima, Magdalena[227]	Lima	Perú	1759	AAL; GHG 249
Lima, Miraflores	Lima	Perú	1813	AAL; GHG 251
Lima, San Marcelo	Lima	Perú	1772	AAL; GHG 249
Lima, San Marcelo	Lima	Perú	1768	AAL; GHG 249
Lima, San Marcelo	Lima	Perú	1764	AAL; GHG 249
Lima, San Marcelo	Lima	Perú	1766	AAL; GHG 249
Lima, San Marcelo	Lima	Perú	1784	AAL; GHG 251
Lima, Santa Ana	Lima	Perú	1790	AAL; GHG 251
Lima, Santa Ana	Lima	Perú	1808	AAL; GHG 251
Lima, Surco	Lima	Perú	1840	AAL; GHG 252
Lunahuana	Lima	Perú	1778	AAL; GHG 250
Lunahuana	Lima	Perú	1813	AAL; GHG 251
Lunahuana	Lima	Perú	1829	AAL; GHG 252
Lurigancho	Lima	Perú	1790	AAL; GHG 251
Omas	Lima	Perú	1813	AAL; GHG 251
Omas	Lima	Perú	1808	AAL; GHG 252
Omas	Lima	Perú	1840	AAL; GHG 252
Pacaraos	Lima	Perú	1784	AAL; GHG 251
Pacaraos	Lima	Perú	1813	AAL; GHG 251
Paccho	Lima	Perú	1698	AAL; GHG 249
Paccho	Lima	Perú	1813	AAL; GHG 252
Paccho	Lima	Perú	1840	AAL; GHG 252
Pachangara	Lima	Perú	1777	AAL; GHG 249
Parac	Lima	Perú	1840	AAL; GHG 252
Pari	Lima	Perú	1813	AAL; GHG 251
Pari	Lima	Perú	1813	AAL; GHG 251
Pari	Lima	Perú	1840	AAL; GHG 252
Pari	Lima	Perú	1784	AAL; GHG 251
Piuche	Lima	Perú	1814	AAL; GHG 252
Santa María	Lima	Perú	1778	AAL; GHG 250
Sayán	Lima	Perú	1813	AAL; GHG 252

[226] San José de Chorrillos.
[227] This is a *padrón* of Indians.

Locality	Province	Country	Year(s)	Reference
Sayán	Lima	Perú	1815	AAL; GHG 252
Viso	Lima	Perú	1777	AAL; GHG 250
Ichuna	Moquegua	Perú	1828–1852	1389141
Chacayán	Pasco	Perú	1777	AAL; GHG 249
Conoc	Pasco	Perú	1813	AAL; GHG 251
Pallanchacra	Pasco	Perú	1778	AAL; GHG 250
Pasco	Pasco	Perú	1777	AAL; GHG 250
Paucartambo	Pasco	Perú	1779	AAL; GHG 250
Paucartambo	Pasco	Perú	1778	AAL; GHG 250
Paucartambo	Pasco	Perú	1813	AAL; GHG 252
Racracancha	Pasco	Perú	1813	AAL; GHG 251
Amotape	Piura	Perú	1783	1083257
Huancabamba	Piura	Perú	1783	1083257
Acora	Puno	Perú	1574	VHP
Chucuito	Puno	Perú	1574	VHP
Ilave	Puno	Perú	1574	VHP
Juli	Puno	Perú	1574	VHP
Pomata	Puno	Perú	1574	VHP
Yunguyo	Puno	Perú	1574	VHP
Zapita	Puno	Perú	1574	VHP

PUERTO RICO

The 1900 census of Puerto Rico has not been located. Although it was taken as part of the U.S. general census, Puerto Rico having come under U.S. jurisdiction after the 1898 Spanish-American War, it is uncertain whether or not it has survived. None of the island-wide Spanish censuses prior to 1898 have been found either.

Locality	Province	Country	Year(s)	Reference
		P.Rico	----	GHG 258
		P.Rico	1866–1872	AGP
Adjuntas		P.Rico	1910	1375769
Aguada		P.Rico	1910	1375769
Aguadilla		P.Rico	1910	1375770
Aguas Buenas		P.Rico	1910	1375769
Ahasco		P.Rico	1910	1375771
Aibonito		P.Rico	1910	1375770
Arecibo		P.Rico	1910	1375771-1375772
Arroyo		P.Rico	1910	1375771
Barceloneta		P.Rico	1910	1375772
Barranquitas		P.Rico	1910	1375770
Barros		P.Rico	1910	1375772-1375773
Bayamón		P.Rico	1910	1375773
Bayamón		P.Rico	1860	AGP
Cabo Rojo		P.Rico	1910	1375774
Caguas		P.Rico	1910	1375773-1375775
Camuy		P.Rico	1910	1375775
Carolina		P.Rico	1910	1375775
Cayey		P.Rico	1910	1375776
Ciales		P.Rico	1910	1375776
Cidra		P.Rico	1910	1375777
Coamo		P.Rico	1910	1375777
Comerío		P.Rico	1910	1375777
Corado		P.Rico	1910	1375775
Corozal		P.Rico	1910	1375778
Culebra		P.Rico	1910	1375769
Fajardo		P.Rico	1910	1375778
Guayama		P.Rico	1910	1375779
Guayanilla		P.Rico	1910	1375779
Gurabo		P.Rico	1910	1375779
Hatillo		P.Rico	1910	1375780

Locality	Province	Country	Year(s)	Reference
Humacao		P.Rico	1910	1375780
Isabela		P.Rico	1910	1375781
Juana Díaz		P.Rico	1910	1375781-1375782
Juncos		P.Rico	1910	1375782
Lajas		P.Rico	1910	1375782
Lares		P.Rico	1910	1375783
Las Marías		P.Rico	1910	1375782
Loiza		P.Rico	1910	1375783
Manabo		P.Rico	1910	1375783
Manatí		P.Rico	1910	1375784
Maranjito		P.Rico	1910	1375786
Maricao		P.Rico	1797	AGP
Maricao		P.Rico	1910	1375778
Mayagüez		P.Rico	1910	1375784-1375785
Moca		P.Rico	1910	1375785
Morovis		P.Rico	1910	1375786
Naguabo		P.Rico	1910	1375786
Patillas		P.Rico	1910	1375786-1375787
Peñuelas		P.Rico	1910	1375787
Ponce		P.Rico	1910	1375787-1375788
Quebradillas		P.Rico	1910	1375789
Rincón		P.Rico	1910	1375785
Río Grande		P.Rico	1910	1375789
Río Piedras		P.Rico	1910	1375789
Sabana Grande		P.Rico	1910	1375790
Salinas		P.Rico	1910	1375790
San Germán		P.Rico	1910	1375790
San Juan		P.Rico	1910	1375791-1375792
San Juan, La Marina		P.Rico	1839–1841	AGP
San Juan, Santa Bárbara		P.Rico	1833	AGP
San Juan, Santa Bárbara		P.Rico	1840	AGP
San Juan, Santo Domingo		P.Rico	1833	AGP
San Lorenzo		P.Rico	1910	1375792
San Sebastián		P.Rico	1910	1375792
Santa Isabel		P.Rico	1910	1375793
Toa Alta		P.Rico	1910	1375793
Toa Baja		P.Rico	1910	1375793
Toa Baja (electoral)		P.Rico	1892	AGP
Trujillo Alto		P.Rico	1910	1375793
Utado		P.Rico	1910	1375794
Vega Alta		P.Rico	1910	1375795
Vega Baja		P.Rico	1910	1375795

Locality	Province	Country	Year(s)	Reference
Vieques		P.Rico	1910	1375795
Yabacoa		P.Rico	1910	1375793
Yauco		P.Rico	1910	1375795-1375796

EL SALVADOR

Locality	Province	Country	Year(s)	Reference
Ahuachapan	Ahuachapan	E.Salvador	1813	763382
Apaneca	Ahuachapan	E.Salvador	1821	763383
Atiquizaya	Ahuachapan	E.Salvador	1821	763383
Concepción de Ataco	Ahuachapan	E.Salvador	1813	763382
Osicala	Morazán	E.Salvador	1820	763384
Perquin	Morazán	E.Salvador	1820	763384
San Fco. Goterra	Morazán	E.Salvador	1820	763384
San Simon	Morazán	E.Salvador	1820	763384
Sensembra	Morazán	E.Salvador	1820	763384
Torola	Morazán	E.Salvador	1820	763384
Yamabel	Morazán	E.Salvador	1820	763384
Yoloaiquin	Morazán	E.Salvador	1820	763384
Amapala	San Miguel	E.Salvador	1790	741887
Amapala	San Miguel	E.Salvador	1803	741887
Chinameca	San Miguel	E.Salvador	1732	741888
Chinameca	San Miguel	E.Salvador	1732	746867
Chinameca	San Miguel	E.Salvador	1813	763384
Ciudad Barrios	San Miguel	E.Salvador	1790	741887
Ciudad Barrios	San Miguel	E.Salvador	1803	741887
Apopa	S.Salvador	E.Salvador	1813	763382
Cuscatancingo	S.Salvador	E.Salvador	1755	741887
El Paisnal	S.Salvador	E.Salvador	1813	763382
Guazapa	S.Salvador	E.Salvador	1813	763382
Nejapa	S.Salvador	E.Salvador	1813	763382
Panchimalco	S.Salvador	E.Salvador	1813	763381
Apastepeque	S.Vicente	E.Salvador	1755	746869
Apastepeque	S.Vicente	E.Salvador	1756	741890
Coatepeque	Santa Ana	E.Salvador	1755	741890
Masahuat	Santa Ana	E.Salvador	1750	741889
Masahuat	Santa Ana	E.Salvador	1821	763383
Metapan	Santa Ana	E.Salvador	1755	741887
Metapan	Santa Ana	E.Salvador	1755	746867
Metapan	Santa Ana	E.Salvador	1787	741887
Metapan	Santa Ana	E.Salvador	1787	746865
Metapan	Santa Ana	E.Salvador	1813	763381
Santa Ana	Santa Ana	E.Salvador	1714	746827
Santa Ana	Santa Ana	E.Salvador	1813	763381
Caluco	Sonsonate	E.Salvador	1821	763383
Izalco	Sonsonate	E.Salvador	1813	763381

Locality	Province	Country	Year(s)	Reference
Juayua	Sonsonate	E.Salvador	1821	763383
Nahuizalco	Sonsonate	E.Salvador	1813	763381
Nahuizalco	Sonsonate	E.Salvador	1821	763383
Nahulingo	Sonsonate	E.Salvador	1755	747058
Nahulingo	Sonsonate	E.Salvador	1821	763383
Salcoatitan	Sonsonate	E.Salvador	1821	763383
Sonsonate	Sonsonate	E.Salvador	1821	763383
Sonzacate	Sonsonate	E.Salvador	1821	763383
Tecapa	Usalatán	E.Salvador	1813	763384
San Carlos	?	E.Salvador	1820	763384
San Fernando	?	E.Salvador	1820	763384
San Jacinto	?	E.Salvador	1813	763381
Santa Lucia	?	E.Salvador	1746	746867

URUGUAY

Locality	Province	Country	Year(s)	Reference
		Uruguay	1782	GHG 133
		Uruguay	1801	GHG 133
		Uruguay	1811	?
	Achucarro	Uruguay	1773–1839	GHG 263
	La Rosa	Uruguay	1773–1839	GHG 263
	Sacramento	Uruguay	?	URU
	Sacramento	Uruguay	?	IAC 11:106-122
Cerro Largo	Cerro Largo	Uruguay	1852	GHG 263
Cerro Largo	Cerro Largo	Uruguay	1773–1839	GHG 263
Durazno	Durazno	Uruguay	1773–1839	GHG 263
La Florida	La Florida	Uruguay	1773–1839	GHG 263
Minas	Lavalleja	Uruguay	1773–1839	GHG 263
Maldonado	Maldonado	Uruguay	1773–1839	GHG 263
Montevideo	Montevideo	Uruguay	1726	LEA 27-29
Montevideo	Montevideo	Uruguay	1743	AGI Charcas 33
Montevideo	Montevideo	Uruguay	1773–1839	GHG 263
Montevideo	Montevideo	Uruguay	1836	GHG 263
Montevideo	Montevideo	Uruguay	1860	GHG 263
Paysandú	Paysandú	Uruguay	1773–1839	GHG 263
S.José	S.J.de Mayo	Uruguay	1773–1839	GHG 263
Salto	Salto	Uruguay	1773–1839	GHG 263
Canelones	Santa Lucia	Uruguay	1773–1839	GHG 263
Mercedes	Soriano	Uruguay	1832–1833	GHG 263
Soriano	Soriano	Uruguay	1773–1839	GHG 263
Soriano	Soriano	Uruguay	1832–1833	GHG 263
Tacuarembo	Tacuarembo	Uruguay	1773–1839	GHG 263

VENEZUELA

Locality	Province	Country	Year(s)	Reference
		Venezuela	1756–1798	1162408-1162418
		Venezuela	1873	GHG 267
		Venezuela	1873	Centro Nac. de Estad.
		Venezuela	1881	GHG 267
		Venezuela	1881	Centro Nac. de Estad.
		Venezuela	1891	GHG 267
		Venezuela	1891	Centro Nac. de Estad.
		Venezuela	1920	GHG 267
		Venezuela	1920	Centro Nac. de Estad.
		Venezuela	1926	GHG 267
		Venezuela	1936	GHG 267
		Venezuela	1941	GHG 267
		Venezuela	1950	GHG 267
		Venezuela	1960	GHG 267
		Venezuela	1970	GHG 267
	Cumarebo	Venezuela	1761	1162410:36
	Cumarebo	Venezuela	1780	1162410:27
	Perija	Venezuela	1767	1162410:28
Puerto Cabello	Carabobo	Venezuela	1761	1162418:3
Puerto Cabello	Carabobo	Venezuela	1767	1162417:8
Puerto Cabello	Carabobo	Venezuela	1784	1162418:3
Puerto Cabello	Carabobo	Venezuela	1788	1162417:6
Caracas	D.F.	Venezuela	1756–1798	1162408-1162418
Caracas, Altagracia	D.F.	Venezuela	1754	1162408:24
Caracas, Altagracia	D.F.	Venezuela	1766	1162417:5
Caracas, Altagracia	D.F.	Venezuela	1770	1162417:5
Caracas, Altagracia	D.F.	Venezuela	1770	1162418:1
Caracas, Altagracia	D.F.	Venezuela	1792	1162408:21
Caracas, Altagracia	D.F.	Venezuela	1805	1162408:22
Caracas, Altagracia	D.F.	Venezuela	1813	1162408:23
Caracas, Candelaria	D.F.	Venezuela	1758	1162413:15
Caracas, Candelaria	D.F.	Venezuela	1761	1162413:14
Caracas, Candelaria	D.F.	Venezuela	1762	1162413:19
Caracas, Candelaria	D.F.	Venezuela	1766	1162413:21
Caracas, Candelaria	D.F.	Venezuela	1767	1162413:18
Caracas, Candelaria	D.F.	Venezuela	1768	1162413:23
Caracas, Candelaria	D.F.	Venezuela	1773	1162409:25
Caracas, Candelaria	D.F.	Venezuela	1774	1162409:26
Caracas, Candelaria	D.F.	Venezuela	1776	1162409:24

Locality	Province	Country	Year(s)	Reference
Caracas, Candelaria	D.F.	Venezuela	1776	1162409:38
Caracas, Candelaria	D.F.	Venezuela	1778	1162413:13
Caracas, Candelaria	D.F.	Venezuela	1781	1162409:37
Caracas, Candelaria	D.F.	Venezuela	1786	1162413:12
Caracas, Candelaria	D.F.	Venezuela	1787	1162409:30
Caracas, Candelaria	D.F.	Venezuela	1788	1162409:34
Caracas, Candelaria	D.F.	Venezuela	1790	1162409:32
Caracas, Candelaria	D.F.	Venezuela	1791	1162409:33
Caracas, Candelaria	D.F.	Venezuela	1792	1162409:31
Caracas, Candelaria	D.F.	Venezuela	1794	1162409:30
Caracas, Candelaria	D.F.	Venezuela	1795	1162409:28
Caracas, Candelaria	D.F.	Venezuela	1796	1162409:35
Caracas, Candelaria	D.F.	Venezuela	1798	1162409:35
Caracas, Catedral	D.F.	Venezuela	1751	1162411:54-55
Caracas, Catedral	D.F.	Venezuela	1758	1162411:50-52
Caracas, Catedral	D.F.	Venezuela	1766	1162411:53
Caracas, Catedral	D.F.	Venezuela	1767	1162409:47-48
Caracas, Catedral	D.F.	Venezuela	1767	1162411:49
Caracas, Catedral	D.F.	Venezuela	1768	1162409:43-44
Caracas, Catedral	D.F.	Venezuela	1769	1162409:42
Caracas, Catedral	D.F.	Venezuela	1770	1162409:45
Caracas, Catedral	D.F.	Venezuela	1772	1162409:41
Caracas, Catedral	D.F.	Venezuela	1774	1162409:46
Caracas, Catedral	D.F.	Venezuela	1778	1162409:39-40
Caracas, Catedral	D.F.	Venezuela	1781	1162411:70
Caracas, Catedral	D.F.	Venezuela	1786	1162411:69
Caracas, Catedral	D.F.	Venezuela	1787	1162411:66-68
Caracas, Catedral	D.F.	Venezuela	1788	1162411:63-65
Caracas, Catedral	D.F.	Venezuela	1790	1162411:58,60
Caracas, Catedral	D.F.	Venezuela	1791	1162411:59,63
Caracas, Catedral	D.F.	Venezuela	1792	1162411:61-62
Caracas, San Pablo	D.F.	Venezuela	1766	1162417:7
Caracas, San Pablo	D.F.	Venezuela	1768	1162417:9
Chaguaramal	Guarico	Venezuela	1782	1162410:43
Chaguaramal	Guarico	Venezuela	1796	1162410:44
Chaguaramal	Guarico	Venezuela	1798	1162410:45
Chaguaramas	Guarico	Venezuela	?	1162410:38
Chaguaramas	Guarico	Venezuela	?	1162410:43
Chaguaramas	Guarico	Venezuela	1758	1162410:36
Chaguaramas	Guarico	Venezuela	1767	1162410:37
Chaguaramas	Guarico	Venezuela	1772	1162410:41
Chaguaramas	Guarico	Venezuela	1782	1162410:42
Santa Ana del Serric	Guarico	Venezuela	1768	1162410:46
Santa María	Guarico	Venezuela	1759	1162410:37
	Lara	Venezuela	1759	1162408:1-17

Locality	Province	Country	Year(s)	Reference
Araguita in Carora	Lara	Venezuela	1769	1162413:8
Araguita in Carora	Lara	Venezuela	1792	1162413:9
Aregue	Lara	Venezuela	1791	1162413:10
Aregue	Lara	Venezuela	1794	1162413:11
Barquisimeto	Lara	Venezuela	17--	1162414:49
Barquisimeto	Lara	Venezuela	1758	1162414:55
Barquisimeto	Lara	Venezuela	1767	1162414:58-59
Barquisimeto	Lara	Venezuela	1768	1162414:61
Barquisimeto	Lara	Venezuela	1782	1162418:48
Barquisimeto	Lara	Venezuela	1786	1162414:65
Barquisimeto	Lara	Venezuela	1817	1162414:68
Buria	Lara	Venezuela	1784	1162414:67
Mitagache	Lara	Venezuela	1617	HOP 1:113-120
Santa Lucia	Lara	Venezuela	1795	1162414:50
Santa Rosa	Lara	Venezuela	?	1162414:51
Santa Rosa	Lara	Venezuela	1758	1162414:63
Santa Rosa	Lara	Venezuela	1768	1162414:56
Santa Rosa	Lara	Venezuela	1781	1162414:60
Santa Rosa	Lara	Venezuela	1784	1162414:52
Santa Rosa	Lara	Venezuela	1786	1162414:53
Santa Rosa (indios)	Lara	Venezuela	1758	1162414:64
Sarare	Lara	Venezuela	1768	1162414:61
Chacao	Miranda	Venezuela	1770	1162410:34
Chacao	Miranda	Venezuela	1772	1162410:34
Chacao	Miranda	Venezuela	1781	1162410:34
Chacao	Miranda	Venezuela	1782	1162410:35
Chacao	Miranda	Venezuela	1790	1162410:35
Chacao	Miranda	Venezuela	1791	1162410:35
Charallave	Miranda	Venezuela	1764	1162410:29
Charallave	Miranda	Venezuela	1767	1162410:28
Charallave	Miranda	Venezuela	1768	1162410:28
Charallave	Miranda	Venezuela	1770	1162410:29
Charallave	Miranda	Venezuela	1772	1162410:33
Charallave	Miranda	Venezuela	1776	1162410:28
Charallave	Miranda	Venezuela	1777	1162410:28
Charallave	Miranda	Venezuela	1778	1162410:27
Charallave	Miranda	Venezuela	1778	1162410:33
Charallave	Miranda	Venezuela	1781	1162410:32
Charallave	Miranda	Venezuela	1781	1162410:33
Charallave	Miranda	Venezuela	1782	1162410:33
Charallave	Miranda	Venezuela	1786	1162410:32
Charallave	Miranda	Venezuela	1790	1162410:32
Charallave	Miranda	Venezuela	1794	1162410:31
Charallave	Miranda	Venezuela	1795	1162410:31
Charallave	Miranda	Venezuela	1796	1162410:30

Locality	Province	Country	Year(s)	Reference
Charallave	Miranda	Venezuela	1798	1162410:30
Charallave	Miranda	Venezuela	1799	1162410:29
Charallave	Miranda	Venezuela	1800	1162410:30
Petare	Miranda	Venezuela	1761	1162418:4
Petare	Miranda	Venezuela	1767–1768	1162418:2
Bagueche	R.Tocuyo	Venezuela	1617	HOP 1:113-116
Querealle	R.Tocuyo	Venezuela	1617	HOP 1:117-118
Aparicion[228]	Portuguesa	Venezuela	1745	1162412:61
Araure	Portuguesa	Venezuela	1758	1162412:50
Araure	Portuguesa	Venezuela	1770	1162412:48
Araure	Portuguesa	Venezuela	1782	1162412:49
Aruare	Portuguesa	Venezuela	1791	1162413:1
Aruare	Portuguesa	Venezuela	1794	1162412:64
Aruare	Portuguesa	Venezuela	1798	1162413:2
Carimoto in Tucupido	Portuguesa	Venezuela	1760	1162412:55-57
Carimoto in Tucupido	Portuguesa	Venezuela	1761	1162412:59
Carimoto in Tucupido	Portuguesa	Venezuela	1792	1162412:60
Pueblo Nuevo	Portuguesa	Venezuela	1758	1162412:51-52
Zaragoza	Portuguesa	Venezuela	1758	1162412:62
Zaragoza	Portuguesa	Venezuela	1782	1162412:49
Zaragoza (indios)	Portuguesa	Venezuela	?	1162412:53
	Trujillo	Venezuela	1771	1162308:18

---

[228] Aparición de la Corteza.